VALUES EDUCATION SOURCEBOOK

Values Education Sourcebook

Conceptual Approaches, Materials Analyses, and an Annotated Bibliography

Douglas P. Superka
Christine Ahrens
Judith E. Hedstrom
with Luther J. Ford
and Patricia L. Johnson

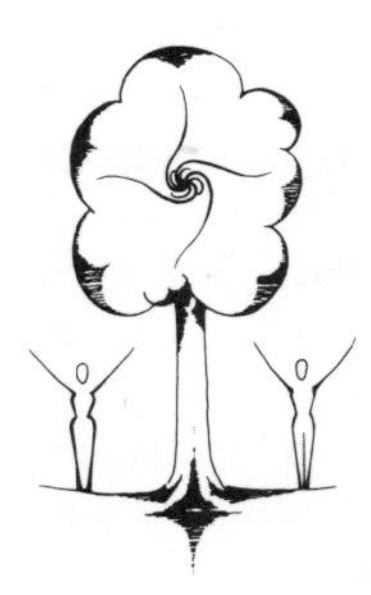

Social Science Education Consortium
ERIC Clearinghouse for Social Studies/
Social Science Education
1976

Ordering Information

This publication is available from: Social Science Education Consortium, Inc., 855 Broadway, Boulder, Colorado 80302. Request SSEC Publication No. 176.

Also available from Pennant Educational Materials, 8265 Commercial Street, Suite 14, La Mesa, California 92041

It is also listed in *Resources in Education* and can be obtained in microfiche and hard copy from the ERIC Document Reproduction Service, identified as ED 118 465. See *Resources in Education* for ordering information and ED number.

The material in this publication was prepared pursuant to a contract with the National Institute of Education, U.S. Department of Health, Education, and Welfare. Contractors undertaking such projects under government sponsorship are encouraged to express freely their judgment in professional and technical matters. Prior to publication, the manuscript was submitted to the National Council for the Social Studies for critical review and determination of professional competence. Points of view or opinions, however, do not necessarily represent the official view or opinions of either the National Council for the Social Studies or the National Institute of Education.

Book and jacket design: Rick Julliard

ACKNOWLEDGEMENTS: We thank the following persons for making significant contributions to this publication: Irving Morrissett, for his thoughtful suggestions and enthusiastic support during all phases of the development of the manuscript; Janet Jacobs, for her considerable and competent editing and rewriting efforts during the revision and integration stages of the work; Robert D. Barr, Jack R. Fraenkel, Alan L. Lockwood, and Jack K. Henes, for their critical comments and reviews of various aspects of the book; Karen Wiley and Faith Rogers, for their careful editing of the final manuscript; Nancy Dille and Joan Russell, for their continuing coordination of the typing; and Judy Gamble, Linda Branch, Betsy Gyger, Rick Julliard, and Carol Rayburn, for their speedy and accurate typing of various versions and sections of the publication.

table of contents

foreword

In response to numerous requests for information about values education, ERIC/ChESS undertook two studies — one concerned with alternative approaches to this subject, the other with selection and analysis of a wide variety of educational materials dealing directly with values issues. We were fortunate in having a staff member, Douglas Superka, who had already made a thorough study of various approaches to values education, and a number of staff members with substantial experience in the analysis of educational materials. In addition to the persons listed as authors of this publication, many others have contributed to these studies, as the authors indicate in their acknowledgments.

The two studies have now been combined in this volume. We hope this sourcebook will serve as a useful reference to ways in which values education may be approached and to materials that are useful in values education, as well as a guide to other useful references in the growing literature on this field.

Irving Morrissett
Director, ERIC/ChESS
Executive Director
Social Science Education Consortium

The artifacts and actions of our hands are emblematic of our values.

preface

Values education is currently one of the most exciting and explosive areas in education. Although educators have not completely neglected this area in previous decades, there has been in the last several years a spectacular upsurge of interest in and emphasis on "values" and "valuing" in education. This increased interest and activity has affected the entire educational spectrum from elementary to graduate school.

Values education has attracted the interest and involvement not only of teachers and students but also of psychologists, social psychologists, sociologists, philosophers, and political scientists. Their ideas have been communicated through books, articles, newsletters, films, workshops, conferences, inservice programs, methods courses, and informal conversation. A wide variety of materials, including films, filmstrips, records, tapes, handbooks, storybooks, minicourses, and entire curricula have been produced and distributed for the explicit purpose of facilitating the teaching of values and valuing.

However, several interrelated problems have persisted or developed in the midst of this energetic, wide-ranging activity. The major problems include (1) confusion and conflict about the meaning of the key terms used in values education—*values* and *valuing;* (2) lingering doubts on the part of many teachers, administrators, and parents concerning the role of the school in teaching values; (3) classroom norms among the students that discourage open, trusting value activity; (4) uncertainty of teachers about how self-disclosing, probing, and accepting they should be; (5) a generally inadequate level of teacher training in values education; (6) a tremendous influx into the values education movement of relatively inexperienced persons conducting workshops and developing materials; (7) lack of reliable, valid, and usable evaluation procedures and instruments to measure values development in students; and (8) the difficulty of intelligently and systematically selecting from the overwhelming amount of curriculum and teacher background materials being produced and disseminated.

This book will focus primarily on alleviating the last problem—the difficulty of comprehending and choosing from the plethora of values education materials. In order to help educators evaluate the enormous quantity of resources explicitly designed to teach values and valuing, we have formulated and explained a scheme of values education approaches by which materials are categorized according to rationale, purpose, and methodology. In addition, we have developed an analytical framework to guide educators in critically examining values education resources. We gathered over 100 sets of materials related to values education and the major portion of this publication is devoted to the analysis of 84 of these curriculum packages.

Designed to be a resource guide primarily for teachers, curriculum coordinators, and other educators, the *Values Education Sourcebook* is an outgrowth and amplification of an earlier work, *Values Education: Approaches and Materials,* a joint publication of the ERIC Clearinghouse for Social Studies/Social Science Education (ERIC/ChESS) and the Social Science Education Consortium (SSEC). The earlier publication contains a typology of values education approaches, analyses of 13 sets of materials, and an annotated bibliography of over 150 sets of student curricula, teacher resources, and theoretical background materials in values education. The content of the earlier work has been incorporated into this volume to provide an overview of values education approaches, teaching procedures, and curriculum materials and enable readers to select appropriate materials.

The Introduction to this book outlines and explains the guidelines used to formulate and organize the analyses of values education materials. It includes definitions of terms and a discussion of the criteria used to analyze the resources. Chapter I provides an overview of the typology of values education approaches developed in the first publication and three procedures designed to help readers apply the analytical system.

The next five chapters (II through VI) contain the analyses of curriculum resources. Each chapter focuses on one of five values education approaches: inculcation, moral development, analysis, clarification, and action learning. Each is divided into three sections: a detailed explanation of the approach; analyses of student materials reflecting that approach; and analyses of teacher materials reflecting that approach.

Chapter VII describes and explains two other approaches to values education—evocation and union—for which there are few curriculum materials presently available. These two approaches are explained in terms of their rationale, purpose, and methods. In addition, sample learning activities and educational programs related to these two approaches are discussed.

An annotated bibliography of over 400 materials and resources is found in Chapter VIII. The Afterword attempts to place our work in perspective and discuss other efforts needed in the area of values education.

Before proceeding any further, we think it appropriate at this point to discuss what we consider the essential nature of the work. We intend this book to be primarily an objective description and analysis of values education. No attempt is made to be prescriptive or evaluative. It is not our purpose here to recommend a particular approach or to determine the worth of a specific set of materials. Rather, it is to provide significant information and a useful framework in which to process data that will help readers make evaluative decisions. It is our belief, however, that every human endeavor, including the writing of this book, inevitably involves some basic assumptions and values. (That statement itself is, of course, an assumption.) Rather than pretend total objectivity, we would like to describe the four basic assumptions on which our work is based:

1) Individuals are continually involved in choosing, developing, and implementing their own values in real-life situations.

2) The process of valuing is mainly social. People are influenced by and act in particular social contexts. These contexts tend to impose certain values while, at the same time, they respond to value change.

3) Values development is a lifelong process. It is not confined to the earliest years and fixed by childhood socialization. Rather, it involves periodic testing and restructuring of one's value system in light of reflection on and experience in a changing culture.

4) Valuing can involve both rational and nonrational ways of knowing.

Finally, in completing our work, we came across one problem in particular that we feel merits attention, that of the lack of communication among persons working in values education throughout the country. In order to promote a better exchange of information, we urge you to send us your critical comments concerning this publication. Suggestions for improvement are especially welcome. If you have used a set of materials analyzed in this book and believe that the data in our analyses are inaccurate, write us about your perception. Further, since our analyses were done from an "armchair" perspective, we are especially eager to know how the materials *really* work with students. Are they interesting and exciting? What problems arise in using the materials? What is the most effective method of implementation? Finally, if you have analyzed or evaluated any values education resources not summarized in this publication, we would like a copy of your work. Please send all information to Values Education Project, ERIC Clearinghouse for Social Studies/Social Science Education, 855 Broadway, Boulder, Colorado 80302.

D.P.S.
C.A.
L.J.F.
J.H.
P.L.J.

introduction

What's available for teaching values education? Which are the best materials? These are the two questions on values education materials that seem to be of most concern to teachers and curriculum coordinators. We hope this book will help to answer the first question. The second question, however, is much more difficult, if not impossible, to answer. Frankly, we do not know which are the best values education resources. Choosing the "best" depends on individual purposes, goals, and values in relation to values education in particular, to education in general, and to life in even more general terms. We believe, therefore, that you as an educator must make your own decisions concerning which materials are best for your particular goals, needs, and values.

We can help you to some extent by providing information on the range of materials available and the characteristics of specific sets of materials. That is the purpose of this book. We have presented this information in a systematic format to aid you in making comparisons among materials and between your needs and the materials. But you, of course, must fill in half of the equation—information on the needs of your students, your school, your community, and yourself—and make the match between materials and needs.

The remainder of this introduction explains the terminology and criteria used in analyzing the 84 sets of values education materials for this book. Chapter I discusses the various values education approaches reflected in existing materials. Chapters II through VI contain the analyses of the materials. Chapter VII discusses two values education approaches that have not yet been used to any substantial extent in curriculum materials. And Chapter VIII contains an extensive bibliography of values education resources.

What Is Meant by Values and Valuing?

Much of the confusion in values education has resulted from the vagueness that surrounds the terms *values* and *valuing*. There appear to be as many definitions as there are writers. Throughout the values education literature, *values* has been defined as everything from eternal ideas to behavioral actions, while *valuing* has been considered the act of making value judgments, an expression of feeling, or the acquisition of and adherence to a set of principles.

Teachers who have to confront the value issues that arise every day in schools may not be concerned with the problem of defining these terms; but they must deal with values regardless of what they are called. Because this book is aimed at helping educators deal with the practical problems of teaching and learning values, we do not feel that this is the appropriate place to try to solve this definitional problem.* We do think it necessary, however, to define the key terms as we have used them in this book. We do not claim that our definitions are better than any others that have been formulated. The goal is simply to facilitate the reader's understanding of our vocabulary.

Values: criteria for determining levels of goodness, worth, or beauty. (For example, if someone dislikes a politician because he or she is dishonest, then that person would possess the value of honesty.)

Valuing: the process of developing or actualizing values.

Values education: the explicit attempt to teach about values and/or valuing.

Values education approach: a general orientation toward teaching about values and/or valuing.

Instructional model: a system of procedures used by teachers to facilitate the process of valuing with students.

Values education materials: student and teacher curriculum resources explicitly designed to deal with values and/or valuing. (Materials such as novels or films, which are heavily laden with values and value issues but which have not been developed for educational purposes, have not been considered.)†

What Materials Are Included?

When we began to work on this publication, we were aware of approximately 130 sets of student and teacher resources explicitly designed to teach values and valuing processes. We reviewed a major portion of these materials and, in order to limit the number of analyses, we combined into one analytical summary similar works produced by the same publisher or developer. For example, the entire *Holt Social Studies Curriculum* is analyzed in one summary, as are the McDougal, Littell *Values Education Series* and several of the Center for the Humanities sound-slide programs. Thus, we were able to reduce the number of analyses to 84. Since our initial collection effort, we have become aware of other materials. Although time did not permit their analysis, we have included these later discoveries in the bibliography.

What Information Is Included in the Analyses?

We tried to consider the amount and kind of information that would be most useful to teachers and other educators. Using the *Social Studies Curriculum Materials Data Book* (1971—) as a model, we developed an analysis framework that included descriptive data (title, publisher, cost, etc.) as well as analytical information such as rationale, objectives, content, and procedures. The analyses of student materials are presented by means of a checklist and a brief narrative. The analyses of teacher materials are presented in narrative form only, as the variations in structure and purpose of these materials did not fit the checklist format.

At the beginning of each student material, information for ordering the materials from the publisher is provided. Analytical information is provided at the end. This information is divided into four major categories—Descriptive Characteristics, Preconditions, Substantive Characteristics, and Evaluation Information. The items in

*For a more detailed discussion of definitions with respect to values in each of the following areas, see the corresponding references: sociology—F. Adler (1956); psychology—Dukes (1955) and Tisdale (1961); behavioral sciences—Handy (1969); Educational psychology—Trow (1953); social studies education—Bond (1970); philosophy—Lepley (1949); philosophy and theology—appendix of Canning (1970).

†Other publications of SSEC and ERIC/ChESS have focused on games and simulations, so we will not analyze these resources here. For information on games and simulations, see Charles and Stadsklev (1972).

Descriptive Characteristics (cost,* time, components) and Evaluation Information (fieldtest data) were easy to apply to the materials and require little explanation. Those in the other two categories are, in some cases, less obvious. Our criteria for analysis in these areas are described below:

Preconditions: This category identifies some conditions teachers need to consider before implementing the materials. The three items included under this heading were marked in accordance with the following interpretations:

1) *Amount of Reading:* No attempt was made to assess the reading level capabilities needed by students who use the materials. Rather, attention was focused on the amount of reading the materials require students to do—much, moderate, or very little. For example, a textbook series would be marked as "much reading," while an audiovisual program would be labeled "very little reading."
2) *Teacher Training:* No effort was made to judge whether training is needed. Rather, we identified the degree to

Checklist used to analyse student values education materials:

DESCRIPTIVE CHARACTERISTICS

Grade Level

___ K-3
___ 4-6
___ 7-8
___ 9-10
___ 11-12

Materials

___ Student materials
___ Teacher guide
___ A-V kit
___ Tests
___ Other: ________________
____

Time

___ Curriculum (2 or more years)
___ Course (one year)
___ Semester (half year)
___ Minicourse (6-9 weeks)
___ Units (1-3 weeks)
___ Supplementary
___ Other: ________________
____

Medium Used

___ Readings
___ Worksheets
___ Films
___ Filmstrips
___ Records or tapes
___ Charts or posters
___ Transparencies
___ Other: ________________
____

PRECONDITIONS

Amount of Reading

___ Much
___ Moderate
___ Very little

Teacher Training

___ Provided in materials
___ Suggested by developers
___ Not mentioned
___ Other: ________________

Prejudice/Stereotyping

Much evidence = M
Some evidence = S

___ Racial or Ethnic
___ Sexrole
___ Other: ________________
____

EVALUATION INFORMATION

Provision for Student Evaluation

___ Instruments specified
___ Procedures specified
___ Guidelines suggested
___ Nothing provided
___ Other: ________________

Materials Evaluation

Materials tested = T
Results available = A

___ Fieldtested before publication
___ Fieldtested after publication
___ User feedback solicited
___ Other: ________________
___ Not evaluated

SUBSTANTIVE CHARACTERISTICS

Values Education Approach

___ Inculcation
___ Moral development
___ Analysis
___ Clarification
___ Action learning
___ Other: ________________
____

Values Education Emphasis

___ Major focus
___ One of several concerns
___ A minor concern

Process/Content Emphasis

___ Process of valuing
___ Content of valuing

Objectives

___ Stated specifically
___ Stated generally
___ Not stated

Student Activities

Used or stressed frequently = F
Used or stressed occasionally = O

___ Reading
___ Writing
___ Class discussion
___ Small-group discussion
___ Games
___ Simulations
___ Role playing
___ Action projects
___ Other: ________________

* Prices are current as of the publication date.

which such training is provided in the materials or elsewhere.

3) *Prejudice/Stereotyping:* The following questions were asked in order to judge whether prejudice or stereotyping exists in the materials: Are persons from various racial and ethnic groups and both sexes represented? Are these persons depicted in various positions—traditional and nontraditional, low status and high status? Depicting persons from another culture in what Americans would term "traditional roles" was not necessarily considered stereotyping.* Other kinds of stereotyping for which one could also look, but which we did not examine systematically, are occupational (for example, a business person is better than a factory worker); physical (fat people are jovial; blondes have more fun); classification (professors are absent minded; barbers are talkative); sectional (Southerners are racially prejudiced); and religious (Catholics are sexually inhibited).†

Substantive Characteristics: This category contains information about the values education approach reflected in the materials, the degree to which values education is treated, the type of values emphasis (process or content), the objectives, and the kind of student activities provided. While most of the items under this heading are self-explanatory, three require discussion:

1) *Values Education Emphasis:* Only materials that deal with values education in a "major" way or as "one of several concerns" were considered for inclusion in this book. Most materials analyzed focus on values education, but some, such as the *Holt Social Studies Curriculum* (Holt, Rinehart and Winston), the Taba Program (Addison-Wesley), and the *Valuing Approach to Career Education* (Education Achievement Corporation), have other objectives as well.

2) *Process/Content Emphasis:* If the materials are more concerned with procedures (such as prizing and feeling) for dealing with value issues than with specific values, "process of valuing" is checked. If the materials stress certain values or value topics (such as prejudice, friendship, or competition) rather than any particular processes or procedures, "content of values" is marked. Both "content" and "process" are checked if the materials place emphasis on both specific values and valuing processes.

3) *Objectives:* This item was designed to indicate the degree of specificity of the objectives provided by the developer. If the resource includes objectives or purposes for each lesson or chapter, "stated specifically" is checked. An objective does not have to be stated in strict behavioral terms to be judged specific.
Materials that enumerate general goals or purposes for the entire program or for major units, but not for specific lessons, are marked "stated generally." Those materials that provide both general and specific objectives are only checked "stated specifically." For those materials that provide only general rationale statements or a brief, general sentence on the purpose of the entire program, "not stated" is checked. Those resources that contain no statement of rationale or purpose are also marked "not stated."

In addition to the checklist, each set of student materials is summarized in a short narrative that provides an overview of the materials and describes their learning objectives, content focus, main teaching procedures and learning activities, and fieldtest data. Other relevant information, such as evidence of stereotyping and provisions for teacher training, may also be mentioned in the narrative.

---

*Use of the masculine pronoun (he/his/him) was not seen as a basis for judging materials to be prejudiced or stereotyped. Since many of the materials were developed in the late sixties and early seventies—a period in which the use of masculine pronouns was not an issue—it seemed inappropriate to indicate their appearance as evidence of sex-role stereotyping. For current developments, however, we feel it is an important issue to be considered and remedied by developers and publishers.

†These four types of stereotyping are embodied in a materials analysis instrument developed and used by the Educational Products Information Exchange Institute (EPIE).

How Are the Analyses Organized?

The analyses are categorized according to the five values education approaches on which the bulk of our work is based. Thus, each set of materials is labeled according to one of five approaches—inculcation, moral development, analysis, clarification, and action learning. These, as well as two other approaches (evocation and union), are explained briefly in Chapter I and in depth in Chapters II through VII. It should be noted here, however, that the inculcation approach, by its very nature, is evident in every set of materials. Usually inculcation is implicit in the intent and activities of the package. For the purposes of our work, we did not classify materials under inculcation unless the developers have explicitly stated that there are certain values they want students to adopt and have provided activities to accomplish this goal.

The number of resources analyzed for each approach is as follows:

Inculcation 10	
Student Materials	4
Teacher Materials	6
Moral Development 9	
Student Materials	5
Teacher Materials	4
Analysis 23	
Student Materials	17
Teacher Materials	6
Clarification 39	
Student Materials	26
Teacher Materials	13
Action Learning 3	
Student Materials	1
Teacher Materials	2

You will note that most of the materials analyzed embody either the analysis or the clarification approach. This is an accurate representation of the full range of available values education resources. Several factors may be responsible for the preponderance of the analysis and clarification approaches. These include the extensive efforts by Simon and his associates to introduce the clarification approach to educators through workshops and conferences; the widespread support of the analysis approach among social studies educators; the ease with which these two approaches can be integrated into traditional teaching styles; the primary focus of Kohlberg and the moral development advocates on research rather than curriculum development and instruction; and the relative newness of the action learning approach.

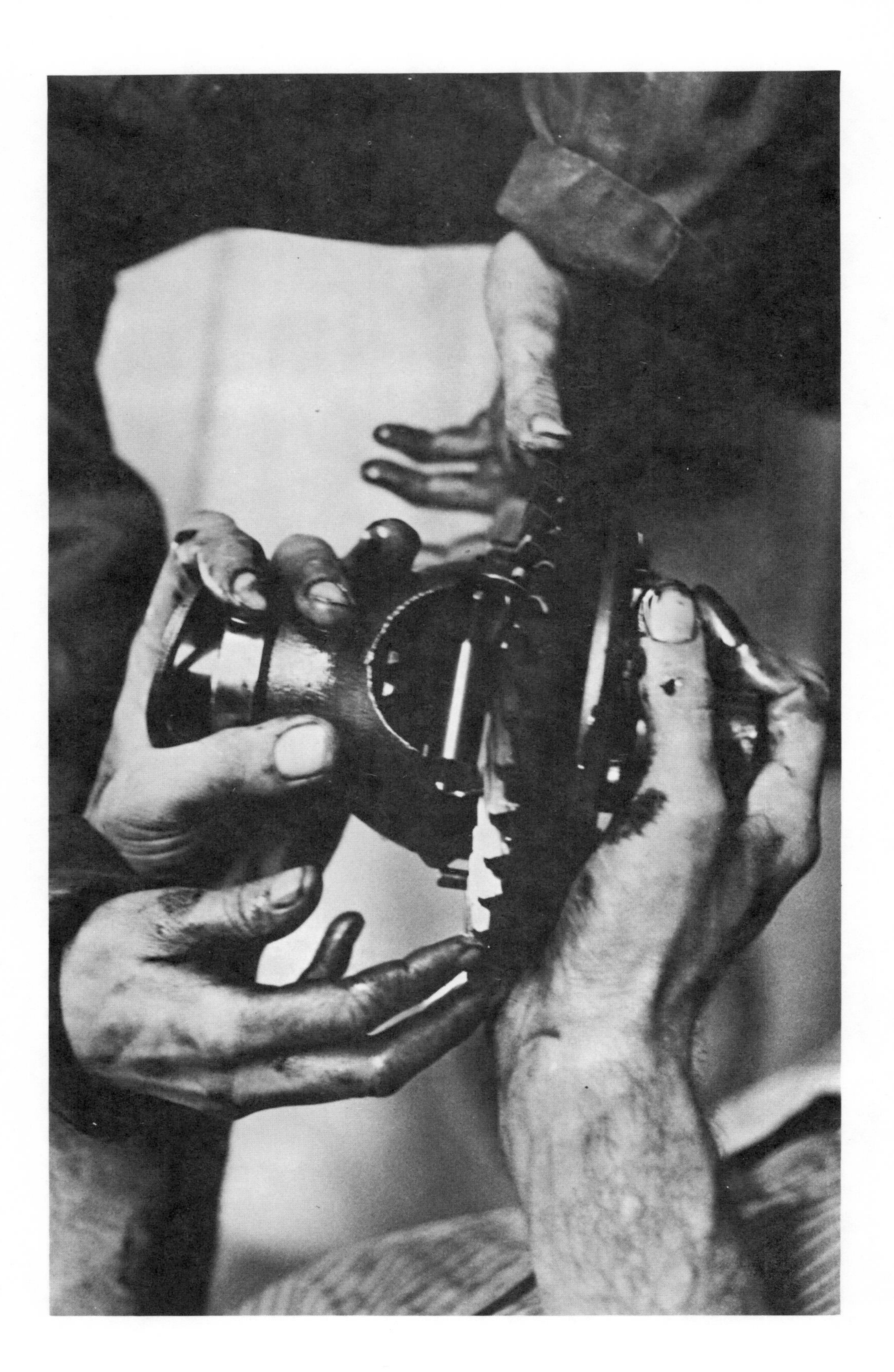

I

a typology of values education approaches

As values education has become increasingly important, various approaches to teaching values and valuing have developed. This chapter describes seven of these approaches, five of which are found in existing curriculum materials and two of which have been used only slightly in materials. Also included are three exercises to help readers clarify their priorities in values education.

Development of the Typology

This typology of values education approaches was initially formulated by Superka in a doctoral dissertation (1973). While reviewing the descriptive and empirical literature on values in psychology, sociology, philosophy, and education, he discovered a vast and confusing amount of data that seemed to be in need of some kind of organization. Although a few other writers had provided some guidelines, no systematic classification of values literature existed. This classification task became the theme of Superka's dissertation.

The typology was originally constructed around eight approaches. For each approach, a theory of value development was identified. From subsequent discussions with several educators, a number of conflicts and inconsistencies in the original typology were discovered. Curriculum materials did not exist for at least two of the value approaches, so these were eliminated. Two other approaches were combined into one because of the similarity and overlap of purpose and methods. We have, therefore, reduced the typology to five approaches and added a separate discussion section to deal with the two that were eliminated.

Although rigorous efforts to determine the reliability and validity of the typology were not made, two procedures were used to ensure that the typology would be helpful to educators. An overview of the typology was sent to ten values scholars. These included research psychologists, social psychologists, philosophers, and educators. Of the six who responded, four indicated that the categories were distinguishable from one another and that the typology could be useful. Two of the scholars did not believe that creating a classification system was practically or empirically meaningful.

The second validation procedure involved a larger number of persons in a more concrete application of the typology. In two conferences held in October 1974, 64 educators were commissioned to analyze more than 200 sets of elementary and secondary social studies materials.*

*The conferences were sponsored by the

Part of their task was to classify the materials according to the values education approaches presented in the typology. Once again, only a brief overview of the typology was used. Preliminary examination of those materials analyzed at the conferences indicated that the analysts could apply the typology and classify materials with reasonable reliability. For each set of materials there were two independent analysts; when checked against one another, the analysts demonstrated a surprisingly high rate of congruity on the values section of their evaluations. Further, when the analysts' categorizations were checked against our work, the classification system again proved to be reliable.

At this time there is no statistical validation of the typology. We still view the classification scheme and the concepts underlying it as working hypotheses subject to experimentation and revision. The procedures described above, however, have convinced us that the typology in its present form is a useful framework for organizing the vast number of values education materials.

Overview of the Typology

An overview of the typology, briefly describing the characteristics of each approach, is presented in the chart which follows. The five values education approaches that compose the typology are *inculcation, moral development, analysis, clarification,* and *action learning*. The chart outlines the purposes and methods of each approach and cites several sets of curriculum materials that use that approach. The chart is intended to provide a summary of the five approaches most often applied to values education resources. An in-depth discussion of each approach is provided in Chapters II through VI.

As previously mentioned, two approaches for which no curriculum materials presently exist have been excluded from the typology. These are *evocation* (to help students express their values as personal moral emotions without thought or hesitation) and *union* (to help students perceive themselves and act not as separate egos but as parts of a larger, interrelated whole). Both approaches are discussed extensively in Chapter VII.

Educational Products Information Exchange Institute (EPIE) and the Social Science Education Consortium (SSEC).

Using the Typology and Analyses

Because of the vast amount of information presented in the analyses of values approaches and materials, we felt that we needed to provide some means to help readers process this data. Exercises 1 and 2 are suggested to help readers decide which approach to values education and which criteria for selecting materials are most important to them. Exercise 3 suggests a systematic process for using this sourcebook to select particular values education resources.

Exercise 1

1) Answer *each* of the following questions with a yes or no.

a) Are there certain values and value positions that you want your students to adopt?

b) Do you want to help students examine their personal feelings and actions in order to increase their awareness of their own values?

c) Do you want to provide definite opportunities for your students to act individually and in groups according to their values?

d) Do you want to stimulate your students to develop higher forms of reasoning about values?

e) Do you want to help your students use logical thinking and scientific investigation to analyze social value issues?

2) If you responded "no" to all the above

questions, then probably none of the five approaches represents your view of values education. Another possibility is that you do not want to work with values at all as a teacher.

3) Each question, a) through e), represents one of the five approaches described in this chapter. If you responded "yes" to only one question, you probably gravitate toward that approach. The five questions correlate with the five approaches as follows:

a = inculcation
b = clarification
c = action learning
d = moral development
e = analysis

4) If you responded "yes" to more than one question, then take those questions and rank them according to their importance to you. (#1 = goal most important to you.) The approach that corresponds to the question you ranked #1 would be the one you are most likely to use. The #2 approach in your ranking would also reflect your goals and probably would relate to the #1 approach. For example, if analysis = #1 and inculcation = #2, then analysis would be the approach you most desire to use; in addition, you probably are interested in inculcating the values underlying the analysis approach—rationality, intellectual curiosity, the scientific method, etc. The #2 approach could relate to your first choice in another way. If, for instance, you selected clarification = #1 and action learning = #2 it might mean that you believe that persons must clarify their values before acting upon them.

Exercise 2

If you are interested in choosing from among various sets of values education materials, what are the most important questions to ask about each resource? Eighteen "key questions" are suggested below. Read this list of questions now. If you have any other questions you think are important to ask about curriculum materials, add them to the list. Then from this list choose the nine questions that seem to be the most important to you—that would be of most help to you in providing significant information to make a decision. Place an asterisk (*) beside each of those nine questions. Next, divide these questions into three groups by placing a "1" beside the three questions of greatest importance, and a "2" beside those of secondary importance, and a "3" beside those of tertiary importance.

__ Is the approach embodied in the materials similar to the approach you believe is the best?

__ Are the objectives clearly stated somewhere in the materials?

__ Do the rationale and objectives fit your own?

__ Is the reading level appropriate to your students? (A)

__ Is there little or no racial or ethnic bias and sterotyping in the materials?

__ Is there little or no sexual bias and stereotyping in the materials?

__ Is special teacher training required to use the materials? (B) If so, is it provided?

__ Will obtaining school or community acceptance for using the materials be a problem? (B)

__ Is the time sequence of materials suited to your needs?

__ Will the content and activities involve and interest your students? (B)

__ Do the materials emphasize the process of valuing instead of the content?

__ Do the materials stress personal as well as social value questions? (B)

__ Do the materials use a variety of teaching methods and learning activities?

__ Does the teacher's guide (if provided) offer guidelines for applying the procedures or strategies?

__ Are the rights of learners to withhold personal information protected? (A)

__ Are specific evaluation procedures or instruments provided to determine student growth?

Overview of Typology of Values Education Approaches

Approaches	Purposes	Methods	Examples of Materials: Title	Examples of Materials: Developers
Inculcation	To instill or internalize certain values in students To change the values of students so they more nearly reflect certain desired values	modeling; positive and negative reinforcement; mocking; nagging; manipulating alternatives; providing incomplete or biased data; games and simulations; role playing; discovery learning	*Human Values Series* *Coronado Plan: Teacher's Guides*	Blanchette *et al.* (1970) Bensley (1974)
Moral Development	To help students develop more complex moral reasoning patterns based on a higher set of values To urge students to discuss the reasons for their value choices and positions, not merely to share with others, but to foster change in the stages of reasoning of students	moral dilemma episodes with small-group discussion relatively structured and argumentative	*First Things: Values* "Teaching Strategies for Moral Dilemmas"	Kohlberg and Selman (1970) Galbraith and Jones (1975)
Analysis	To help students use logical thinking and scientific investigation to decide value issues and questions To help students use rational, analytical processes in interrelating and conceptualizing their values	structured rational discussion that demands application of reasons as well as evidence; testing principles; analyzing analogous cases; debate; research	*Public Issues Series* *Analysis of Public Issues Program* *Values Education*	Oliver and Newmann (1967-72) Shaver and Larkins (1973) Metcalf (1971)

Clarification	To help students become aware of and identify their own values and those of others To help students communicate openly and honestly with others about their values To help students use both rational thinking and emotional awareness to examine their personal feelings, values, and behavior patterns	role-playing games; simulations; contrived or real value-laden situations; in-depth self-analysis exercises; sensitivity activities; out-of-class activities; small group discussion	*Decisions and Outcomes* *Values and Teaching* *Values Clarification* *Values in Action* Scholastic *Contact* Series *A Probe into Values*	Gelatt *et al.* (1973) Raths *et al.* (1966) Simon *et al.* (1972) Shaftel and Shaftel (1970) Goodykoontz (1968-74) Church (1973)
Action Learning	Those purposes listed for analysis and clarification To provide students with opportunities for personal and social action based on their values To encourage students to view themselves as personal-social interactive beings, not fully autonomous, but members of a community or social system	the methods listed for analysis and clarification as well as action projects within the school and community and skill practice in group organizing and interpersonal relations	*Finding Community* *Social Action*	Jones (1971) Newmann (1972)

__ Have the materials been and do they continue to be fieldtested or learner verified?

__ Do the materials contain carefully planned, detailed lessons or are they basically a resource that teachers can use any way they see fit?

(Space for your own questions:)

____

____

____

____

The above items followed by an "A" are questions for which our analyses do not provide any information. You would have to examine and perhaps fieldtest the materials yourself to make those judgments. The items followed by a "B" are questions that our analyses do not answer directly, but for which some information is provided that would enable you to formulate tentative judgments. A look at the content and procedures sections of analysis narratives, for instance, should enable you to infer whether "the materials stress personal as well as social value questions." If, for example, on the environmental issue the materials ask questions such as, What have you done lately to reduce air pollution?, in addition to those such as, What law should be passed to reduce air pollution?, then both personal and social questions are asked. The analyses in this work do provide direct answers to the questions not followed by an "A" or a "B."

Now, as you read the analyses of the various values education materials, focus your attention on the items in them that give you some information about the nine questions you marked with asterisks—especially the three of greatest importance. You might establish a general rule for serious consideration of a set of materials. One might be that each of the three questions you considered to be of greatest importance must be answered to your satisfaction, while two of the three secondary questions and one of the three tertiary questions must be answered to your satisfaction.

Exercise 3

If you are just beginning to get into values education because of individual interest or because you represent your school or district, the sheer quantity of materials designed to teach values and valuing processes is especially overwhelming. To help you use this publication for selecting resources, we have devised the following procedure. It could be followed by one teacher, a curriculum coordinator, or a committee of teachers. In any case, it can be modified and varied to fit individual needs and goals.

1) Complete Exercise 1.

2) Complete Exercise 2.

3) Check off the chapters in the Table of Contents of this work that most closely correspond to the values education approaches toward which you seem oriented based on Exercise 1.

4) To confirm your interest in them, read the descriptions of those approaches at the beginning of the appropriate chapters.

5) Read the brief description of the other approaches at the beginning of each chapter (II through VI) to confirm your lesser interest in them. If you change your mind, check any additional approaches that appeal to you.

6) Now apply one or two criteria that will enable you to narrow quickly the number of analyses you will have to read. (Grade level may be such a criterion.) Turning to the alphabetical list of materials at the end of the book, place a check beside each material for which you want to read the analysis.

7) Keeping in mind the questions you determined to be most important by doing Exercise 2, read the analyses of those materials.

8) Read the annotations in the bibliography for other materials reflecting your preferred approaches.

9) Divide the materials you have read about into three groups:

   a) those you think you want to order and use,

   b) those about which you need more information before making a decision, and

   c) those you definitely do not want to order or use.

10) Order the materials in groups (a) and (b) on an examination basis.

11) When they arrive, examine and fieldtest them.

II

inculcation

Because it is both consciously and unconsciously applied, inculcation is probably the most extensively used approach to values education. This chapter begins with a detailed explanation of the rationale, purpose, teaching methods, and instructional model of the inculcation approach. Then a learning activity is provided to illustrate the application of the approach in the classroom. A discussion of the educational materials and programs that reflect the inculcation approach follows. This discussion focuses on the curriculum materials that have been analyzed in this chapter. The last two sections of the chapter present the analyses of four sets of student materials and six teacher resources that use the inculcation approach to values education.

Explanation of the Approach

Rationale and Purpose. The purpose of the inculcation approach is to instill or internalize certain values that are considered desirable. According to this approach, values are viewed as standards or rules of behavior the source of which is a society or culture. Valuing is considered a process of identification and socialization whereby a person, sometimes unconsciously, takes standards or norms from another person, group, or society and incorporates them into his or her own value system. Depending on the goal of the course and the orientation of the teacher, social, personal, moral, political, scholarly, and/or other values might be inculcated into students.

Regardless of the particular values being instilled, proponents of the inculcation approach take a view of human nature in which the individual is treated, during the inculcation process, as a reactor rather than as an initiator. Extreme advocates of inculcation believe that the needs and goals of society transcend and even define the needs and goals of individuals.* Maintenance and development are viewed as goals of society, and recruitment and replacement of people in various positions is seen as a major need. The task of values education, therefore, is to instill the values that people must have to assume efficiently the roles prescribed by society.

Educators who consider an individual to be a free, self-fulfilling participant in society tend to inculcate values as well, especially values such as freedom to learn, human dignity, justice, and self-exploration. Inculcation, however, is often

*This interpretation is closely related to the views of the sociologist Talcott Parsons (1951) and Freudian psychologists Sears *et al.* (1957) and Whiting (1961).

mistakenly associated with only a narrow concept of human nature and is often considered a negative approach. Yet, this approach is used by persons holding a variety of value positions, including those generally labeled humanistic.

A teacher, for example, may react very deeply and strongly against a student who has just uttered a racial slur to another student in the class. This could take the form of a short but emotional lecture on the evils of racism or a simple expression of disappointment in the student's behavior. At any rate, the teacher is inculcating in this situation. Perhaps this is because he or she believes that the enduring values of human dignity and respect for the individual are essential for the survival of democratic society. This reflects the widespread belief that, in order to insure continuity of culture, certain basic values must be instilled in its members.

A final rationale for inculcation is the notion that certain values are universal and absolute. Thus, one would not have to analyze or clarify those values but merely commit oneself to them. The traditional Western Christian belief that values originate in God would be one example of this orientation. Some social studies educators, however, express a similar position. Oliver and Shaver, for instance, believe that certain values are nearly universal:

> For us the most basic values of the [American] Creed, as they relate to the function of the school in society, are to be treated as more than psychological facts. They describe certain potentially universal characteristics of man which, at least from our particular cultural frame of reference, make him "human"—such as a quest for self-respect, a sense of sympathy and love, a concern for fairness and justice in his dealing with others.

Teaching Methods. Various methods have been used to inculcate values. One of the most widely used and effective methods is reinforcement. This process might involve positive reinforcement, such as a teacher's praising a student for behaving in accordance with a particular value, or negative reinforcement, such as a teacher's punishing a student for behaving contrary to a certain desirable value. It is extremely difficult, if not impossible, for a teacher to avoid using some form of reinforcement. Often merely a smile or a frown will tend to reinforce certain values. But reinforcement can also be applied consciously and systematically, as in behavior modification.* A widely used behavior modification technique is to provide students with "tokens" such as food, play money, or grade points for doing desirable tasks such as solving a math problem, remaining quiet for 20 minutes, or helping another student.

Another extremely effective method of inculcating values is modeling, in which a particular person is a model for desirable values that a teacher might want the students to adopt. The teacher, simply by personifying whatever values he or she holds, is always a model for some values—for example, punctuality or lateness, enthusiasm for learning or boredom. Even if teachers attempt to be objective and conceal their values, they become models for the values of objectivity and hiding one's values. Advocates of the "new social studies" have urged teachers to be examples of inquiry learners and socially active citizens in order to encourage students to adopt similar value orientations. Other students can also serve as models of desirable values. Students assume model roles when a teacher asks an individual to read his or her "A" term paper or essay answer to the class. In most cases the student's work is being singled out as an example to be followed by the rest of the class, instilling in other students the desire to produce similar work and to receive similar recognition.

Some behavioral research has indicated that a combination of reinforcement and modeling can be an effective way to inculcate values.† Students observe a model

*Although not usually considered a values education program, some of the procedures of behavior modification can be used to inculcate values. Many manuals have been developed to help teachers apply these techniques. These include works by Sarason *et al.* (1972), Sarason and Sarason (1974), Meacham and Wiesen (1969), Sulzer and Mayer (1972), and White and Smith (1972).

†For a discussion of these educational studies, see Woody (1969).

(usually another student) being reinforced for behaving according to a certain value. Studies have shown that if the model is positively reinforced or rewarded, then the observers are more likely to behave similarly and, thus, to adopt that value. On the other hand, if the model is negatively reinforced or punished, the observers are less likely to behave that way and to adopt the value underlying that behavior (Sarason and Sarason 1974, pp. 6-7). In the classroom this combination of reinforcement and modeling often occurs naturally and unwittingly. One example would be a teacher's praising a student for doing his or her homework while other students look on. It is hoped that as a result other students will value doing their homework as well.

Another example, which often occurs contrary to the intentions of the teacher, is the student who constantly makes wisecracks in class, causing other students, and sometimes the teacher, to laugh. This response not only reinforces that person's behavior, but frequently stimulates other students to mimic the wisecrack behavior. Although some educators may interpret this reaction merely as imitative, it can also be viewed as the adoption, however superficial, of one or more values associated with that behavior—values such as being a class clown or distracting other students and the teacher.

Despite the possible negative consequences of the combined reinforcement and modeling technique, this strategy can be applied purposefully and systematically to inculcate whatever values are deemed desirable. For example, in relation to educational values, either a thoughtful questioning of or an unbridled respect for school authority could be instilled in students. The choice depends upon the values of the teachers and administrators of the school.

The methods described above, however powerful and effective, are not foolproof ways of instilling values. To stay within the scope of this work, the explanation of these techniques has been simplified. The effective use of reinforcement and modeling is actually more complicated. Specific types of rewards and schedules of reinforcement are significant factors that influence the success of efforts to change behavior and values. Further, although anyone could serve as a model, experience has shown that models who are admired or respected by the observer are most effective. Some models should be similar to the observer, others different, depending on the situation and the rationale for emulating the model. Before implementing these techniques, the reader is urged to use the sources cited in this section and in the bibliography in Chapter VIII.

In addition to reinforcement and modeling, many other techniques have been used to inculcate values into students. Role playing and participation in games and simulations are effective ways to instill certain values. These methods, too, could be used to inculcate any kind of values. Traditionally, the use of games has instilled implicitly the value of competition. Recently, however, games have been constructed that require players to cooperate and, thus, they inculcate the value of cooperation.

Some other inculcation methods seem less ethical to many educators. These include nagging, lecturing, providing incomplete or biased information, and omitting alternatives. Some teachers, for example, knowingly or unwittingly "guide" students to the right answers during a discovery lesson by making only certain evidence available. Although most teachers frown on these methods, they are often used unconsciously but nevertheless effectively.

Instructional Model. Although most value inculcation occurs implicitly and often unintentionally, a specific set of procedures to help teachers apply this approach explicitly and purposefully can be identified. We have formulated such an instructional model by combining and adapting a system of behavior modification (Sulzer and Mayer 1972) with the taxonomy of educational objectives in the affective domain (Krathwohl *et al.* 1964). This model is presented below as a possible guideline for using value inculcation in a systematic manner:

1) *Determine the value to be inculcated:*

Choose the value to be instilled in the students (perhaps in cooperation with students and parents).

2) *Identify the level of internalization desired:* Select the degree of internalization that will be sought:

a) *Receiving*

(1) *Awareness:* Learner (or valuer) takes into account that a phenomenon exists.

(2) *Willingness to receive:* Learner is willing to listen to stimulus.

(3) *Controlled or selected attention:* Learner selects and responds to favored stimuli.

b) *Responding*

(1) *Acquiescence in responding:* Learner complies with requirements.

(2) *Willingness to respond:* Learner volunteers to exhibit an expected behavior.

(3) *Satisfaction in response:* Learner's reaction is associated with enjoyment.

c) *Valuing*

(1) *Acceptance of a value:* Learner's response shows consistent identification with a class of phenomena.

(2) *Preference for a value:* Learner seeks out a particular value because he is committed to it.

(3) *Commitment:* Learner displays conviction or loyalty to a cause.

d) *Organization*

(1) *Conceptualization of a value:* Learner begins to relate one value to other values by means of analysis and synthesis.

(2) *Organization of a value system:* Learner begins to integrate a complex of values into an ordered relationship.

e) *Characterization by a Value or a Value Complex*

(1) *Generalized set:* Learner orders the world around him with a consistent and stable frame of reference.

(2) *Characterization:* Learner formulates a code of conduct and a value system and they are completely internalized.

3) *Specify the behavioral goal:* Specify the behavior and the level of performance required to indicate attainment of the value at the particular level of internalization. This behavior could be in the form of an overt action (such as working for a political candidate) or a certain response to an item on a value or attitude questionnaire.

4) *Select an appropriate method:* Choose a procedure appropriate to the type of behavioral change desired:

a) *Increase a behavior* (positive reinforcement, provision of a model, removal of interfering conditions, games and simulations, role playing).

b) *Teach a new behavior* (shaping, chaining, response differentiation, games and simulation, role playing).

c) *Maintain a behavior* (one or more of several schedules of intermittent reinforcement).

d) *Reduce or eliminate undesirable behavior* (withdrawal of reinforcement, punishment, stimulus change).

5) *Implement the method:*

a) *Determine* the baseline by measuring the dependent behavior (the behavior that is to be changed) before applying the inculcation method.

b) *Apply* the method and measure and record the change.

c) *Conduct* a probe to determine what factor was responsible for the behavioral change by *not* applying the behavioral procedures for several days.

d) *Reapply* the behavioral procedures.

e) *Maintain* the behavioral change.

6) *Graph and communicate the results:* collate the recorded data, graph the data, make inferences concerning internalization of values, and communicate the results to appropriate persons.

This instructional model for inculcating values is very rigorous and detailed. Although teachers may not be able to apply it fully, they may find it a useful guide for influencing the development of certain values in students. Generally, however, most inculcation occurring in the schools today does not, as the following activity illustrates, closely follow every step of this model.

Illustrative Learning Activity. This activity has been adapted from a lesson in the *Analysis of Public Issues Program* (Shaver and Larkins 1973, pp. 349-53).*

Ms. Scott's 12th-grade social studies class has just read an article about Vince Lombardi, late coach of the Green Bay Packers. The passage stresses how deeply Lombardi valued winning and respect for authority. The article also provides some indication that the Packer coach also valued human dignity. Ms. Scott has chosen the article as a way to stimulate students to think rationally about the possible conflict between valuing winning and respect for authority, on the one hand, and human life and compassion, on the other. (By choosing and using the article for this purpose she is already inculcating a value held by many social studies educators—the value of rationally examining value conflicts.)

During the discussion of the article, Ms. Scott asks the class which of the two sets of values they believe to be most important. In order to provoke rigorous thinking, she is prepared to challenge with contrary propositions students who take either position. Thus, when several students affirm that human life and compassion are most important, she posed the idea that, if the Allied soldiers had refused to obey the military command and had not killed any of the Germans during World War II (thereby upholding human life and compassion instead of victory and respect for authority), Hitler might have subjugated half of the world. Students are encouraged to test the validity of that proposition and to re-examine (although not necessarily change) their positions.

Several students then contend that winning and respect for authority are more important. To counter this position, Ms. Scott shows a slide depicting the starving children of Biafra. She then interprets it by stating that those children suffered and died from malnutrition because the soldiers and leaders of Biafra and Nigeria were committed to fighting the war to the end. This, she points out, is an example of what can occur when winning and respect for authority are more highly valued than human life and compassion.

Ms. Scott did use logical propositions to question both value positions. By using the dramatic slide for the second proposition and by interpreting it for the students, however, she has unwittingly shown the former values in a less favorable light than the latter. She has, however unintentionally, interjected elements of inculcation into a basically analytical approach.

Materials and Programs. Inculcation, especially that accomplished through reinforcement and modeling, is the one values education approach that to some extent or another is embodied in all materials and programs and is used, consciously or unconsciously, by all teachers. Usually, however, the procedures are not nearly as rigorous as those presented in the model.

The extent to which certain materials and programs have as their goal the inculcation of values varies greatly. Many programs established by individual school districts in the 1950s and early 1960s were developed to instill by means of identification and socialization certain "correct" values. Pasadena City Schools (1957) developed a program to teach moral and spiritual values in this manner. A more recent example is an effort by the Los Angeles City Schools (1966). Love, respect for law and order, reverence, justice, integrity, and responsibility are frequently among the "correct" values. Current school district curriculum guides still contain lofty statements concerning the development of values such as good citizenship, human dignity, and respect for the country. Most often, however, systematic

*The original lesson in the *Analysis of Public Issues Program* was designed to apply the analysis approach to values education. We have changed it to show how inculcation can be combined in subtle ways with other approaches.

procedures for attaining these goals are not provided.

The student curriculum and teacher resource materials in this chapter have been classified as inculcation because they appear to focus more on instilling certain values into students than on other purposes, such as analyzing or clarifying values. Unlike the vague curriculum guides mentioned above, these resources do contain specific activities. Most of the materials analyzed concentrate on values that most educators would regard as significant ones for persons to hold. Five sets of materials analyzed here have been developed to teach a framework of values originally explicated by Lasswell and later adapted by Rucker. This Lasswell-Rucker value framework identifies eight values as basic, universal human needs: affection, respect, skill, enlightenment, power, wealth, well-being, and responsibility. *Human Values in Education* (Rucker *et al.* 1969) was the original teacher text explicating this program and *The Human Values Series* (Steck-Vaughn) was the first set of student materials designed to develop those eight values. *The Coronado Plan Teacher's Guides* (Bensley 1974), *Becoming Aware of Values* (Simpson 1973), and *Valuing in the Family* (Brayer and Cleary 1972) are more recent teacher resources based on the Lasswell-Rucker value categories. Although analysis in terms of the eight values is a vital part of each of these materials, the purpose of such analysis is clearly to encourage students to internalize these values.

Other groups of values have also been the basis of curriculum materials. *Building Better Bridges with Ben* (Sunny Enterprises) attempts to inculcate 11 of Ben Franklin's 13 virtues, including frugality, industry, humility, and sincerity. *Human Values in the Classroom* (Hawley 1973), while urging some clarification of values, emphasizes the internalization of love, cooperation, trust, compromise, truth, dignity, joy, and reverence. The *Character Education Curriculum* (American Institute for Character Education) also manifests both clarification and inculcation. The major focus of its objectives and activities clearly is to instill values such as being honest, sharing with others, and using time wisely. A sound-slide program by the Center for Humanities attempts to inculcate particular ideas about the interrelationship between freedom and responsibility. Finally a curriculum guide produced by the Dade County Public Schools, *Values: Language Arts,* presents certain models that will stimulate students to develop "an acceptable code of ethical conduct."

In other materials the inculcation of certain values is secondary to other educational objectives. These materials, such as the *Social Science Laboratory Units* (Science Research Associates) and *Public Issues Series* (Xerox) are not analyzed in this section (see Chapter IV, ANALYSIS) although they do attempt to inculcate the values of rational thinking, discussion, and scientific investigation. Similarly, other programs such as *Values Clarification* (Simon *et al.* 1972) and *Values in Action* (Winston Press), deal primarily with the process of valuing and are not included here (see Chapter V, CLARIFICATION), despite their emphasis on certain specific values, such as awareness of emotions, self-actualization, rational choice making, and purposeful behavior.

inculcation: student materials

Title: BUILDING BETTER BRIDGES WITH BEN

Author: Blanche A. Leonard

Publisher: Sunny Enterprises, 2700 Neilson Way, Suite 1521, P.O. Box 5688, Santa Monica, CA 90405

Date: 1974

Grade Level: 4-8

Materials and Cost: Student text and teacher's guide ($5.00)

Building Better Bridges with Ben is a character-building program for upper elementary and junior high grades; it can also be adapted for use with lower elementary and secondary students. The materials are based on Benjamin Franklin's list of 13 virtues. The author felt the need for such a program because of the state of "social upheaval and dissolving values" that exists in our society, as well as the fact that children in school now will have "more options to choose from than any other generation." She feels that there is a need for "rededication to principles and values." Beginning with the belief that actions and decisions are determined by values and attitudes and also that attitudes can be changed, this program attempts to inculcate 11 of Franklin's 13 virtues which, according to the author, will result in moral living. Objectives focus on the adoption and diligent practice of these virtues. It is hoped that children will learn that "doing right is one of the most satisfying experiences in life."

The program consists of a teacher's manual and a student book. The teacher's manual gives the rationale for the program and includes lesson plans, classroom activities, and background information on Benjamin Franklin. The student book is based on a 12-month calendar and includes illustrations, cartoons, wise sayings, and short readings.

The 11 virtues dealt with are silence, order, resolution, frugality, industry, sincerity, justice, moderation, cleanliness, tranquility, and humility. Among the activities intended to develop these virtues are keeping a calendar modeled after Franklin's book, in which students maintain a record of how they are practicing the desired qualities; writing original "wise sayings," such as those in *Poor Richard's Almanac,* that illustrate virtues; making cartoons, similar to those by Norman Rockwell, to illustrate the sayings; making up parables; and having contests based on what students have learned about the life and times of Benjamin Franklin.

There are no suggestions for student evaluation apart from the activities. There is a degree of sex-role stereotyping in the material. Many of Franklin's quotations reflect an old-fashioned, stereotyped view of a woman's role. For example, women are referred to as the "softer sex" and their place is definitely seen to be in the home. This was undoubtedly the accepted opinion during Franklin's time, but nothing has been done to bring the materials up to date concerning this matter.

According to the publishers, the materials have been informally tested in two California classrooms and the results of these fieldtests have been very favorable. However, no details are available.

DESCRIPTIVE CHARACTERISTICS

Grade Level

___ K-3
_X_ 4-6
_X_ 7-8
___ 9-10
___ 11-12

Materials

_X_ Student materials
_X_ Teacher guide
___ A-V kit
___ Tests
___ Other: ________________

Time

___ Curriculum (2 or more years)
___ Course (one year)
___ Semester (half year)
___ Minicourse (6-9 weeks)
___ Units (1-3 weeks)
_X_ Supplementary
___ Other: ________________

Medium Used

_X_ Readings
_X_ Worksheets
___ Films
___ Filmstrips
___ Records or tapes
___ Charts or posters
___ Transparencies
___ Other: ________________

PRECONDITIONS

Amount of Reading

___ Much
_X_ Moderate
___ Very little

Teacher Training

___ Provided in materials
___ Suggested by developers
_X_ Not mentioned
___ Other: ________________

Prejudice/Stereotyping

Much evidence = M
Some evidence = S

___ Racial or Ethnic
_S_ Sexrole
___ Other: ________________

EVALUATION INFORMATION

Provision for Student Evaluation

___ Instruments specified
___ Procedures specified
___ Guidelines suggested
_X_ Nothing provided
___ Other: ________________

Materials Evaluation

Materials tested = T
Results available = A

___ Fieldtested before publication
_T_ Fieldtested after publication
___ User feedback solicited
___ Other: ________________
___ Not evaluated

SUBSTANTIVE CHARACTERISTICS

Values Education Approach

_X_ Inculcation
___ Moral development
___ Analysis
___ Clarification
___ Action learning
___ Other: ________________

Values Education Emphasis

_X_ Major focus
___ One of several concerns
___ A minor concern

Process/Content Emphasis

___ Process of valuing
_X_ Content of valuing

Objectives

_X_ Stated specifically
___ Stated generally
___ Not stated

Student Activities

Used or stressed frequently = F
Used or stressed occasionally = O

_F_ Reading
_F_ Writing
_O_ Class discussion
___ Small-group discussion
_O_ Games
___ Simulations
___ Role playing
___ Action projects
_O_ Other: Drawings

Curriculum: CHARACTER EDUCATION CURRICULUM: LIVING WITH ME AND OTHERS

Publisher: The American Institute for Character Education, 342 West Woodlawn, San Antonio, TX 78212 (Mailing address: P.O. Box 12617)

Date: 1974

Grade Level: K-5

Materials and Cost: Multimedia kit including teacher's handbook, teacher's guide, posters, activity sheets, illustrations, and tests (each grade level—$16.95)

The *Character Education Curriculum* is a kindergarten through fifth-grade program designed to help children attain certain affective objectives. The curriculum is primarily concerned with helping children attain a deep sense of self-worth and develop values clarification and decision-making skills. This rationale, as well as many of the suggested teaching strategies, objectives, and student activities, reflects the clarification approach. However, the program aims to inculcate certain values, such as honesty, generosity, kindness, tolerance, courage, responsibility, and good citizenship. Throughout the program users will find a mixture of the two approaches. This is reflected in the lesson objectives. An example of the inculcation approach is an objective for the first grade: "students should exhibit politeness, helpfulness, generosity, and kindness to their peers and adults in their classroom." On the other hand, there are a number of clarification objectives, such as "students should be able to state alternative solutions to problems and the consequences of each." Most of the objectives seem to be of the inculcation variety. Suggested strategies and activities are, however, in many cases open ended.

For each of the grade levels the program provides a teacher's handbook or introduction to the curriculum, a teacher's guide, student worksheets, illustrations, evaluation instruments, and posters. The materials are divided into units on the following topics: courage and convictions; generosity, kindness, and helpfulness; honesty and truthfulness; honor; justice and tolerance; use of time and talents; freedom of choice; freedom of speech and citizenship; the right to be an individual; and the right to equal opportunity and economic security. The teacher's guide contains specific objectives for each lesson, as well as a list of materials needed and lesson plans. At the end of each unit there is a list of resource materials including books, films, filmstrips, and records for use in the classroom. For the most part, activities and questions tend to be open ended. For example, there are many "what would you do?" situations where students role play their own solutions. Many of the lessons, however, include leading questions or statements such as, "What are some ways you can be more generous?" or "Tell the children that a good citizen is usually helpful and courteous. Have the children identify some things they can do to be polite. . ." Posters are used in conjunction with the lessons in a variety of ways. Poster guidelines are provided for each grade and include such activities as problem solving, role playing, and creative art and writing. A "Freedom's Code" poster is also included for each grade level. It lists the standards of "Informed and Responsible Men of Good Will."

Student evaluation sheets are provided. They are intended to measure the extent to which students have reached specific objectives. Having desired outcomes in mind, the developers have included answer sheets. The following are two sample test items: "You can choose to get angry at someone if that person does something you don't like. Do you feel good if you are angry? Yes or No?" The answer is "No." "If you see Jerry doing something wrong, you should: A. Ask Jerry not to do it, B. Hit Jerry, C. Forget about Jerry." The answer is "A."

The first editions of the curriculum were fieldtested by approximately 5,000 teachers. Feedback from these tests has been incorporated into the revised editions. In the teacher's guide, there are suggestions for implementation and teaching strategies that were received from teachers who used the original program. The results of this study indicated that the "AICE character education program apparently had beneficial impact on students at the Kindergarten and third grade levels but no demonstrable benefit at grade six." The areas of most influence between experimental and control groups in the early grades were honesty, truthfulness, kindness, generosity, and helpfulness. Reports of this study and copies of the instruments used are available from the developer upon request.

This program was also evaluated in the October 1974 issue of *Thrust*–a publication of the Association of California School Administrators (Burlingame, California). The character education materials rated higher than Simon's values clarification, Kohlberg's moral development, and the *Lifeline* series on the four criteria used: "(1) affective as well as cognitive goals are set; (2) adequate value specificity is attained; (3) the program is well designed for student comprehension, interest, and involvement; and (4) the goals for teachers are meaningful and attainable."

DESCRIPTIVE CHARACTERISTICS

Grade Level

X K-3
X 4-6
__ 7-8
__ 9-10
__ 11-12

Materials

X Student materials
X Teacher guide
__ A-V kit
X Tests
__ Other: ______

Time

X Curriculum (2 or more years)
__ Course (one year)
__ Semester (half year)
__ Minicourse (6-9 weeks)
__ Units (1-3 weeks)
__ Supplementary
__ Other: ______

Medium Used

__ Readings
X Worksheets
__ Films
__ Filmstrips
__ Records or tapes
X Charts or posters
__ Transparencies
__ Other: ______

PRECONDITIONS

Amount of Reading

__ Much
X Moderate
__ Very little

Teacher Training

__ Provided in materials
__ Suggested by developers
X Not mentioned
__ Other: ______

Prejudice/Stereotyping

Much evidence = M
Some evidence = S

__ Racial or Ethnic
__ Sexrole

EVALUATION INFORMATION

Provision for Student Evaluation

X Instruments specified
__ Procedures specified
__ Guidelines suggested
__ Nothing provided
__ Other: ______

Materials Evaluation

Materials tested = T
Results available = A

A Fieldtested before publication
__ Fieldtested after publication
__ User feedback solicited
A Other: Journal review
__ Not evaluated

SUBSTANTIVE CHARACTERISTICS

Values Education Approach

X Inculcation
__ Moral development
__ Analysis
X Clarification
__ Action learning

Values Education Emphasis

X Major focus
__ One of several concerns
__ A minor concern

Process/Content Emphasis

X Process of valuing
X Content of valuing

Objectives

X Stated specifically
__ Stated generally
__ Not stated

Student Activities

Used or stressed frequently = F
Used or stressed occasionally = O

O Reading
O Writing
F Class discussion
F Small-group discussion
__ Games
__ Simulations
F Role playing
__ Action projects
O Other: Artwork
F listening

Title: FREEDOM AND RESPONSIBILITY: A QUESTION OF VALUES

Publisher: The Center for Humanities, Inc., Two Holland Ave., White Plains, NY 10603

Date: 1973

Grade Level: 9-12

Materials and Cost: Audiovisual kit including 160 slides in 2 carousel cartridges, 2 cassettes or 2 records, 1 teacher's guide, and 30 student activity cards ($104.50)

Freedom and Responsibility is a two-part sound-slide program composed of illustrations from various works of literature. It is designed to help students understand and clarify the concepts of freedom and responsibility. Defining freedom as "the opportunity to make choices within limits," this program stresses the interrelationship between freedom and responsibility. The developers believe that the more freedom one has, the more responsibility one has to others and to oneself. Thus, a central goal is to demonstrate to students "that they become accountable to community, family, and self in direct proportion to the amount of freedom they have."

Part I focuses on freedom and shows how human potentialities are limited by "social and moral controls, physical necessities, natural law, and individual motivations." This point is illustrated through various examples from literature, including *The Grapes of Wrath, Moby Dick, No Exit,* and *The Crucible*. Captain Ahab, for instance, is seen to be a prisoner of his own compulsive revenge against Moby Dick. The ability and inability to make choices is dramatized by John Proctor in Miller's *The Crucible* and by Garcin in Sartre's *No Exit.* Part II centers on the concept of responsibility. The consequences of accepting responsibility for one's choices are demonstrated by authors such as Robert Frost, Ernest Hemingway, and Eldridge Cleaver. The program concludes by stressing that assuming responsibility for one's relatively free choices is an inevitability.

The teacher's guide for *Freedom and Responsibility* contains suggested discussion questions and research activities, in addition to full transcripts of the narrative. Inquiry questions focusing on the artistic content of particular slides and student activity cards containing five exercises related to the program are also provided. Discussion questions reflect the analysis approach ("What kinds of freedoms did the Athenians value so highly?" "How do freedom and responsibility enter into the idea of revenge?") and the clarification approach ("Do you feel that the responsibility of preserving freedom is worth the price of one's own life?" "Do you feel you have to use a special talent or are you free not to?"). These seem directed, however, toward leading students to the major conclusions about freedom and responsibility that the program emphasizes.

According to the publisher, both prepublication fieldtest data and informal teacher feedback were obtained. The results, however, are not available.

DESCRIPTIVE CHARACTERISTICS

Grade Level

___ K-3
___ 4-6
___ 7-8
X 9-10
X 11-12

Materials

X Student materials
X Teacher guide
X A-V kit
___ Tests
___ Other: ______

Time

___ Curriculum (2 or more years)
___ Course (one year)
___ Semester (half year)
___ Minicourse (6-9 weeks)
___ Units (1-3 weeks)
X Supplementary
___ Other: ______

Medium Used

___ Readings
___ Worksheets
___ Films
___ Filmstrips
X Records or tapes
___ Charts or posters
___ Transparencies
X Other: Slides, activity cards

PRECONDITIONS

Amount of Reading

___ Much
___ Moderate
X Very little

Teacher Training

___ Provided in materials
___ Suggested by developers
X Not mentioned
___ Other: ______

Prejudice/Stereotyping

Much evidence = M
Some evidence = S

___ Racial or Ethnic
___ Sexrole
___ Other: ______

EVALUATION INFORMATION

Provision for Student Evaluation

___ Instruments specified
___ Procedures specified
___ Guidelines suggested
X Nothing provided
___ Other: ______

Materials Evaluation

Materials tested = T
Results available = A

T Fieldtested before publication
___ Fieldtested after publication
T User feedback solicited
___ Other: ______
___ Not evaluated

SUBSTANTIVE CHARACTERISTICS

Values Education Approach

X Inculcation
___ Moral development
X Analysis
X Clarification
___ Action learning
___ Other: ______

Values Education Emphasis

X Major focus
___ One of several concerns
___ A minor concern

Process/Content Emphasis

___ Process of valuing
X Content of valuing

Objectives

___ Stated specifically
X Stated generally
___ Not stated

Student Activities

Used or stressed frequently = F
Used or stressed occasionally = O

___ Reading
O Writing
F Class discussion
___ Small-group discussion
___ Games
___ Simulations
___ Role playing
___ Action projects
___ Other: ______

Curriculum: THE HUMAN VALUES SERIES

Titles: *The Human Values Series Teaching Pictures* (grade K); *About Me (1); About You and Me (2); About Values (3); Seeking Values (4); Sharing Values (5);* and *Thinking with Values (6)*

Developers: Zelda Beth Blanchette, V. Clyde Arnspiger, James A. Brill, and W. Ray Rucker

Publisher: Steck-Vaughn Company, P.O. Box 2028, Austin, TX 78767

Dates: 1970, 1973

Grade Levels: K-6

Materials and Cost: Student text ($5.43 each grade level); teacher's edition ($5.43 each grade level); eight 3' X 4' posters ($8.00); teacher's kit for levels K and 1 including pictures, rationale, lesson plans, and suggestions for value analysis of stories ($21.00)

Reflecting an inculcation approach to values education, the *Human Values Series* provides "specific examples of moral standards and ethical behavior that are compatible with the democratic view." Having identified eight value categories—affection, respect, well-being, wealth, power, rectitude, skills, and enlightenment—the developers specifically state objectives for each grade level that relate to the value categories described in the rationale. For example, in *About You and Me,* the story "The Big Dolphin's Friend" attempts to foster the values of respect and affection.

Brief stories present personal value issues and problems related to the eight value categories. In *Sharing Values,* students who read "An Eye for an Eye" learn about rectitude and well-being. Focusing on the theme of justice, the story "demonstrates how ideas of right and wrong vary from one part of the world to another." The teacher's edition suggests that the students be encouraged to express their own opinions about justice (judging or treating others fairly) after reading the story. Generally, the stories for all grade levels end with a specified or implied moral. For instance, "That Guilty Feeling," a fourth-grade story, stresses two points: "dishonesty, in the long run, is too great a price to pay for a temporary enhancement of affection" and "most people are eager to forgive and to go out of their way to reward a penitent person."

Special training for using these materials is available through workshops sponsored by the Value Education Consultants Clearinghouse, P.O. Box 947, Campbell, CA 95008. The materials provide no evaluation assistance. Instruments, however, can be found in other sources: Rucker *et al.* (1969, pp. 278, 281-85), *Simpson Perception of Values Inventory* (PVI), *Gardner Analysis of Personality Survey* (GAP), *Murphy Inventory of Values* (MIV), and *Values Inventory of Behavioral Responses* (VIBR). These instruments are available from Pennant Educational Materials, 4680 Alvarado Canyon Rd., San Diego, CA 92120.

The series was systematically fieldtested before and after publication and some of the results are presented in the *Learner Verification Report: The Human Values Series,* which is available from Steck-Vaughn. Two studies cited in that report indicate that the fifth- and sixth-grade texts of this series were somewhat effective in increasing reading comprehension and academic achievement.

DESCRIPTIVE CHARACTERISTICS

Grade Level

X K-3
X 4-6
___ 7-8
___ 9-10
___ 11-12

Materials

X Student materials
X Teacher guide
___ A-V kit
___ Tests
X Other: Posters

Time

___ Curriculum (2 or more years)
X Course (one year)
___ Semester (half year)
___ Minicourse (6-9 weeks)
X Units (1-3 weeks) (each title)
___ Supplementary
___ Other: ___

Medium Used

X Readings
___ Worksheets
___ Films
___ Filmstrips
___ Records or tapes
X Charts or posters
___ Transparencies
___ Other: ___

PRECONDITIONS

Amount of Reading

X Much
___ Moderate
___ Very little

Teacher Training

___ Provided in materials
___ Suggested by developers
___ Not mentioned
X Other: Available elsewhere

Prejudice/Stereotyping

Much evidence = M
Some evidence = S

___ Racial or Ethnic
___ Sexrole
___ Other: ___

EVALUATION INFORMATION

Provision for Student Evaluation

___ Instruments specified
___ Procedures specified
___ Guidelines suggested
___ Nothing provided
X Other: Available elsewhere

Materials Evaluation

Materials tested = T
Results available = A

A Fieldtested before publication
A Fieldtested after publication
___ User feedback solicited
___ Other: ___
___ Not evaluated

SUBSTANTIVE CHARACTERISTICS

Values Education Approach

X Inculcation
___ Moral development
X Analysis
___ Clarification
___ Action learning
___ Other: ___

Values Education Emphasis

X Major focus
___ One of several concerns
___ A minor concern

Process/Content Emphasis

___ Process of valuing
X Content of valuing

Objectives

X Stated specifically
___ Stated generally
___ Not stated

Student Activities

Used or stressed frequently = F
Used or stressed occasionally = O

F Reading
___ Writing
F Class discussion
___ Small-group discussion
___ Games
___ Simulations
___ Role playing
___ Action projects
___ Other: ___

inculcation: teacher materials

Title: BECOMING AWARE OF VALUES

Author: Bert K. Simpson

Publisher: Pennant Educational Materials, 4680 Alvarado Canyon Rd., San Diego, CA 92120

Date: 1973

Grade Levels: K-12

Materials and Cost: Teacher's guide ($4.95)

Becoming Aware of Values brings together a sample of the variety of educational materials for all grade levels that are based on the Lasswell-Rucker value framework (Rucker *et al.* 1969). This framework identifies eight values as universal human needs which all persons should possess, enhance, and share with others. These are affection, respect, skill, enlightenment, influence, wealth, well-being, and responsibility. Three dimensions of the valuing process are identified in this framework: developing within each person each of these basic values or needs; participating in the sharing and shaping of the eight values in other persons; and recognizing the ways in which others influence the sharing and shaping of these needs within oneself. Simpson emphasized the need to instill through the educational system a strong sense of these eight values and intends that his guidebook will provide the principles, activities, and leads to other strategies and techniques necessary for applying this program in the classroom.

The guidebook is divided into three sections. Section One discusses this conception of valuing and its applications, dimensions, principles, procedures, and the overall processes. The author uses Rucker's Value Deprivation-Enhancement Continuum to show the fluidity of the eight universal value areas (human needs). For example, a person can move from the point of alienation to intimacy in the affection category, thus indicating a high degree of value enhancement. In an effort to demonstrate how to gain a balance of values, five principles of valuing are cited—enhancement and deprivation (gaining and losing), base and scope (instrumental and terminal values), the balanced life, the democratic goal (widespread sharing), and shaping and sharing one's values continuously. Various processes related to valuing are also explained, including goal setting, problem solving, modeling, decision making, and active listening.

Section Two presents and describes materials and activities based on the Lasswell-Rucker value framework. The first part of the section discusses six games that have been developed, including "The Balanced Life in a Cruel Cruel World," "Timao," and "Value Bingo." Each game is explained in terms of its basic purpose, central concepts, key procedures, and follow-up questions. The last part of Section Two presents activities related to each of the eight value categories and the interrelationships among the values. Some value categories have lists of 14 to 20 activities; others have over 40. Several student worksheets are also provided. The activities include keeping a diary, choosing a secret friend and showing respect to that person, reading a story from the *Human Values Series* (see preceding Student Materials section), discussing how one has been enhanced in or deprived of influence, and listing nine words that show well-being.

Section Three consists of various kinds of data that the author hopes will be useful to teachers. A note to the principal describes a way to involve the administrator in implementing this method of valuing and provides guidelines for such implementation. A short description of four evaluation instruments that can be used to measure student growth in achieving the eight values is provided. Two lists conclude the book. One classifies various children's books according to the eight values; the other identifies research studies related to this method of values education.

Title: CORONADO PLAN: TEACHER'S GUIDES

Developer: Marvin L. Bensley

Publisher: Pennant Educational Materials, 4680 Alvarado Canyon Rd., San Diego, CA 92120

Date: 1974

Grade Levels: K-12

Materials and Cost: Teacher's guides, K-3, 4-6, 7-8, 9-12 ($2.50 each), advertising guide ($1.50), set of all 5 books ($10.95)

The *Coronado Plan* consists of four teacher's guides and one unit guide on advertising. It is designed to fuse drug abuse instruction with the valuing program based on the Lasswell-Rucker categories (Rucker *et al.* 1969). The *Coronado Plan* grew out of an attempt by educators in San Diego to find solutions to the problem of drug abuse prevalent in the middle-class suburb of Coronado, California. Concluding that several factors contributed to the problem—home conflicts, peer group pressure, low self-esteem, and advertising—it was decided that increased communication and self-awareness were avenues for significant redirection. The teacher's guides were developed by members of the Coronado school community to provide guidelines for teachers to help students identify and develop certain values, goals, and ideals. The values are the eight categories of the Lasswell-Rucker framework, including affection, skill, enlightenment, and well-being. In addition, four other goals were identified: "develop a positive self-image," "provide opportunities for decision making and learning problem-solving skills," and "understand [the] function and techniques of advertising."

The teacher's guides are divided into four books (K-3, 4-6, 7-8, 9-12). Each guide contains background information on the problems of today's youth, the relationship between valuing and drug abuse, and the Lasswell-Rucker value framework. The major section of each guide consists of lesson plans, including objectives, techniques, activities, and resources, designed to integrate the teaching of this valuing program with the regular curriculum. The K-3 guide, for example, is organized according to the five basic goals of the *Coronado Plan*. To develop well-being, students are urged to "make a mural of a happy day or week." The 7-8 and 9-12 guides, on the other hand, focus on subject areas, such as social studies, English, and science. Suggestions are made, for instance, on how to develop the eight values in a unit on post-World War I history. Student activities stressed throughout include reading, writing, discussion, role playing, and action projects. A supplementary guide on advertising is also available. It is designed to lead to an in-depth exploration of the many-faceted techniques of advertising. Such questions as "To whom is advertising aimed?" and "Why do people buy?" force a reexamination of the pattern of purchasing and consumption of goods and services.

Several instruments to evaluate student growth in terms of the eight value categories were developed both as a part of this project in Coronado and out of dissertation work at United States International University. Four of these are summarized by Simpson (1973). Workshops for the Coronado program are conducted by Bensley and others through Value Education Consultants Clearinghouse, P.O. Box 947, Campbell, CA 95005. Reports of research studies related to the Coronado Plan are also available at prices ranging from $2.50 to $5.00 per report.

Title: HUMAN VALUES IN EDUCATION

Authors: W. Ray Rucker, V. Clyde Arnspiger, and Arthur J. Brodbeck

Publisher: Kendall/Hunt Publishing Co., 2460 Kerper Blvd., Dubuque, IA 52001

Date: 1969

Grade Levels: K-12

Materials and Cost: Teacher's guide ($6.00)

Human Values in Education is the original teacher's text for incorporating the Lasswell-Rucker value framework into the educational program. That framework identifies eight basic values which the authors see as universal human needs: affection, respect, skill, enlightenment, power, wealth, well-being, and rectitude. The goal of this kind of values-oriented instruction is to help students develop these values and "distribute" them among other persons. "Suggested practices," according to the authors, "are designed to contribute increasingly to the wide distribution of human values to all people who accept responsibility for participating in value sharing as the basis of a humanistic way of life." It is believed that participation in achieving wide access to these eight basic values will "contribute to the overriding objective of the free society—the realization of human dignity on a grand scale."

This practice-oriented book is divided into four parts. The first part defines the eight value categories and identifies numerous classroom practices that can contribute to the development and distribution of each value. To share affection, for instance, it is suggested that the teacher should always return a child's friendly greeting. Another is that "children who do not follow practices of fair play on the playground are asked to play alone for awhile." The last chapter of Part I, "A Descriptive Science of Values," outlines a rationale for using this method of value teaching. Topics discussed include the role of values in the social process, the relation between human dignity and child development, and the importance of experiencing alternatives in order to develop values.

The four chapters composing Part II, "The Release of Learning Potential," discuss and describe methods and techniques for promoting discipline and order in the classroom, enhancing self-image through development of the eight human values, analyzing one's past experiences in terms of deprivation or enhancement of those values, and extending this analysis into the appraisal of moods and feelings. Specific case studies of teachers and students and several coding instruments are provided to illustrate these topics.

In the third part, the authors define and illustrate the ways in which the systematic thinking required by this value framework can be incorporated in the process of problem solving. Five types of thinking are identified and stressed: goal (clarification of goal), trend (analysis and appraisal of past events), condition (analysis of relevant existing conditions), projective (estimate of probable future developments), and alternative (creating alternative ways of achieving the goal).

Most of the last part of the book is devoted to explaining and illustrating, with a case study, the prototype of a school that adheres to scheme of value shaping and sharing. Interviews with teachers involved in such a project make up most of Chapter 12. Chapter 13, "Transforming the Individual," focuses on the personality development of children in terms of value deprivation and emphasizes that the goal of a democratic school is to develop "multi-valued individuals" who are endowed with all eight basic values. Procedures and instruments for evaluating growth toward this "multi-valued personality" are discussed and provided in the final chapter.

Title: HUMAN VALUES IN THE CLASSROOM: TEACHING FOR PERSONAL AND SOCIAL GROWTH

Author: Robert C. Hawley

Publisher: Education Research Associates, Box 767, Amherst, MA 01022

Date: 1973

Grade Levels: K-12

Materials and Cost: Teacher's guide ($3.75)

Human Values in the Classroom suggests how teachers can teach basic values such as love, trust, interdependence, dignity, and joy as survival skills. Stressing the need to shift from a competitive, divisive value system to a cooperative, unifying one, the author believes that schools can and should play a significant role in facilitating this change. The teacher's role is to create opportunities in which students may practice and acquire skill in those values and to be a genuine model of the values he or she holds. The ultimate goal of education, according to the author, is to help students achieve "social self-actualization."

The book is divided into three parts. The first discusses briefly the relationship between human values and needs and education. It emphasizes values as survival skills. Maslow's hierarchy of needs is then explained and discussed as a basis for defining personal-social growth.

Part Two presents a sequence of teaching concerns that the author has found useful to consider in planning lessons, units, and programs that focus on teaching human values. Each chapter in this part treats one of the following concerns: orientation ("Why have we all gathered here?"); community-building ("How can we get to know each other better so that we can work together better?"); achievement motivation ("What are our goals?" "What procedures and conditions are needed?"); open communication ("How can we communicate more openly and understand each other better?"); information seeking, gathering, and sharing ("What do we know and what do we want to know?"); value exploration and clarification ("What do we value?" "What choices can we make which will reflect our values?"); and planning for change ("How do we want to change?" "How can we decide which alternatives and which resources to use?" "How can we act on our decisions?"). Each chapter contains general comments and specific suggestions for implementing each step in the sequence of concerns. In Chapter VII, for instance, the author identifies and explains ways to communicate supportively rather than negatively. These include being descriptive rather than evaluative, cooperative rather than controlling, and provisional rather than certain.

"Part Three: Notes on Teaching for Personal and Social Growth" is composed of short essays containing ideas and suggestions on a variety of topics related to teaching human values. These topics are grades and evaluation, discipline and classroom control, utilization of space in the classroom, creative thinking, role playing, the authoritarian personality, and means and end values. The appendices include suggestions for further reading, an instrument for rating the openness of a teacher's communication behavior, and a conversation among teachers and the author concerning experiences in applying some of the techniques described in the book.

Title: VALUES: LANGUAGE ARTS

Author: Richard B. Hargraves

Publisher: Division of Instruction, Dade County Public Schools, Miami, FL (available only through ERIC—see Materials and Cost below)

Date: 1971

Grade Levels: 7-12

Materials and Cost: Curriculum guide available only from ERIC Document Reproduction Service, Box 190, Arlington, VA 22210 (order ED 064 738: microfiche—$.76, xerography—$1.95 plus postage)

Values: Language Arts is a junior and senior high school curriculum guide for a nine-week course aimed at helping the student identify, understand, and develop a personal value system. After examining a wide range of pertinent literature, the student should be able to synthesize various concepts and modes that the author feels are beneficial in the establishment of one's own system of values. The purpose, according to the author, is not to attempt to regiment student moral behavior, but rather to present through literature "models for study and emulation" that will motivate students to develop "an acceptable code of ethical conduct." The authors recognize that such a code should contain certain universal values that serve as guides to conduct in our society. Nine performance objectives for the course are given: (1) "the consideration of a positive self-concept"; (2) "the differentiation between tolerant and intolerant acts"; (3) "the investigation of the role of mental preparedness"; (4) "the generalization of the importance of freedom based on personal independence"; (5) "the synthesization of the concept [of] justice based on truth and reconciliation"; (6) "the demonstration of a developing awareness of aesthetics"; (7) "the identification of the variables of good and evil"; (8) "the examination of the role of religion"; and (9) "the proposal of reasons for attaining social tranquility fostered by peace and nonviolence."

Each week's study focuses on one of the nine performance objectives. Suggested learning activities include reading, viewing films, taking field trips, completing value sheets, role playing, discussing, and participating in projects. There are at least seven of these various activities, and sometimes as many as 22, for each of the nine objectives, allowing teachers to choose those suitable to the interests, needs, and abilities of their own particular students. Various literary works, including *Siddhartha, Raisin in the Sun, Walden,* and *Anne Frank: The Diary of a Young Girl,* are suggested as possible course readings. In addition, a major portion of the course outline is composed of a listing of student and teacher resource materials for possible use with the course.

Title: VALUING IN THE FAMILY: A WORKSHOP GUIDE FOR PARENTS

Authors: Herbert O. Brayer and Zella W. Cleary

Publisher: Pennant Educational Materials, 4680 Alvarado Canyon Rd., San Diego, CA 92120

Date: 1972

Grade Levels: K-12

Materials and Cost: Parent's/teacher's guide ($3.95)

Valuing in the Family is a workshop guide appropriate for use with teachers and, especially, parents. "It is designed to help parents implement the valuing process in the home, encouraging respect and self-esteem in family relations." Although intended to aid parents in understanding their children's needs and in devising methods to meet those needs, the guide also included methods through which parents can better understand themselves. Structured in cookbook fashion, the book is intended for busy parents who need ready access to a reference but do not want to be burdened with theory. The purpose of the guide is to help parents begin new patterns of communication and activity with their children. The authors do not believe that a complete change of family procedure is required, but they emphasize ways parents can utilize ordinary, daily family contact to develop mutual affection and respect.

The book contains nine chapters, eight of which focus on the values identified by Rucker and his colleagues (Rucker *et al.* 1969). The introductory chapter discusses the guidelines and problems encountered by the authors in conducting family drug abuse workshops using this valuing approach. Chapter Two, "Affection," deals with ways to establish and maintain a deep sense of emotional security, caring, love, and congeniality in all phases of individual and group life. "Respect," Chapter Three, lists ways of achieving a recognized social role and self-esteem without fear of undeserved deprivation or penalties from others. Chapter Four, "Enlightenment," suggests methods for providing each child the opportunity to learn, inquire, and discover truth in many everyday situations. Chapter Five, "Skill," is aimed at helping the parents to encourage their children to develop talents to the limits of their ability, both at home and in the community. "Power," Chapter Six, discusses means of participating in and influencing important decision making within the family and when working with others. "Wealth," Chapter Seven, focuses upon getting the young person to understand the economics of life. "Well-Being," the eighth chapter, deals with attainment and maintenance of a high degree of mental and physical health. Finally, "Rectitude" has to do with attitudes and standards of behavior such as honesty, justice, and compassion.

Each chapter consists of an outline of specific activities through which the desired values may be enhanced. For example, to develop the value of power in young people, the parents are urged to allow their children to participate actively "in making important decisions affecting their life in and with the family." These decisions could include family chores, friends, clothes, hobbies, and pets. As children mature, the authors suggest that the range, nature, and importance of their decisions be increased.

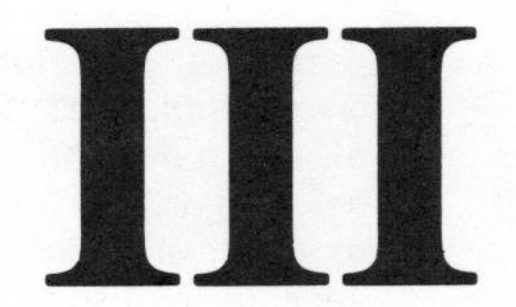

moral development

The moral development approach is based on the theory and research of cognitive developmental psychologists such as Jean Piaget and Lawrence Kohlberg. The first section of this chapter explains this approach by elaborating on its basic rationale, purpose, teaching methods, and instructional model. A sample learning activity from a recent educational project based on Kohlberg's work is also provided. The materials and programs that apply the moral development approach are discussed and analyzed. These include five sets of student materials and four teacher resources.

Explanation of the Approach

Rationale and Purpose. The moral reasoning approach to values education attempts to stimulate students to develop more complex moral reasoning patterns through successive and sequential stages. Proponents of this approach do not use the term *valuing* and do not define the term *values*. The emphasis on reasoning and thinking, however, indicates that values are conceived to be cognitive moral beliefs or concepts. This approach focuses primarily on moral values, such as fairness, justice, equality, and human dignity. Other types of values (social, personal, and aesthetic) are usually not considered.*

Kohlberg's (1966, 1972) theory of moral development is the one most frequently used to provide a rationale for this approach. Expanding on Piaget's (1962) clinical studies of moral judgment in children and conducting his own extensive, cross-cultural research, Kohlberg has formulated a three-level, six-stage theory of the development of moral reasoning:†

> ***Preconventional Level***–At this level the child is responsive to such rules and labels as good or bad and right or wrong. He interprets these labels in purely physical or hedonistic terms: If he is bad, he is punished; if he is good, he is rewarded. He also interprets the labels in terms of the physical power of those who enunciate them—parents, teachers and other adults. The level comprises the following two stages:

*Recently, however, a colleague of Kohlberg, Robert Selman, has postulated a theory of social reasoning ("perspective taking") and has developed curriculum materials to help students progress through four stages of social development (Selman *et at.* 1974). Because this program is similar to programs based on Kohlberg's work and because there are few materials that reflect the moral development approach, the social reasoning resources have been included in this chapter.

†From "Understanding the Hidden Curriculum," by Lawrence Kohlberg with Phillip Whitten. Reprinted by special permission of *Learning, The Magazine for Creative Teaching,* December 1972, © 1972 by Education Today Company, Inc., 530 University Avenue, Palo Alto, California 94301.

Stage 1: *punishment and obedience orientation*. The physical consequences of action determine its goodness or badness regardless of the human meaning or value of these consequences. Avoidance of punishment and unquestioning deference to power are valued in their own right, not in terms of respect for an underlying moral order supported by punishment and authority, the latter being stage 4.

Stage 2: *instrumental relativist orientation*. Right action consists of that which instrumentally satisfies one's own needs and occasionally the needs of others. Human relations are viewed in terms similar to those of the marketplace. Elements of fairness, of reciprocity and equal sharing are present, but they are always interpreted in a pragmatic way. Reciprocity is a matter of "you scratch my back and I'll scratch yours," not of loyalty, gratitude or justice.

Conventional Level–At this level maintaining the expectations of the individual's family, group or nation is perceived as valuable in its own right, regardless of immediate and obvious consequences. The attitude is one not only of conformity to the social order but of loyalty to it, of actively maintaining, supporting and justifying the order, and of identifying with the persons or group involved in it. This level comprises the following two stages:

Stage 3: *interpersonal concordance or "good boy-nice girl" orientation*. Good behavior is that which pleases or helps others and is approved by them. There is much conformity to stereotypical images of what is majority or "natural" behavior. Behavior is frequently judged by intention: "He means well" becomes important, and one earns approval by "being nice."

Stage 4: *"law and order" orientation*. Authority, fixed rules and the maintenance of the social order are valued. Right behavior consists of doing one's duty, showing respect for authority and maintaining the social order for its own sake.

Postconventional Level–At this level there is a clear effort to reach a personal definition of moral values—to define principles that have validity and application apart from the authority of groups or persons and apart from the individual's own identification with these groups. This level again has two stages:

Stage 5: *social-contract legalistic orientation*. Generally, this stage has utilitarian overtones. Right action tends to be defined in terms of general individual rights and in terms of standards that have been critically examined and agreed upon by the whole society. There is a clear awareness of the importance of personal values and opinions and a corresponding emphasis on procedural rules for reaching consensus. Other than that which is constitutionally and democratically agreed upon, right is a matter of personal values and opinion. The result is an emphasis both upon the "legal point of view" and upon the possibility of making rational and socially desirable changes in the law, rather than freezing it as in "law and order" stage 4. Outside the legal realm, free agreement is the binding element of obligation. This is the "official" morality of the U. S. government and the Constitution.

Stage 6: *universal ethical-principle orientation*. Right is defined by the conscience in accord with self-chosen ethical principles, which in turn are based on logical comprehensiveness, universality and consistency. These principles are abstract and ethical (the golden rule, the categorical imperative); they are not concrete moral rules like the Ten Commandments. At heart, these are universal principles of justice, of the reciprocity and equality of human rights, and of respect for the dignity of human beings as individual persons.

Kohlberg has identified 25 "basic moral concepts" that he uses as the foundations for formulating hypothetical moral dilemmas posed to research subjects. Kohlberg's (1966, pp. 8-9) explication of how a child at each stage would define one of these concepts (the "value of human life") clarifies the differences among his six stages:

Stage 1: The value of a human life is confused with the value of physical objects and is based on the social status or physical attributes of its possessor.

Stage 2: The value of a human life is seen as instrumental to the satisfaction of the needs of its possessors or of other persons.

Stage 3: The value of a human life is based on the empathy and affection of family members and others towards its possessor.

Stage 4: Life is conceived as sacred in terms of its place in a categorical moral or religious order of rights and duties.

Stage 5: Life is valued both in terms of its relation to community welfare and in terms of life being a universal human right.

Stage 6: Belief in the sacredness of human life as representing a universal human value of respect for the individual.

Several other theorists, such as Bull (1969) and Perry (1970), have posited similar schemes of moral development. These, however, have not been applied as directly to education as has Kohlberg's theory, and they will not be considered here. Moreover, regardless of the specific differences among these theorists, they share with Kohlberg several common beliefs about the nature of moral development:

1) There exist structural bases within each person that determine how he or she will perceive a value.
2) These bases develop in a sequential series of stages. No stage may be skipped.
3) Some persons go faster and farther through the stages than others.
4) Movement from stage to stage is a long-term process. Progression is not automatic, but dependent upon the person's interaction with the environment.
5) The general direction of this movement is from no morality to social morality to autonomous morality.
6) All persons in all cultures develop through these stages.
7) Moral reasoning is related to moral behavior.*

In addition to these beliefs, Kohlberg contends that students can comprehend reasoning patterns one stage below and one stage above their own level and that exposure to the next higher stage of moral reasoning is essential for enhancing moral development. Furthermore, Kohlberg (1966, p.19) contends that movement from one stage to another involves not instilling an external value (as in inculcation) but encouraging the formation of value patterns toward which the students are already tending.

The view of human nature reflected in the rationale for this approach seems to be similar to that manifested in the ideas of Erikson, Loevinger, and other developmental psychologists.† In contrast to the inculcation approach, the moral development approach views the person as an active initiator and a reactor within the context of his or her environment. The individual cannot fully change the environment, but neither can the environment fully mold the individual. A person's actions are the result of his or her feelings, thoughts, behaviors, and experiences. Although the environment can determine the content of one's experiences, it cannot determine its form. Genetic structures already inside the person are primarily responsible for the way in which a person internalizes that content, and organizes and transforms it into personally meaningful data.††

Teaching Methods. The technique most characteristic of the moral development approach is to present a hypothetical or factual value dilemma story which is then

*Some of these contentions are disputed by other psychologists, especially those of a non-developmental orientation. Specifically, contentions 6 and 7 are the most controversial, but 2 has also been criticized as too rigid.

†These theorists postulate that human growth occurs in sequential stages of development. Some psychologists have attempted to formulate developmental theories of the entire personality. Such theorists are usually termed *ego development theorists*. Sullivan *et al.* (1957) and Loevinger *et al.* (1970) are examples. Other developmental psychologists seem to have concentrated on specific aspects of human growth: Piaget (Inhelder and Piaget 1958)—intellectual development; Erikson (1950)—psycho-sexual development; Harvey, Hunt, and Schroder (1961)—conceptual development; and Peck and Havighurst (1960)—character development. Those theorists who have concentrated on value development have been called moral development theorists, and these include McDougall (1908), Piaget (1962), Kohlberg (1966), and W. G. Perry (1970).

††Generally, this view of human nature can be termed *interactive*, in contrast to *reactive* or *active* conceptions of the person. The moral development theory of human nature, however, can be distinguished from the interactive conception of human nature which underlies the action learning approach to values education (see Chapter VI). Although interaction between person and environment is seen as fundamental in both conceptions, the moral development theory can conceive of the person, with his or her innate cognitive and moral structures, as separate from the environment or society. The theories underlying the action learning approach, on the other hand, contend that the person can not be defined out of his or her environmental or societal context.

discussed in small groups. Through a short reading, filmstrip, or film, students are presented with a story involving one or more characters confronted with a moral dilemma. Students are urged to state a position on what the person in the story should do, to provide reasons for this position, and to discuss these reasons with others. Kohlberg's research indicates that exposing students to higher levels of reasoning through group discussion stimulates them to reach the next stage of moral development.

Galbraith and Jones (1975) have experimented with many moral dilemma exercises in the classroom as part of a project at Carnegie-Mellon University. They have concluded that three variables are crucial to an effective group discussion of a moral dilemma, and thus, to the enhancement of moral development in students. These are (1) a story that presents "a real conflict for the central character," includes "a number of moral issues for consideration," and "generates differences of opinion among students about the appropriate response to the situation"; (2) "a leader who can help to focus the discussion on moral reasoning"; and (3) "a classroom climate which encourages students to express their moral reasoning freely" (Galbraith and Jones 1975, p. 18).

Instructional Model. A sequential instructional model to help teachers use this approach to values education has also been formulated in the Carnegie-Mellon project. The version presented below has been adapted from Galbraith and Jones (1975, pp. 19-22):

1) *Confronting a moral dilemma*
   a) Introduce the dilemma.
   b) Help students to define the terms used in the dilemma.
   c) State the nature of the dilemma.

2) *Stating a position on the original or alternative dilemma*
   a) Help students establish their individual positions on the action.
   b) Establish the class response to the position on the action. (If there is not enough conflict, introduce an alternative dilemma.)
   c) Help students establish the reasons for their individual positions.

3) *Testing the reasoning for a position on the moral dilemma*
   a) Select an appropriate strategy for grouping the students (small groups consisting of students who agree on the action but for different reasons or small groups of students who do not agree on the action).
   b) Help students examine individual reasons with the group or class.
   c) Ask probe questions to elicit additional reasoning about the moral problem or to focus on a particular issue involved in the dilemma.
   d) Examine reasons as they relate to the probe questions.

4) *Reflecting on the reasoning*
   a) Ask students to summarize the different reasons that they have heard.
   b) Encourage the students to choose the reason that they feel represents the best response to the moral dilemma.
   c) Ask students if they believe there is a best answer for this problem.
   d) Add any additional reasons that did not occur from student discussions; these should be added not as the "best" reasons but as additional reasons to ponder.

Illustrative Learning Activity. This activity has been adapted and condensed from Galbraith and Jones (1975, pp.18-21). The teacher hands out a short reading entitled "Helga's Dilemma" and introduces it in such a way that it relates to recent classwork. The students read the passage.

HELGA'S DILEMMA

Helga and Rachel had grown up together. They were best friends despite the fact that Helga's family was Christian and Rachel's was Jewish. For many years, this religious difference didn't seem to matter much in Germany, but after Hitler seized power, the situation changed. Hitler required Jews to wear armbands with the Star of David on them. He began to encourage his followers to destroy the property of Jewish people and to beat them on the street. Finally, he began to arrest Jews and deport

> them. Rumors went around the city that many Jews were being killed. Hiding Jews for whom the Gestapo (Hitler's secret police) was looking was a serious crime and violated a law of the German government.
>
> One night Helga heard a knock at the door. When she opened it, she found Rachel on the step huddled in a dark coat. Quickly Rachel stepped inside. She had been to a meeting, she said, and when she returned home, she had found Gestapo members all around her house. Her parents and brothers had already been taken away. Knowing her fate if the Gestapo caught her, Rachel ran to her old friend's house.
>
> Now what should Helga do? If she turned Rachel away, the Gestapo would eventually find her. Helga knew that most of the Jews who were sent away had been killed, and she didn't want her best friend to share that fate. But hiding the Jews broke the law. Helga would risk her own security and that of her family if she tried to hide Rachel. But she had a tiny room behind the chimney on the third floor where Rachel might be safe.
>
> Question: Should Helga hide Rachel?

The teacher helps students to define terms that might need explanation. Then he or she helps the class to establish the nature of the dilemma (Should Helga hide her long-time Jewish friend, Rachel, from the Nazi Gestapo or turn her away?). The students are then asked what Helga should do and why. Some may believe Helga should hide her friend; others may believe she should turn Rachel over to the Gestapo. Students may also disagree about the reasons, while agreeing about the action. For example, one student might believe that Helga should tell the Nazis because she might get into trouble if she doesn't (this is Stage 2 reasoning). Another might support the same action because Helga has an obligation to protect her family (Stage 3) or to obey the laws of the government (Stage 4).

The teacher then divides the class into several discussion groups, each composed of members who agree on Helga's action but disagree on the reasons. The teacher moves from group to group to facilitate discussion and to keep the focus on moral reasoning rather than on less important details. In order to do this, the teacher might propose alternative dilemmas. (For example, suppose Helga had only met Rachel once and did not know her well. What should she do then?) Or the teacher could pose other probe questions such as, Should a person ever risk the welfare of relatives for the welfare of friends? Why? Through discussion and reflection, students are encouraged to express a reasonable value position rather that to come to a consensus by adopting other points of view. "When a good moral discussion class ends," wrote Galbraith and Jones (1975, p. 15), "students should feel that it is incomplete. They should leave the classroom still wondering about the best response to a difficult moral problem."

This sample lesson has been condensed for the purposes of illustration. Educators interested in using the moral development approach should consult the materials cited in the next section.

Materials and Programs. Efforts to implement the moral development approach began as part of several research studies including one by Blatt (1969). His original curriculum, used in Sunday schools and public high schools, consisted of a battery of written moral dilemmas and a few probe questions to stimulate thought. Recent curriculum development in this area has produced more effective use of other media, including films, filmstrips, and records. The approach has also been implemented at the elementary level and in some prison education programs as well (Kohlberg *et al.* 1973). A recent effort has been established by the Center for Moral Development and Education at Harvard University to coordinate communication among those involved in teaching and research in moral education. In addition to publishing a newsletter, *Developmental Moral Education,* the Center has instituted an attempt to create a National Consortium in Moral Education to help establish various moral education centers and project clusters throughout North America.

A concise review of materials and programs based on Kohlberg's theory of moral reasoning is presented by Rest (1974, pp. 250-51):

> Kohlberg and his students have made a

> number of additional innovations which have extended the original program ideas and materials . . . A moral education course for college undergraduates included not only the discussion-of-dilemmas format but also readings and discussions of classic moral philosophers . . . , thus extending the resources available in the curriculum . . . The Moral Education Project of the Ontario Institute for Studies in Education is an ongoing research and development project for curriculum materials, teaching methods, teacher training, and theory elaboration. This ambitious, broad-gauge enterprise has set up moral education programs in elementary and high schools in Canada and has published books containing many practical suggestions and possible topics and materials for moral education . . .

In the pages that follow, we have analyzed nine moral development resources. *First things: Values* (Guidance Associates), a filmstrip series for elementary students, was the first published set of student materials directly based on Kohlberg's work. This was followed by *First Things: Social Reasoning* (Guidance Associates), curriculum materials based on the theory of social reasoning ("perspective thinking") developed by a colleague of Kohlberg, Robert Selman. Both of these resources contain teacher training components. In addition to these materials, the recently revised version of the *Holt Social Studies Curriculum* (Holt, Rinehart, and Winston) has incorporated moral dilemma objectives and activities based on Kohlberg's theory, as well as some values clarification goals and questions. *Photo Study Cards: Meaning and Values* (Greenhaven Press) also uses both the moral development and clarification approaches. Because of the lack of materials reflecting the former approach and a multitude of clarification resources, these analyses have been included in this chapter. Similarly, *Moral Reasoning,* one of the unit booklets of the *Public Issues Series* (Xerox), is included in this chapter since it also focuses on moral reasoning.

The teacher resources analyzed include *How to Assess the Moral Reasoning of Students* (Porter and Taylor 1972), a guide to evaluating moral development; *Getting It Together* (Mattox 1975), a guidebook for leading group discussions of moral dilemmas; and the teacher training kits that accompany *First Things.* A training manual for teaching the Kohlberg moral dilemmas has been developed at Carnegie-Mellon University. This work has not been analyzed because the final version was not available in time. The training manual will be completed and published by Greenhaven Press early in 1976.

moral development: student materials

Curriculum: FIRST THINGS: SOCIAL REASONING

Titles: *How Can You Work Things Out?; How Would You Feel?; How Do You Know What's Fair?; How Do You Know What Others Will Do?;* and *A Strategy for Teaching Social Reasoning*

Developers: Robert L. Selman, Diane F. Byrne, and Lawrence Kohlberg

Publisher: Guidance Associates, 757 Third Ave., New York, NY 10017

Date: 1974

Grade Levels: 1-5

Materials and Cost: 5 audiovisual kits, each including filmstrips, records or cassettes, and teacher's guide (with records—$19.50 each, with cassettes—$21.50 each)

First Things: Social Reasoning is a series of sound-filmstrip programs designed to help elementary students improve and use their ability to reason about social interactions. The programs are based on the psychological theory that a child's ability to reason develops through a sequence of universal stages. According to Selman, as a child reaches each new stage of social reasoning, he or she develops a new theory about the nature of people and human interactions. The new theory greatly influences his or her social awareness, social judgment, social ability, and social maturity. The primary goals of this set of materials are to encourage the development of social reasoning through four perspective-taking levels and to encourage humane, fair, and considerate use of higher levels of reasoning. The objective for *How Can You Work Things Out?* is to help children understand perspective-taking as a key factor in communication. *How Do You Know What's Fair?* is intended to help students employ perspective taking as a means of resolving ethical problems. In *How Would You Feel?* children are encouraged to recognize and honor the feelings of others. To help children predict behavior by analyzing the thoughts, feelings, and motives of others is the objective of *How Do You Know What Others Will Do?*

Each of the four student programs includes two filmstrips that present open-ended social dilemmas with which elementary students can identify. The areas covered by the dilemmas are solving social problems, understanding others' feelings, making fair decisions, and communicating and persuading. For example, in one of the dilemmas a boy is feeling sorrow over his lost dog and his friend can not decide whether a new puppy will make a good birthday gift or an inappropriate one. The filmstrip character provides reasons for making his choice—reasons that children can add to and discuss.

Teacher training for *First Things: Social Reasoning* is provided in a separate program, *A Strategy for Teaching Social Reasoning,* which is analyzed in the Teacher Materials section of this chapter.

Fieldtesting was done both before and after the kits were published. Results of the first fieldtest are available; those of the second are forthcoming. The materials were also evaluated in a pilot study by Robert Enright (for further information, contact Enright at N 548 Elliott Hall, University of Minnesota, Minneapolis, MN 55455). The results will be published within a year. Preliminary examination of the data suggests that sixth-grade students who have participated in discussions related to these filmstrips and to other similar dilemmas have progressed in social reasoning more than control group students. Since the experimental treatment consisted of several other activities, one cannot conclude that the *Social Reasoning* materials were primarily responsible for that growth.

DESCRIPTIVE CHARACTERISTICS

Grade Level

X K-3
X 4-6
___ 7-8
___ 9-10
___ 11-12

Materials

___ Student materials
X Teacher guide
X A-V kit
___ Tests
___ Other: ________________

Time

___ Curriculum (2 or more years)
___ Course (one year)
___ Semester (half year)
___ Minicourse (6-9 weeks)
X Units (1-3 weeks)
X Supplementary
___ Other: ________________

Medium Used

___ Readings
___ Worksheets
___ Films
X Filmstrips
X Records or tapes
___ Charts or posters
___ Transparencies
___ Other: ________________

PRECONDITIONS

Amount of Reading

___ Much
___ Moderate
X Very little

Teacher Training

X Provided in materials
___ Suggested by developers
___ Not mentioned
___ Other: ________________

Prejudice/Stereotyping

Much evidence = M
Some evidence = S

___ Racial or Ethnic
___ Sexrole
___ Other: ________________

EVALUATION INFORMATION

Provision for Student Evaluation

___ Instruments specified
___ Procedures specified
___ Guidelines suggested
X Nothing provided
___ Other: ________________

Materials Evaluation

Materials tested = T
Results available = A

A Fieldtested before publication
T Fieldtested after publication
T User feedback solicited
T Other: Pilot study
___ Not evaluated

SUBSTANTIVE CHARACTERISTICS

Values Education Approach

___ Inculcation
X Moral development
___ Analysis
___ Clarification
___ Action learning
___ Other: ________________

Values Education Emphasis

X Major focus
___ One of several concerns
___ A minor concern

Process/Content Emphasis

X Process of valuing
X Content of valuing

Objectives

___ Stated specifically
X Stated generally
___ Not stated

Student Activities

Used or stressed frequently = F
Used or stressed occasionally = O

___ Reading
___ Writing
O Class discussion
F Small-group discussion
___ Games
___ Simulations
F Role playing
___ Action projects
___ Other: ________________

Curriculum: FIRST THINGS: VALUES

Titles: *The Trouble with Truth; That's No Fair!; You Promised!; But It Isn't Your. . .; What Do You Do about Rules?;* and *A Strategy for Teaching Values*

Developers: Lawrence Kohlberg and Robert Selman

Publisher: Guidance Associates, 757 Third Ave. New York, NY 10017

Date: 1972

Grade Levels: 1-5

Materials and Cost: 6 audiovisual kits, each including filmstrips, records or cassette tapes, and teacher's guide (with records—$19.50 each, with cassettes—$21.50 each)

First Things: Values is a series of six sound filmstrips designed to help elementary students reason about moral issues. The rationale is based on Kohlberg's research on moral development and the series stresses the importance of having good reasons for moral actions. Since this research has indicated "that the most effective way to develop moral reasoning involves the use of open-ended dilemmas," the developers believe that sustained, spontaneous discussion of such dilemmas, which elicit reasoning from various stages, will help students move to higher stages of moral development

Each unit contains two moral dilemmas and focuses on a topic of importance to elementary students—keeping promises, telling the truth, respecting property rights, sharing, taking turns, and understanding the reasons for rules. Students are asked to make their own moral choices for resolving each dilemma. In the first situation of each unit, filmstrip characters present reasons for and against the choices they make in a dilemma—reasons that reflect different stages of moral development and that students can evaluate in addition to presenting their own reasons. The second dilemma is presented without providing reasons; the children must develop their own justification for making personal moral choices. For example, in *The Trouble with Truth,* Debbie can have a birthday visit to the fair if she says she is a year younger. The students consider whether she should lie or tell the truth.

Special teacher training for using these materials is provided in a unit accompanying these materials, *A Strategy for Teaching Values*. (See the Teacher Materials section of this chapter for an analysis of this inservice training component.) The materials do not, however, provide any help for evaluating student progress. One instrument that is available to help measure growth in terms of Kohlberg's stages of moral development is the guide produced by the Ontario Institute for Studies in Education, called *How to Assess the Moral Reasoning of Students* (Porter and Taylor 1972; analyzed in the Teacher Materials section of this chapter). Another test, "Opinions About Social Problems," has been used in research by James Rest at the University of Minnesota but is not generally available at this time.

First Things: Values was fieldtested before and after publication; the results, both general and favorable, are available from the publisher. In addition, user feedback was solicited through teacher interviews and the materials were further evaluated at the UCLA Curriculum Inquiry Center. The Bay Area Media Evaluation Guild has stated that "the children's voices and actions [on the filmstrips] are very real, and children will identify immediately with them." The Educational Facilities Center in Chicago rated the quality of the objectives and content "excellent."

DESCRIPTIVE CHARACTERISTICS

Grade Level

X K-3
X 4-6
___ 7-8
___ 9-10
___ 11-12

Materials

___ Student materials
X Teacher guide
X A-V kit
___ Tests
___ Other: ____________

Time

___ Curriculum (2 or more years)
___ Course (one year)
___ Semester (half year)
___ Minicourse (6-9 weeks)
X Units (1-3 weeks)
X Supplementary
___ Other: ____________

Medium Used

___ Readings
___ Worksheets
___ Films
X Filmstrips
X Records or tapes
___ Charts or posters
___ Transparencies
___ Other: ____________

PRECONDITIONS

Amount of Reading

___ Much
___ Moderate
X Very little

Teacher Training

X Provided in materials
___ Suggested by developers
___ Not mentioned
___ Other: ____________

Prejudice/Stereotyping

Much evidence = M
Some evidence = S

___ Racial or Ethnic
___ Sexrole
___ Other: ____________

EVALUATION INFORMATION

Provision for Student Evaluation

___ Instruments specified
___ Procedures specified
___ Guidelines suggested
___ Nothing provided
X Other: Available elsewhere

Materials Evaluation

Materials tested = T
Results available = A

A Fieldtested before publication
A Fieldtested after publication
T User feedback solicited
A Other: Critical review
___ Not evaluated

SUBSTANTIVE CHARACTERISTICS

Values Education Approach

___ Inculcation
X Moral development
___ Analysis
___ Clarification
___ Action learning
___ Other: ____________

Values Education Emphasis

X Major focus
___ One of several concerns
___ A minor concern

Process/Content Emphasis

X Process of valuing
X Content of valuing

Objectives

___ Stated specifically
___ Stated generally
X Not stated

Student Activities

Used or stressed frequently = F
Used or stressed occasionally = O

___ Reading
___ Writing
O Class discussion
F Small-group discussion
___ Games
___ Simulations
___ Role playing
___ Action projects
___ Other: ____________

Curriculum: HOLT SOCIAL STUDIES CURRICULUM

Titles: *Comparative Political Systems; Comparative Economic Systems; The Shaping of Western Society; Tradition and Change in Four Societies; A New History of the United States; The Humanities in Three Cities; Introduction to the Behavioral Sciences*

General Editor: Edwin Fenton

Publisher: Holt, Rinehart and Winston, Inc., 383 Madison Ave., New York, NY 10017

Dates: 1969-75

Grade Levels: 9-12

Materials and Cost: For each title, student text ($4.95-$8.82 each); teacher's guide ($2.85-$4.95 each); multimedia kit including filmstrips, records, class handouts, student activity components, student readings, transparencies, testing program, and teacher-training filmstrip ($112.50-$180.00 each)

The *Holt Social Studies Curriculum* was developed by the Carnegie-Mellon University Social Studies Project. The program consists of seven courses, each including five components: a textbook developed around readings and pictures; audiovisual materials; a detailed teacher's guide; a testing program; and an individual and group activity component. The overall objective of the program is to help students develop their abilities to think independently and to realize their responsibilities as citizens. More specifically, the materials are designed to help students (1) develop a constructive attitude toward learning; (2) acquire a positive self-concept; (3) value; (4) develop learning skills; (5) develop inquiry skills: and (6) attain knowledge. For each lesson these objectives are stated even more specifically. For example, in *The Shaping of Western Society*, the lesson on "Nazism in Practice" has the following valuing objectives: "to state one's position on a value question and offer reasons for adopting that position" and "to test one's own position on a value question by responding to arguments made by other students."

The content of the curriculum is based upon a conceptual pyramid. At the highest level are universal concepts such as culture and society. Forming the second level are concepts such as social system and political system. The third level contains more specific concepts, including social class, cultural change, and decision making. Each course in the curriculum is based on this pyramid. In the ninth-grade course students compare the political and economic systems of primitive and traditional societies, the United States, and the Soviet Union. The two tenth-grade programs focus on world history and the effects on four countries of political change, economic development, race relation, and urbanization. United States history is the subject of study for the 11th-grade course, while 12th-grade students study the humanities and the behavioral sciences.

Lessons are organized around student readings and class discussion. Students read two or more case studies in which social or personal values are often at issue. The teacher asks directed questions, suggested in the teacher's guide, in order to bring the issue into focus. Students must make decisions after examining the facts and their own feelings. A variety of activities are suggested to supplement the lessons. The moral development approach is reflected in the use of value dilemmas patterned after those of Kohlberg. The teacher's guides include brief explanations of the teaching of moral dilemmas as well as typical responses at each level for the dilemmas presented. Student activities that reflect the clarification approach are also included. For example, students are asked to clarify and state their positions on "the value of human life when national honor is involved."

Student tests, provided on duplicating masters, are primarily designed to evaluate progress in learning inquiry skills and content mastery. Occasionally, students will be asked in essay exams "to make judgments or to clarify their attitudes toward a controversial issue." A teacher training component is provided for each course in the form of a sound-filmstrip. In some cases, additional readings are also suggested. The pilot editions of the curriculum were fieldtested in classrooms using seven different testing devices. In the area of content mastery and general skill development, measured by standardized tests, these materials did not have a significantly greater effect than other materials. However, in the development of social studies inquiry skills, this curriculum proved to be much more effective than other materials. Results are provided in *Final Report: A High School Social Studies Curriculum for Able Students: Project Numbers HS-041 and H-292,* available through the ERIC system (ED 030 672). The latest revisions of the materials are based upon informal feedback gathered over a period of four years.

DESCRIPTIVE CHARACTERISTICS

Grade Level

__ K-3
__ 4-6
__ 7-8
X 9-10
X 11-12

Materials

X Student materials
X Teacher guide
X A-V kit
X Tests
__ Other: ________

Time

X Curriculum (2 or more years)
__ Course (one year)
__ Semester (half year)
__ Minicourse (6-9 weeks)
__ Units (1-3 weeks)
__ Supplementary
__ Other: ________

Medium Used

X Readings
X Worksheets
__ Films
X Filmstrips
X Records or tapes
X Charts or posters
X Transparencies
X Other: Activity books

PRECONDITIONS

Amount of Reading

X Much
__ Moderate
__ Very little

Teacher Training

X Provided in materials
__ Suggested by developers
__ Not mentioned
__ Other: ________

Prejudice/Stereotyping

Much evidence = M
Some evidence = S

__ Racial or Ethnic
__ Sexrole
__ Other: ________

EVALUATION INFORMATION

Provision for Student Evaluation

X Instruments specified
__ Procedures specified
__ Guidelines suggested
__ Nothing provided
__ Other: ________

Materials Evaluation

Materials tested = T
Results available = A

A Fieldtested before publication
__ Fieldtested after publication
T User feedback solicited
__ Other: ________
__ Not evaluated

SUBSTANTIVE CHARACTERISTICS

Values Education Approach

__ Inculcation
X Moral development
__ Analysis
X Clarification
__ Action learning
__ Other: ________

Values Education Emphasis

__ Major focus
X One of several concerns
__ A minor concern

Process/Content Emphasis

X Process of valuing
__ Content of valuing

Objectives

X Stated specifically
__ Stated generally
__ Not stated

Student Activities

Used or stressed frequently = F
Used or stressed occasionally = O

F Reading
O Writing
F Class discussion
O Small-group discussion
__ Games
__ Simulations
O Role playing
O Action projects
__ Other: ________

Title: MORAL REASONING: THE VALUE OF LIFE *(Public Issues Series)*

Author: Alan Lockwood

Publisher: Xerox Education Publications, Education Center, Columbus, OH 43216

Date: 1972

Grade Levels; 9-12

Materials and Cost: Student text ($.50); teacher's guide (free with purchase of 10 or more student books)

Moral Reasoning: The Value of Life, a part of the *Public Issues Series,* consists of dilemmas and discussion questions designed to help students ''formulate, clarify, and justify [their] thinking about the value of life in general and the value of life in difficult conflict situations.'' The material does not provide a set of closed solutions to current social ills or persisting historical problems. Rather, it is intended to challenge the student to formulate his or her own positions and choose courses of action suitable for citizens in a free society.

The content of this booklet is developed around the question, ''What is the value of life [and] under what circumstances, if any, is it right to take a life?'' The student is presented with a number of factual and fictional moral dilemmas and with specific discussion questions related to the situation. These dilemmas include the practice of allowing babies with major physical deficiencies to die, the Eskimo practice of leaving old people to die, capital punishment, and the killing of baby seals. The author states that, as students peruse the material and discuss the dilemmas, they confront values of life that seem to be in conflict with such values as obedience to law and authority, family obligations, political loyalties, and cultural diversity.

Many opportunities are provided for individuals to express preferences in relationship to a given dilemma and explain why that choice was made. One section of the book briefly explains Kohlberg's theory of moral development. The teacher's role is one of facilitating class discussions and aiding students with any difficulties encountered. A teacher's guide accompanies the student book and discusses Kohlberg's theory of moral development and its application in the classroom.

Although no formal student evaluation materials are provided, questions at the end of each selection may be used to check students' understanding and/or serve as a springboard for discussing the material. Informal prepublication fieldtesting was done. Due to the nature of the tests, however, results are not available.

DESCRIPTIVE CHARACTERISTICS

Grade Level

__ K-3
__ 4-6
__ 7-8
X 9-10
X 11-12

Materials

X Student materials
X Teacher guide
__ A-V kit
__ Tests
__ Other: ________

Time

__ Curriculum (2 or more years)
__ Course (one year)
__ Semester (half year)
__ Minicourse (6-9 weeks)
X Units (1-3 weeks)
__ Supplementary
__ Other: ________

Medium Used

X Readings
__ Worksheets
__ Films
__ Filmstrips
__ Records or tapes
__ Charts or posters
__ Transparencies
__ Other: ________

PRECONDITIONS

Amount of Reading

X Much
__ Moderate
__ Very little

Teacher Training

__ Provided in materials
__ Suggested by developers
X Not mentioned
__ Other: ________

Prejudice/Stereotyping

Much evidence = M
Some evidence = S

__ Racial or Ethnic
__ Sexrole
__ Other: ________

EVALUATION INFORMATION

Provision for Student Evaluation

__ Instruments specified
__ Procedures specified
__ Guidelines suggested
X Nothing provided
__ Other: ________

Materials Evaluation

Materials tested = T
Results available = A

T Fieldtested before publication
__ Fieldtested after publication
T User feedback solicited
__ Other: ________
__ Not evaluated

SUBSTANTIVE CHARACTERISTICS

Values Education Approach

__ Inculcation
X Moral development
X Analysis
__ Clarification
__ Action learning
__ Other: ________

Values Education Emphasis

X Major focus
__ One of several concerns
__ A minor concern

Process/Content Emphasis

X Process of valuing
__ Content of valuing

Objectives

X Stated specifically
__ Stated generally
__ Not stated

Student Activities

Used or stressed frequently = F
Used or stressed occasionally = O

F Reading
__ Writing
F Class discussion
__ Small-group discussion
__ Games
__ Simulations
__ Role playing
__ Action projects
__ Other: ________

Title: PHOTO STUDY CARDS: MEANING AND VALUES

Authors: David Bender and Gary McCuen

Publisher: Greenhaven Press, Inc., Box 831, Anoka, MN 55303

Date: 1974

Grade Levels: 8-12

Materials and Cost Kit: Five different Photo Study Cards: 10 or more copies of single Photo Study Card ($1.65 per copy); 5 to 9 copies of single Photo Study Card ($1.95 per copy). (Option A—kit containing 35 student copies of each of the 5 Photo Study Cards and teacher's guide for each card ($57.75); Option B—kit containing 18 student copies of each of the 5 Photo Study Cards and teacher's guide for each card ($29.70).

The Photo Study Cards are designed to "help students clarify their values through analyzing and comparing photos that present different and often conflicting values." The authors feel such materials are needed because of the rapid social change in our society and the current challenges to traditional values. They feel young people today are seeking meaning and purpose for their own lives. Objectives include the clarification of values, feelings, and attitudes, and the advancement to higher stages of moral reasoning. The program therefore reflects the theories of both Lawrence Kohlberg and Sidney Simon.

The five different photo cards are entitled "Who Are You?", "Who Would You Like to Be?", "What Do You Value?", "You and Authority," and "You and Social Responsibility." Each card has pictures and activities on both sides. Photographs depict scenes ranging from John and Jacquelyn Kennedy playing with Caroline to the burning of South Vietnamese Buddhists. The front side of each card deals with affective behavior—clarifying values, feelings, and attitudes. Students examine powerful photographs that portray values in conflict. Open-ended questions for class discussion related to the photos are provided. The reverse side of each card deals with cognitive behavior—moral reasoning. Most of the activities on this side involve moral dilemmas with no right or wrong solutions. Students working individually or in small groups are asked to make a decision and examine the reasoning behind their decision.

Each activity includes simple, concise instructions. The teacher's role is one of facilitating discussion. In the teacher's guide there is a brief summary of Kohlberg's six stages of moral reasoning as well as suggestions for classroom applications. A key correlating student responses for many of the activities with the six stages is also included. No teacher training is mentioned. However, the authors suggest that teachers unfamiliar with Kohlberg's theory should study his ideas carefully before using the materials in the classroom. A bibliography for this purpose is included in the teacher's guide.

There has been no systematic fieldtesting of the materials before or after publication. User feedback has been solicited at professional conferences, but no results are available. A favorable review in *Media & Methods* (April 1975) stated that the photographs stimulate student enthusiasm and discussion.

DESCRIPTIVE CHARACTERISTICS

Grade Level

- ___ K-3
- ___ 4-6
- X 7-8
- X 9-10
- X 11-12

Materials

- X Student materials
- X Teacher guide
- ___ A-V kit
- ___ Tests
- ___ Other: ______

Time

- ___ Curriculum (2 or more years)
- ___ Course (one year)
- ___ Semester (half year)
- ___ Minicourse (6-9 weeks)
- X Units (1-3 weeks)
- X Supplementary
- ___ Other: 4-5 week course

Medium Used

- ___ Readings
- ___ Worksheets
- ___ Films
- ___ Filmstrips
- ___ Records or tapes
- X Charts or posters
- ___ Transparencies
- ___ Other: ______

PRECONDITIONS

Amount of Reading

- ___ Much
- X Moderate
- ___ Very little

Teacher Training

- ___ Provided in materials
- ___ Suggested by developers
- X Not mentioned
- ___ Other: ______

Prejudice/Stereotyping

Much evidence = M
Some evidence = S

- ___ Racial or Ethnic
- ___ Sexrole
- ___ Other: ______

EVALUATION INFORMATION

Provision for Student Evaluation

- ___ Instruments specified
- ___ Procedures specified
- ___ Guidelines suggested
- X Nothing provided
- ___ Other: ______

Materials Evaluation

Materials tested = T
Results available = A

- ___ Fieldtested before publication
- ___ Fieldtested after publication
- T User feedback solicited
- A Other: Critical review
- ___ Not evaluated

SUBSTANTIVE CHARACTERISTICS

Values Education Approach

- ___ Inculcation
- X Moral development
- ___ Analysis
- X Clarification
- ___ Action learning
- ___ Other: ______

Values Education Emphasis

- X Major focus
- ___ One of several concerns
- ___ A minor concern

Process/Content Emphasis

- X Process of valuing
- ___ Content of valuing

Objectives

- ___ Stated specifically
- X Stated generally
- ___ Not stated

Student Activities

Used or stressed frequently = F
Used or stressed occasionally = O

- O Reading
- O Writing
- F Class discussion
- F Small-group discussion
- ___ Games
- ___ Simulations
- ___ Role playing
- ___ Action projects
- ___ Other: ______

moral development: teacher materials

Title: GETTING IT TOGETHER: DILEMMAS FOR THE CLASSROOM

Author: Beverly A. Mattox

Publisher: Pennant Educational Materials, 4680 Alvarado Canyon Rd., San Diego, CA 92120

Date: 1975

Grade Levels: 1-12

Materials and Cost: Teacher's guide ($3.95)

Getting It Together is designed "to provide the working-level educator with an understanding of what the Kohlberg approach is and how to use it in the classroom." The author intends this paperback to serve as a starting point for working with Kohlberg's moral development approach to values education. In a brief introduction, Kohlberg's theory is outlined, based on the following ideas: morality develops in stages; everyone passes through the same stages of moral development; moral reasoning is related to behavior; and discussion is needed for moral growth. Brief descriptions of the orientation of each stage in the theory are listed for stages one through six, respectively: "avoid punishment," "self-benefit," "acceptance by others," "maintain the social order," "contract fulfillment," and "ethical principle." The author states that moral education is relevant for today's students since it can help them "discover what is meaningful to them, how values influence their actions, and the importance of decision-making based upon careful examination of issues." She feels that, ideally, moral education will encourage and equip individual students to function at the level of morality to which each has grown.

The first three chapters provide a brief introduction to the Kohlberg approach, list reasons for moral education, and discuss the opportunities moral education affords educators. In the fourth chapter, Kohlberg's stages of moral development are explained, along with the four factors that influence decision making at each stage. These factors are identified as the rules, pragmatic, justice, and conscience orientations. In addition, the author cites Kohlberg's exploration of a seventh stage, one which might be viewed as having a faith orientation. According to the author, this stage describes a modification to a wider view of life in which the emphasis is on the cosmos rather than the individual. Stage seven "entails unity with an independent reality beyond the self and a resolution to the ultimate questions of life and death." (This seventh stage seems similar to the union approach to values education discussed in Chapter VII of this book.) Chapter 5 describes various teaching techniques to develop moral awareness: dilemma, fish-bowl discussion, simulation, and role play. The teacher's role and classroom climate are topics covered in Chapter 6. The seventh and eighth chapters present 45 classroom dilemmas classified as primary, elementary, or secondary level, and the ninth chapter provides suggestions for students and teachers interested in writing their own dilemmas. In Chapter 10, the author presents a brief comment on the future.

Title: HOW TO ASSESS THE MORAL REASONING OF STUDENTS

Authors: Nancy Porter and Nancy Taylor

Publisher: Ontario Institute for Studies in Education, 252 Bloor St. West, Toronto 5, Ontario, Canada

Date: 1972

Grade Levels: 4-12

Materials and Cost: Teacher's guide ($1.95)

How to Assess the Moral Reasoning of Students is a teacher's guide for determining the stage of moral development of students according to Kohlberg's theory. As a result of work on moral development at the Ontario Institute's Moral Education Project, the authors felt a strong need to provide teachers with "a reliable method for measuring the degree of moral development reached by their students." To meet this need, the authors modified Kohlberg's original research questionnaire and devised guidelines to use it. The authors believe that although the book would be of greatest use in a course on moral philosophy, it could also be incorporated into social studies, English, science, and health classes.

The introduction briefly explains Kohlberg's six-stage theory of moral development, drawing implications for education. The next section offers guidelines for using moral dilemma stories that compose the Kohlberg questionnaire and for scoring student responses. Suggestions for using the instrument with elementary and secondary students are provided, in addition to a numerical scoring system for interpreting the responses. The final section of the book contains five of Kohlberg's original nine stories for which the scoring system is most highly developed. The stories involve value conflicts such as stealing a drug to save the life of a close relative, mercy killing, reporting an escaped convict who had rehabilitated himself, giving up earned money, and gaining money under false pretenses.

After each story there are approximately seven questions that students answer through discussion or writing. An explanation with sample responses showing how persons at each of the six stages would react to each story is also provided in the guide. In the story about mercy killing, for instance, one of the questions asked is, "Should the doctor do what a patient asks and give her the drug that will make her die? Why?" A Stage 1 response would be, "No, her death might be blamed on him. He could be charged with murder." This demonstrates the Stage 1 tendency to reason in terms of punishment and obedience. A Stage 4 response, on the other hand, might be, "No, because even if he knew that the lady was suffering terribly I don't think anyone should be given the right to take a human life." This reflects the Stage 4 tendency to appeal to rules relevant to the situation.

Title: A STRATEGY FOR TEACHING SOCIAL REASONING

Developers: Robert L. Selman, Diane F. Byrne, and Lawrence Kohlberg

Publisher: Guidance Associates, 757 Third Ave., New York, NY 10017

Date: 1974

Grade Levels: 1-5

Materials and Cost: Audiovisual kit including teacher's guide, 2 filmstrips, and 1 record or cassette (with record—$19.00, with cassette—$21.50)

A Strategy for Teaching Social Reasoning is an inservice training unit that elaborates the basic theory upon which the curriculum series *First Things: Social Reasoning* is based. The series, composed of four sound-filmstrip units for elementary students and one unit for teacher training, clearly reflects the moral development approach to values education and was designed "to help children develop and use their ability to reason about social interactions." (See Student Materials section of this chapter for analysis of these student materials.) The filmstrips and teacher's guide present background information in social development theory and developmental psychology and advise teachers about running effective classroom discussion groups.

Part 1, "The Strategy," deals with the theory behind the series and shows some areas of behavior in the classroom that are affected by levels of social reasoning. It is intended that, with this knowledge, primary teachers can learn to use the principles of developmental psychology outlined in the teacher's guide "to encourage pupils to think about others both in the context of the filmstrip dilemmas and in other areas of classroom life." For example, in one section, entitled "Theoretical Background," Selman and Byrne's research in social development—the theoretical underpinning of the entire series—is discussed. Their research has focused on perspective-taking ability—the way children reason about their social experience—and has revealed four different levels that characterize the different types of perspectives children take: egocentric (about ages four to six), informational (about ages six to eight), self-reflective (about ages eight to ten), and mutual (about ages ten to twelve). According to the researchers, these perspective-taking abilities affect a child's development of social concepts. A child's movement from one level to another is "thought to occur through two basic mechanisms—conceptual conflict and exposure to reasoning one level above the child's own level." Such movement requires a long-term process and it occurs only when children have a firm command of the level of reasoning.

Part 2 describes the teacher's role: "to arrange for conditions that encourage open peer discussions, to keep the discussions going and keep them challenging, and to encourage children to take the point of view of each character in the story." Suggestions for implementing discussion include modeling a discussion for the class, breaking the class into small groups, balancing sides, challenging ideas, and keeping discussion relevant. Role playing is examined as a classroom technique and teachers are encouraged to provide follow-up activities.

Title: A STRATEGY FOR TEACHING VALUES

Author: Thomas Lickonia, with consultants Lawrence Kohlberg and Robert Selman

Publisher: Guidance Associates, 757 Third Ave., New York, NY 10017

Date: 1972

Grade Levels: 1-5

Materials and Cost: Audiovisual kit including discussion guide, 3 filmstrips, and 2 records or cassettes (with records— $19.00, with cassettes—$21.50.)

A Strategy for Teaching Values is an inservice training unit with sound-filmstrips "demonstrating optimum application for the *First Things: Values* series," a program designed to help elementary students more adequately develop their moral reasoning by discussing open-ended dilemmas. (See the Student Materials section of this chapter for the analysis of these materials.) The three parts of *Strategy* explain to teachers, counselors, administrators, and parents the moral development approach to values education and show some practical ways to apply it.

Part 1, "The Strategy," outlines some of the problems of traditional values education and presents, as one solution, Kohlberg's theory. The essential findings of Kohlberg's research are presented as follows: all children's moral reasoning develops through a series of six stages; these stages cannot be skipped; some children go faster and farther through the stages; moral reasoning is related to behavior; moral growth may be viewed as the development of a sense of fairness; and the movement from stage to stage is a long-term process and is not automatic. According to the developers, "the process of moral development can be stimulated by presenting children with moral dilemmas" such as those provided in the series. These dilemmas have no one correct solution; rather they encourage children to seek their own solutions. By thinking through the dilemmas and being exposed to the reasoning of others, the children's moral development will be stimulated. Through this process "children can be helped to progress faster and farther through the stages, helped toward more mature moral reasoning and better resolution of moral problems."

Part 2, "The Teacher's Role," shows how a teacher can apply the theory of moral development to the classroom. In this filmstrip a teacher uses the first part of *You Promised!,* an activity from *First Things: Values,* to stimulate a moral discussion with primary-grade students. The group discussions and the teacher's comments are provided. Suggestions are listed to help teachers facilitate small-group discussion. These include selecting discussion groups with care, focusing on reasons, encouraging children who are undecided, teaching the children to teach themselves, keeping the arguments balanced, and modifying the dilemma. The information presented in Part 3, "A Classroom Model," can be used in the classroom or in workshops to make clear the logistics of classroom discussion and debate. It illustrates two methods for discussing a moral dilemma—small-group discussion and debate. Additional questions, workshop suggestions, and filmstrip scripts are also included in the kit.

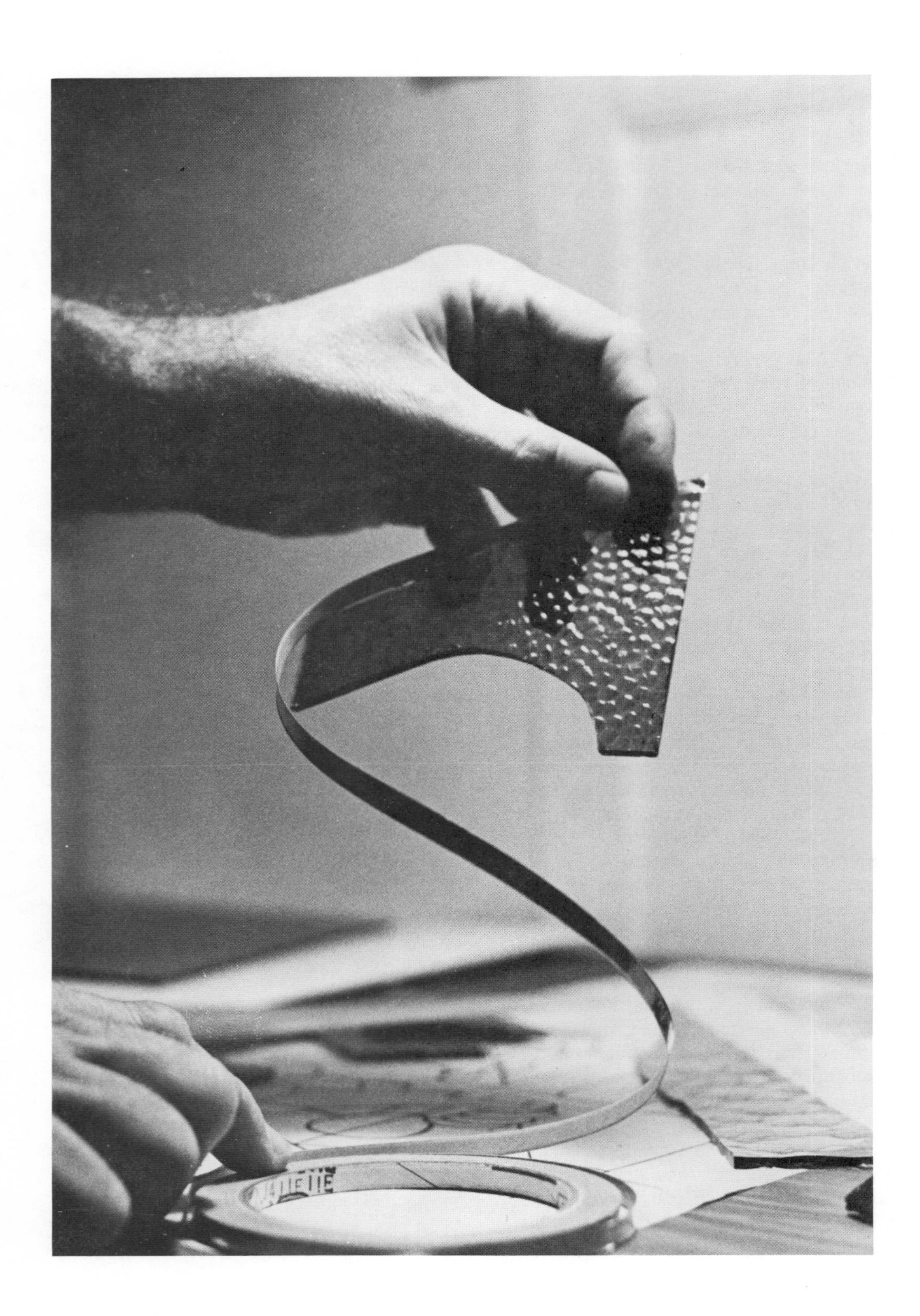

IV

analysis

Analysis is the approach to values education advocated by most of today's leading social science educators, including Hunt, Metcalf, Oliver, Shaver, and Fraenkel. This chapter describes the rationale, purpose, teaching methods, and instructional model of this approach. A sample learning activity is provided to illustrate the use of value analysis in the social studies classroom. Seventeen sets of student materials and six teacher resources are analyzed.

Explanation of the Approach

Rationale and Purpose. The purpose of the analysis approach is to help students use logical thinking and scientific investigation procedures in dealing with value issues. Like moral development, this approach also emphasizes rationality. Students are urged to provide verifiable facts about the goodness or worth of phenomena. Valuing is the cognitive process of determining and justifying those facts. Unlike the moral development approach, value analysis concentrates primarily on social value issues rather than on personal moral dilemmas. Thus, the process of valuing can and should be, according to proponents* of this approach, conducted under the "total authority of facts and reason" (Scriven 1966, p. 232) and "guided not by the dictates of heart and conscience, but by the rules and procedures of logic" (Bond 1970, p. 81).

The human being, viewed from this perspective, is a rational actor in the world who can attain the highest good by subordinating feelings and passions to logic and the scientific method, thereby resolving value issues according to reason and science. The philosophical basis for the analysis approach, therefore, seems to be a fusion of the rationalist and empiricist views of human nature.†

Teaching Methods. The teaching methods most frequently used in the analysis approach to values education are individual and group study of social value problems and issues, library and field research, and rational class discussions

*The rationale for the analysis approach to values education relates directly to the ideas of a group of philosophers, known as axiologists, who engage in the objective study of ethics and morality. These axiologists include Moore (1929), Toulmin (1950), Lewis (1962), Blackham (1968), and Scriven (1966). Other value theorists who have postulated similar views of valuing are R.B. Perry (1954), Pepper (1947, 1958), and Handy (1969).

†This concept of human nature is shared by several cognitively oriented psychotherapists. Ellis' (1962) rational-emotive therapy stresses that a person must merely restructure his or her thinking in order to establish rational behavior patterns. Kelly (1955) emphasizes the need to test one's "personal constructs" (values) empirically and experimentally.

(seminar and Socratic style)—techniques common to social studies instruction. Intellectual operations frequently used in value analysis include stating the issues, questioning and substantiating in the relevance of statements, applying analogous cases to qualify and refine value positions, pointing out logical and empirical inconsistencies in arguments, weighing counterarguments, and seeking and testing evidence (Newmann and Oliver 1970, pp. 293-96).

Many analytical instructional models for teaching values in the social studies classroom have been developed. These include the "reflective value analysis" model of Hunt and Metcalf (1968, p. 134), the "Columbia Associates" model described and applied by Massialas and Cox (1966, p. 163), the "jurisprudential" model advocated and applied by Oliver and Shaver (1966, pp. 126-30), the "value inquiry" model outlined by Banks (1973, pp. 459-66), and the "identifying values" model of Taba (Fraenkel 1973, p. 235). Michaelis (1972) has identified a value analysis model that is a synthesis of the elements common to these valuing models. Some of the models contain aspects reflecting other approaches to values education. Banks' model attempts to incorporate some aspects of the clarification model. All of these models, however, fundamentally embody the analysis approach to values education, with its emphasis on logical thinking and scientific inquiry.

Instructional Model. The model that most clearly reflects this approach is that described in the 41st Yearbook of the National Council for the Social Studies (Metcalf 1971, pp. 29-55). It is summarized below as one possible guide to implementing the value analysis approach:

1) *Identify and clarify the value question:* Call attention to the need to identify the question that is giving rise to discussion about a value issue. Clarify that question by defining terms, by specifying the point of view from which the evaluation is to be made, and by specifying the value object to be judged.

2) *Assemble purported facts:* Help students to gather and organize facts relevant to making a value judgment by insuring that a) value assertions are not mistakenly assembled as part of the body of relevant facts; b) a fairly wide range of facts relevant to judging the value object in question is assembled; and c) fact-gathering is carried out in such a way as not to overwhelm students with the complexity of factual material.

3) *Assess the truth of purported facts:* Encourage students to assess the truth of purported factual assertions by finding supporting evidence and by assessing the source of the purported fact. (Who said this is the case? Why should we believe what this person says?)

4) *Clarify the relevance of facts:* Help students to clarify the relevance of the facts by encouraging them to insure that a) the facts are about the value object in question; and b) the evaluator (student) has criteria (bases) which give the facts a positive or negative valence (desirable or undesirable rating) from the point of view of the value judgment being made.

5) *Arrive at a tentative value decision:* Encourage the student to decide or choose tentatively the answer to the value question.

6) *Test the value principle implied in the decision:* Help students to test the value principle implied in their decision for acceptability in any of the following four ways. a) *New cases test:* Formulate the value principle explicitly, imagine other situations in which it would logically apply, and decide if one can accept its application in these situations. b) *Subsumption test:* Formulate the value principle explicitly and assemble facts (evidence) that show that the value principle is a case of some more general value principle that the evaluator accepts. c) *Role exchange test:* Imaginatively exchange roles with someone else affected by the application of the value principle and consider whether he or she can still

accept the principle as it applies to him or her in this role. d) *Universal consequences test:* Imagine what the consequences would be if everyone in similar circumstances were to engage in the action being evaluated and consider whether one can accept these consequences.

Illustrative Learning Activity. Presented here is an "evidence card" activity which is designed primarily to aid in assessing the relevance of purported facts (Step 4 in the instructional analysis model). This illustration has been adapted from Metcalf (1971, pp. 50-54).*

Some students are trying to decide whether "welfare is a good thing." The teacher can help them literally to "sort out" the problem by using an evidence card activity. To begin, the teacher asks leading questions to help the students identify and clarify the value question: Is it morally wrong for poor people to be supported by public funds through welfare programs? The value object is specified to be "welfare programs" and the point of view is "moral" (as contrasted with aesthetic, economic, or political viewpoints). The students then assemble and assess the truth of purported facts. An evidence card is then used to help determine the relevance of the facts.

The simplest form of an evidence card contains the student's value judgment, his or her fact about the object being evaluated, and the criterion the student has formulated to test the relevance of the fact. A simple form of the evidence card is presented in figure 1. The example in the figure is based on the dilemma discussed above.

The next step is to add a column at the right side of the card to indicate the point of view. In the example described above, the moral point of view is the appropriate one, as indicated in Figure 2.

The next step is to place the specific evidence or backing for the fact on the *back* of the evidence card. There will often be evidence contrary to the fact, and this can also be included. Figure 3 shows this step in the development. Note that the contrary statement brings up the question of what it means to "earn" money.

*From "Teaching Strategies for Value Analysis" by Jerrold R. Coombs and Milton Meux in the 41st *Yearbook Values Education: Rationale, Strategies, and Procedures* edited by Lawrence E. Metcalf, used by permission of the National Council for the Social Studies.

Figure 1. Simple form of evidence card.

Value judgment: Relief is morally wrong.

Fact: Relief gives money to people who haven't earned it.

Criterion: Practices that give money to people who haven't earned it are morally wrong.

Figure 2. Simple form of evidence card with point of view.

	Point of View
Value judgment: Relief is morally wrong.	Moral
Fact: Relief gives money to people who haven't earned it.	
Criterion: Practices that give money to people who haven't earned it are morally wrong.	Moral

Finally, the reasons for and against believing the criterion are placed on the *back* of the evidence card, below the backing and contrary evidence. Examples of such reasons are given in Figure 4. These are, of course, only examples, and the reader may supply his or her own reasons for this case.

Students are then encouraged to weigh their evidence and to make a tentative value decision. Several students might, for example, decide that the evidence supports the criterion—"Practices that give money to people who have not worked for it are morally wrong." Thus, they would conclude that welfare programs are morally wrong.

The teacher next urges the students to test the criteria for their judgments in any of several ways. In order to apply the "new cases test," for instance, the teacher might say, "Some people inherit large amounts of money. They have not worked for it. Is it morally wrong for them to

Figure 3. Back of evidence card, with backing and contrary evidence for fact.

Backing (Positive)	**Contrary (Negative)**
People on relief in Detroit receive $175 per month and have no jobs. People on relief in Chicago get $200 a month and do not have jobs.	Some people on relief work hard even though they don't have a job.

Figure 4. Back of evidence card, with backing and contrary evidence for the facts and reasons for and against the criterion.

Backing (Positive)	**Contrary (Negative)**
People on relief in Detroit receive $175 a month and have no jobs. People on relief in Chicago get $200 a month and do not have jobs.	Some people on relief work hard even though they do not have jobs.
Reasons for believing criterion Such practices lower a person's dignity and self-esteem. Such practices keep a person from trying to improve himself or herself.	**Reasons for not believing criterion** It can't be morally wrong to raise people's standards of living when they are victims of a system over which they have no control.

accept the money?" This should stimulate the students to re-evaluate and refine their criteria and/or judgments.

Materials and Programs. Because the analysis approach to values education is the one most widely advocated by social science educators, it is the approach most frequently embodied in the curriculum materials of the "new social studies." The student materials analyzed in this chapter include major textbook programs, such as *The Taba Program in Social Science* (Addison-Wesley) and *The Social Sciences: Concepts and Values* (Harcourt), and unit booklet series such as *Values and Decisions* (Xerox) and *Opposing Viewpoints* (Greenhaven Press). Other resources, developed by national projects, include *The Analysis of Public Issues Program* (Houghton Mifflin), *Social Science Laboratory Units* (SRA), and *People/Choices/Decisions* (Random House). There are several supplementary kits such as the sound-slide programs from the Center for the Humanities, filmstrip programs from Schloat and Pathescope, and a photography series developed by Scholastic Magazine. Finally, a paperback, *The Moral Imperative* (Alfred Publishing), has been analyzed because of its concrete and systematic development of principles for making rational value judgments.

The teacher resources analyzed in this section include *Values and Youth* (Barr 1971), an anthology of readings which reflects primarily the analysis approach; *Introduction to Value Inquiry* (Nelson 1974), the teacher and student process guide for the *American Values Series* (Hayden); and a self-instructional program that focuses on clarifying value statements in an analytical way (Miller and Vinocur 1972). The National Council for the Social Studies (NCSS) 41st Yearbook, *Values Education* (Metcalf 1971), is also included, as is *Rational Value Decisions and Value Conflict Resolution* (Evans *et al.* 1974), a teacher's handbook for the value analysis model originally explicated in the NCSS Yearbook.

analysis: student materials

Curriculum: AMERICAN VALUES SERIES: CHALLENGES AND CHOICES

Titles: *The Rights of Women; The Environment: A Human Crisis; Dissent and Protest; War and War Prevention; City Life; Urban Growth; Values and Society; Introduction to Value Inquiry: A Student Process Book*

Editor: Jack L. Nelson

Publisher: Hayden Book Company, Inc., 50 Essex St., Rochelle Park, NJ 07662

Date: 1974-75

Grade Levels: 9-12

Materials and Cost: *The Rights of Women, City Life, War and War Prevention, Dissent and Protests, The Environment,* and *Values and Society* ($2.36 each); *Urban Growth* ($2.60); *Introduction to Value Inquiry* (teacher resource, $1.56)

The American Values Series: Challenges and Choices consists of seven books, each dealing with a contemporary American problem. It is the authors' hope that, by raising controversial issues and providing a structure of inquiry, students will develop a questioning attitude toward social issues and make decisions based on facts, value analysis, and projected consequences. All books in the series follow a similar format. Case studies draw attention to a problem and reveal many of its complexities and conflicts. Data banks (short readings, tables, graphs) provide factual material for use in arriving at a decision. Divergent viewpoints show the multiplicity of values and possibilities affecting the issues. Futuristic scenarios enable students to view the future impact of present decisions. Suggestions for student involvement in the community are also provided in each book.

The Rights of Women discusses women from a historical perspective, their status in contemporary society, and the consequences of changes proposed by different groups. *The Environment: A Human Crisis* looks at how planet earth takes care of itself and the problems people cause. It also looks at the environmental options available and possible future effects. *Dissent and Protest* concentrates on anti-war protests, civil disobedience, and the questions of justification and consequences of such behavior. The sociological, economic, historical, and psychological aspects of war and the international agencies that have tried to control and eliminate warfare are examined in *War and War Prevention. City Life* discusses the quality of the city dwellers' lives as they strive to sustain themselves and try to improve their situation, while *Urban Growth* examines how cities start, expand, and are governed and zoned and offers projections for alternative futures.

Values and Society, the final book in the series, focuses on the production of different values by different cultures. In this book students become acquainted with value sources and ways in which values are perpetuated. Various cultures such as the Ik of Uganda and the Swiss are compared with America. Activities include preparing a questionnaire based on the values expressed in the Bill of Rights, using the questionnaire to survey other students and community members, and comparing responses; observing television programs and commercials and noting the values portrayed; and identifying major social institutions of the community (family, school, religious organizations) and conducting interviews with representatives of these institutions.

In addition to the student materials, the series contain a *Student Process Book* (see the Teacher Materials section of this chapter for an analysis of this resource), which can be used as a teacher's guide as well as a medium of transition into the individual unit books.

The series was fieldtested before publication but the results are not available. Although user feedback has been obtained from personal interviews, no data is available.

DESCRIPTIVE CHARACTERISTICS

Grade Level

___ K-3
___ 4-6
___ 7-8
_X_ 9-10
_X_ 11-12

Materials

_X_ Student materials
_X_ Teacher guide
___ A-V kit
___ Tests
___ Other: ________________

Time

___ Curriculum (2 or more years)
_X_ Course (one year)
___ Semester (half year)
___ Minicourse (6-9 weeks)
_X_ Units (1-3 weeks)(each title)
___ Supplementary
___ Other: ________________

Medium Used

_X_ Readings
___ Worksheets
___ Films
___ Filmstrips
___ Records or tapes
___ Charts or posters
___ Transparencies
___ Other: ________________

PRECONDITIONS

Amount of Reading

_X_ Much
___ Moderate
___ Very little

Teacher Training

___ Provided in materials
___ Suggested by developers
_X_ Not mentioned
___ Other: ________________

Prejudice/Stereotyping

Much evidence = M
Some evidence = S

___ Racial or Ethnic
___ Sexrole
___ Other: ________________

EVALUATION INFORMATION

Provision for Student Evaluation

___ Instruments specified
___ Procedures specified
___ Guidelines suggested
_X_ Nothing provided
___ Other: ________________

Materials Evaluation

Materials tested = T
Results available = A

_T_ Fieldtested before publication
___ Fieldtested after publication
_T_ User feedback solicited
___ Other: ________________
___ Not evaluated

SUBSTANTIVE CHARACTERISTICS

Values Education Approach

___ Inculcation
___ Moral development
_X_ Analysis
___ Clarification
___ Action learning
___ Other: ________________

Values Education Emphasis

_X_ Major focus
___ One of several concerns
___ A minor concern

Process/Content Emphasis

_X_ Process of valuing
_X_ Content of valuing

Objectives

___ Stated specifically
___ Stated generally
_X_ Not stated

Student Activities

Used or stressed frequently = F
Used or stressed occasionally = O

_F_ Reading
_O_ Writing
_F_ Class discussion
___ Small-group discussion
___ Games
___ Simulations
___ Role playing
_O_ Action projects
___ Other: ________________

Title: ANALYSIS OF PUBLIC ISSUES PROGRAM

Developers: James P. Shaver and A. Guy Larkins

Publisher: Houghton Mifflin Company, 1 Beacon St., Boston, MA 02107

Date: 1973

Grade Levels: 9-12

Materials and Cost: Student text ($4.80); teacher's guide ($8.97); audiovisual kit ($64.50); duplicating masters ($27.00); problem booklets ($1.65 each)

The *Analysis of Public Issues Program* consists primarily of a student text of readings and a series of problem booklets designed to teach secondary students how to analyze controversial issues critically and rationally. Since the authors believe "that public issues are basically ethical issues—that is, that they involve questions about right or proper aims and actions," the materials focus heavily on values education. Specific objectives reflecting the analysis approach are provided for each "bundle" or series of lessons. One of the objectives for "Bundle Nineteen," for example, is "when asked to take a stand on a political-ethical dispute, the student will state his (or her) position as being contingent on relevant factual information."

The content of the program is based on concepts related to making ethical decisions about public issues. These concepts, outlined extensively in the teacher's guide, emphasize the role of language, facts, and values in making a decision about a particular issue. The value concepts are based on three premises: that "political-ethical decisions are usually justified in terms of the values they will support"; that value conflicts take place "not only between individuals, but within the frames of reference of individuals"; and that "when faced with a political-ethical decision, there are rational ways of choosing the value or values to be supported." Included in the student text are short case studies and value dilemma episodes on a variety of social and personal issues. These deal with such conflicts as the right to representation versus respect for authority, unreasonable laws versus respect for the law, law and order versus human dignity and equality, and friendship and respect for life versus mercy killing.

The accompanying problem booklets contain articles that discuss topics such as the environment, women's rights, students' rights, the riots of the sixties, the relationship between police and Blacks, and the Indian in American history and contemporary society. The teacher facilitates class discussion on these topics using three teaching modes, recitation, socratic, and seminar. Students are frequently required to infer the values underlying a given dilemma, to determine the type of value conflict involved, and to resolve that conflict by investigating factual claims, clarifying any language problems, appealing to a higher third value, or analyzing analogous cases.

Tests are provided in the problem booklets and in a packet of duplicating masters. The tests consist primarily of objective items measuring students' learning of the major value concepts. No evaluative data concerning the effectiveness of the published program with high school students is available. The final report on the project (Shaver and Larkins 1969) that developed the materials, however, can be obtained from ERIC (ED 037 475).

DESCRIPTIVE CHARACTERISTICS

Grade Level

___ K-3
___ 4-6
___ 7-8
_X_ 9-10
_X_ 11-12

Materials

_X_ Student materials
_X_ Teacher guide
_X_ A-V kit
_X_ Tests
___ Other: ____________

Time

___ Curriculum (2 or more years)
_X_ Course (one year)
_X_ Semester (half year)
___ Minicourse (6-9 weeks)
___ Units (1-3 weeks)
___ Supplementary
___ Other: ____________

Medium Used

_X_ Readings
_X_ Worksheets
___ Films
_X_ Filmstrips
_X_ Records or tapes
___ Charts or posters
_X_ Transparencies
___ Other: ____________

PRECONDITIONS

Amount of Reading

_X_ Much
___ Moderate
___ Very little

Teacher Training

___ Provided in materials
___ Suggested by developers
_X_ Not mentioned
___ Other: ____________

Prejudice/Stereotyping

Much evidence = M
Some evidence = S

___ Racial or Ethnic
___ Sexrole
___ Other: ____________

EVALUATION INFORMATION

Provision for Student Evaluation

_X_ Instruments specified
_X_ Procedures specified
___ Guidelines suggested
___ Nothing provided
___ Other: ____________

Materials Evaluation

Materials tested = T
Results available = A

_A_ Fieldtested before publication
___ Fieldtested after publication
___ User feedback solicited
___ Other: ____________
___ Not evaluated

SUBSTANTIVE CHARACTERISTICS

Values Education Approach

___ Inculcation
___ Moral development
_X_ Analysis
___ Clarification
___ Action learning
___ Other: ____________

Values Education Emphasis

_X_ Major focus
___ One of several concerns
___ A minor concern

Process/Content Emphasis

_X_ Process of valuing
___ Content of valuing

Objectives

_X_ Stated specifically
___ Stated generally
___ Not stated

Student Activities

Used or stressed frequently = F
Used or stressed occasionally = O

_F_ Reading
_F_ Writing
_F_ Class discussion
___ Small-group discussion
___ Games
___ Simulations
_O_ Role playing
___ Action projects
___ Other: ____________

Title: I AM THE MAYOR

Authors: Donna S. Allender and Jerome S. Allender

Publisher: Temple University, Center for the Study of Federalism, Philadelphia, PA 19122

Date: 1971

Grade Levels: 4-7

Materials and Cost: 36 folders including student and teacher materials ($35.00). (According to the author, the materials will soon be available from a commercial publisher at a lower price. For further information, contact the Center for the Study of Federalism at Temple University.)

I Am the Mayor is an individualized activity that focuses on city government. Designed to involve intermediate students in the process of inquiry, the major objective is for students to analyze problems and make a decision based on rational examination of a situation. This process includes sensing the problems, formulating questions, searching for information, and finally, making a decision. Each child is given the opportunity to act as an individual and to work at his or her own pace.

Each student who participates in the activity plays the role of the mayor. The student materials are divided into four parts. "The Mayor's Work" consists of letters, phone calls, and reports, each of which call for decision making in relation to an issue such as planting trees, a safety program, building a factory, or repairing city streets. "The Mayor's Questions" and "The Mayor's Files" help the student focus on an issue and find information relevant to it. There are six to ten sets of questions for each issue. Each question leads to a specific file or to a particular piece of information within the files. The files also include city maps, plans, laws, and history, as well as calendars, general information, records and reports of city departments, and financial and budgeting information. An index is provided to help students use this data bank. Finally, in "The Mayor's Decision," there are suggestions for making different types of decisions—doing nothing, getting more information, or taking immediate action—and suggested alternatives for the decision chosen. There are no correct solutions for an issue and it is suggested that teachers give full consideration to each child's choice. However, the teacher should encourage each mayor to defend his or her decision and the rationale behind it.

The materials were fieldtested in classroom and learning center environments over a period of three years. The results are available in a U.S. Office of Education report entitled *The Teaching of Inquiry Skills to Elementary School Children.* This 177-page report is available through the ERIC system (ED 020 805). One finding of that study was that students' inquiry activity increased comparably in both teacher-directed and student-directed settings. The researchers concluded, therefore, "that the teacher was unnecessary [when using *I Am the Mayor*] except to organize the environment and lead discussions when asked."

DESCRIPTIVE CHARACTERISTICS

Grade Level

___ K-3
_X_ 4-6
_X_ 7-8
___ 9-10
___ 11-12

Materials

_X_ Student materials
_X_ Teacher guide
___ A-V kit
___ Tests
___ Other: ________________

Time

___ Curriculum (2 or more years)
___ Course (one year)
___ Semester (half year)
___ Minicourse (6-9 weeks)
_X_ Units (1-3 weeks)
_X_ Supplementary
___ Other: ________________

Medium Used

_X_ Readings
_X_ Worksheets
___ Films
___ Filmstrips
___ Records or tapes
___ Charts or posters
___ Transparencies
___ Other: ________________

PRECONDITIONS

Amount of Reading

_X_ Much
___ Moderate
___ Very little

Teacher Training

___ Provided in materials
___ Suggested by developers
_X_ Not mentioned
___ Other: ________________

Prejudice/Stereotyping

Much evidence = M
Some evidence = S

___ Racial or Ethnic
___ Sexrole
___ Other: ________________

EVALUATION INFORMATION

Provision for Student Evaluation

___ Instruments specified
___ Procedures specified
___ Guidelines suggested
_X_ Nothing provided
___ Other: ________________

Materials Evaluation

Materials tested = T
Results available = A

_A_ Fieldtested before publication
___ Fieldtested after publication
___ User feedback solicited
___ Other: ________________
___ Not evaluated

SUBSTANTIVE CHARACTERISTICS

Values Education Approach

___ Inculcation
___ Moral development
_X_ Analysis
___ Clarification
___ Action learning
___ Other: ________________

Values Education Emphasis

___ Major focus
_X_ One of several concerns
___ A minor concern

Process/Content Emphasis

_X_ Process of valuing
___ Content of valuing

Objectives

___ Stated specifically
_X_ Stated generally
___ Not stated

Student Activities

Used or stressed frequently = F
Used or stressed occasionally = O

_F_ Reading
___ Writing
_O_ Class discussion
___ Small-group discussion
___ Games
_F_ Simulations
___ Role playing
___ Action projects
___ Other: ________________

Title: IMAGES OF MAN I & II

Editor: Sheila Turner

Series Coordinator: Cornell Capa

Publisher: Scholastic Magazines, Inc., School Division, 904 Sylvan Ave., Englewood Cliffs, NJ 07632

Dates: 1972, 1973

Grade Levels: 7-12

Materials and Cost: For each program: audiovisual kit including 4 sound-filmstrips, teacher's guide, and packet of 11'' x 14'' photo reproductions (with records—$75.00; with cassettes—$83.00). Also available as slide/cassette units ($175.00 for all 4 or $50.00 each)

Images of Man is a Concerned Photography Program for secondary students. Based on the works and personal narration of eight well-known photojournalists, the program explores universal themes and underlying values of the human experience. The materials attempt to show things that the photographers feel should be appreciated, as well as things that should be corrected. Using the photographs to arouse social conscience, students will learn to analyze social issues and to deal with questions of values.

The detailed teacher's guide offers suggestions for using the materials in English, social studies, art, and communications classes. The actual content focuses on social issues, social values, and the human experience. War, death, poverty, racial conflict, population, technology, loneliness, and what it means to be civilized are some of the subjects of the first program. The second program deals with everyday life in America—the preservation of the natural environment, lifestyles and values of a variety of traditional cultures, and human emotions. Suggested activities include discussions, written essays, individual or group photo essays, role playing, and a variety of other projects. Through discussion and activities suggested in the teacher's guide, students analyze thoughts, feelings, and values of the photographers and their subjects.

No formal fieldtesting of the programs has been done. However, user feedback is being formally solicited through a questionnaire included in *Images of Man II*. The results have not yet been collated. A preliminary examination of this feedback indicates that the program is being used largely in English and social studies courses in grades 10-12. In addition, unsolicited letters from students and teachers have been favorable. *Images of Man* received a ''Maxi'' award from the readers of *Media & Methods* magazine. This award is given each year to producers of outstanding instructional materials. The program has also been analyzed and evaluated by M. Frances Klein and Louise L. Tyler for the Curriculum Inquiry Center at UCLA. These two educators state that the content is potentially powerful but that the materials lack specification of objectives and evaluation procedures. They conclude, therefore, that *Images of Man* ''has the potential of being a significant learning program for students, but . . . that further development of it is needed.''

DESCRIPTIVE CHARACTERISTICS

Grade Level

___ K-3
___ 4-6
_X_ 7-8
_X_ 9-10
_X_ 11-12

Materials

___ Student materials
_X_ Teacher guide
_X_ A-V kit
___ Tests
___ Other: ________________

Time

___ Curriculum (2 or more years)
___ Course (one year)
___ Semester (half year)
___ Minicourse (6-9 weeks)
___ Units (1-3 weeks)
_X_ Supplementary
___ Other: ________________

Medium Used

___ Readings
___ Worksheets
___ Films
___ Filmstrips
_X_ Records or tapes
_X_ Charts or posters
___ Transparencies
_X_ Other: Photographs

PRECONDITIONS

Amount of Reading

___ Much
___ Moderate
_X_ Very little

Teacher Training

___ Provided in materials
___ Suggested by developers
_X_ Not mentioned
___ Other: ________________

Prejudice/Stereotyping

Much evidence = M
Some evidence = S

___ Racial or Ethnic
___ Sexrole
___ Other: ________________

EVALUATION INFORMATION

Provision for Student Evaluation

___ Instruments specified
___ Procedures specified
___ Guidelines suggested
_X_ Nothing provided
___ Other: ________________

Materials Evaluation

Materials tested = T
Results available = A

___ Fieldtested before publication
___ Fieldtested after publication
_T_ User feedback solicited
_A_ Other: Critical review
___ Not evaluated

SUBSTANTIVE CHARACTERISTICS

Values Education Approach

___ Inculcation
___ Moral development
_X_ Analysis
___ Clarification
___ Action learning
___ Other: ________________

Values Education Emphasis

___ Major focus
_X_ One of several concerns
___ A minor concern

Process/Content Emphasis

_X_ Process of valuing
_X_ Content of valuing

Objectives

___ Stated specifically
___ Stated generally
_X_ Not stated

Student Activities

Used or stressed frequently = F
Used or stressed occasionally = O

___ Reading
_F_ Writing
_F_ Class discussion
_O_ Small-group discussion
___ Games
___ Simulations
_O_ Role playing
_F_ Action projects
___ Other: ________________

Title: LAW AND JUSTICE FOR INTERMEDIATE GRADES: MAKING VALUE DECISIONS

Publisher: Pathescope Educational Films, Inc., 71 Weyman Ave., New Rochelle, NY 10802

Date: 1973

Grade Levels: 4-8

Materials and Cost: Audiovisual kit including 3 filmstrips and teacher's guide (with records—$44.00; with cassettes—$50.00)

The filmstrips in *Law and Justice for Intermediate Grades* were designed to involve students in problems basic to law and justice at a level appropriate to their understanding and range of experience. The analysis approach to values education is emphasized. The materials introduce social issues that are important in the area of law but require personal decisions based on facts and values. The program attempts to develop student inquiry and decision-making skills and to give students practice in looking for evidence. Specific objectives are given for each of the filmstrips. These include "to understand what is meant by the presumption of innocence and the importance of this presumption," "to achieve a better understanding of the possible conflict between personal loyalties and the law," and "to achieve a better understanding of the factors that enter into making an objective decision."

The three filmstrips deal with legal problems and personal decisions. They are open ended and encourage inquiry, presenting provocative questions at various points during the filmstrip when dilemmas or value issues arise. The first story is about a young boy who is wrongly accused of stealing. Questions focus on whether he should have been presumed innocent until proven guilty, what kind of proof was needed to clear him, how the students would have felt if they had been the ones who mistakenly accused him, and how the accused boy would have felt. The point is made that things are not always as they seem to be at first glance and that it is important to get all the facts. The second story deals with conflicting loyalties and the third with the concepts of bias and equal opportunity. All three emphasize the need to look at situations objectively before making decisions.

Suggested projects involve debating an issue or writing about a personal experience related to the dilemma presented in the filmstrip. The major folow-up activity, however, is discussion. Questions that focus directly on the issue at hand are suggested in the teacher's guide. This guide also includes objectives, a summary of the content, and the narration of each filmstrip. The program is intended for use in a social studies class or in a guidance program.

The materials have not been evaluated or fieldtested.

DESCRIPTIVE CHARACTERISTICS

Grade Level

__ K-3
X 4-6
X 7-8
__ 9-10
__ 11-12

Materials

__ Student materials
X Teacher guide
X A-V kit
__ Tests
__ Other: ________

Time

__ Curriculum (2 or more years)
__ Course (one year)
__ Semester (half year)
__ Minicourse (6-9 weeks)
X Units (1-3 weeks)
X Supplementary
__ Other: ________

Medium Used

__ Readings
__ Worksheets
__ Films
X Filmstrips
X Records or tapes
__ Charts or posters
__ Transparencies
__ Other: ________

PRECONDITIONS

Amount of Reading

__ Much
__ Moderate
X Very little

Teacher Training

__ Provided in materials
__ Suggested by developers
X Not mentioned
__ Other: ________

Prejudice/Stereotyping

Much evidence = M
Some evidence = S

__ Racial or Ethnic
__ Sexrole
__ Other: ________

EVALUATION INFORMATION

Provision for Student Evaluation

__ Instruments specified
__ Procedures specified
__ Guidelines suggested
X Nothing provided
__ Other: ________

Materials Evaluation

Materials tested = T
Results available = A

__ Fieldtested before publication
__ Fieldtested after publication
__ User feedback solicited
__ Other: ________
X Not evaluated

SUBSTANTIVE CHARACTERISTICS

Values Education Approach

__ Inculcation
__ Moral development
X Analysis
__ Clarification
__ Action learning
__ Other: ________

Values Education Emphasis

X Major focus
__ One of several concerns
__ A minor concern

Process/Content Emphasis

X Process of valuing
__ Content of valuing

Objectives

X Stated specifically
__ Stated generally
__ Not stated

Student Activities

Used or stressed frequently = F
Used or stressed occasionally = O

__ Reading
O Writing
F Class discussion
__ Small-group discussion
__ Games
__ Simulations
__ Role playing
__ Action projects
__ Other: ________

Title: LAW AND ORDER: VALUES IN CRISIS

Author: Linda Tooni

Publisher: Warren Schloat Productions, Inc., 150 White Plains Rd., Tarrytown, NY 10591

Date: 1971

Grade Levels: 9-12

Materials and Cost: Audiovisual kit including 6 sound-filmstrips and teacher's guide (with records—$120, with cassettes—$138)

Law and Order: Values in Crisis is a multimedia program dealing with the nature of law, values, justice, order, and dissent in America. In the rationale the author notes the divisive forces threatening the existing laws of our society. The program encourages students to analyze objectively the conflicting values behind these forces. According to the author, students also need to examine the values upon which our legal system is based and to relate these to contemporary conflicts.

The content focuses on how social values are reflected in the laws a culture creates and how society is affected if those values change. There are six filmstrips in the series. The first, dealing with the fundamental functions of law, points out how different laws arise from different values, using several primitive societies as examples. It demonstrates how the laws of a society uphold the principles of behavior most important to that society. Next, the series looks at the sources of the values upon which our legal system is based, particularly the belief in human rights and the value of dissent. These are traced to their earliest origins through the Greeks, the Romans, the English, and the Hebrews. The third filmstrip focuses on the present and examines current value conflicts regarding equal rights, personal property, social welfare, patriotism, and wartime atrocities. Part Four, "Strategies for Value Change: Nonviolent Dissent," considers the philosophies of John Quincy Adams, Thomas Jefferson, Henry David Thoreau, Mahatma Ghandi, and Martin Luther King. Value conflicts that produce violent responses, such as the rioting in ghettos and on campuses in recent years, are the subject of the next filmstrip. The question of whether violence is a basic human drive is examined and opposing theories are presented. Concluding the series is "Peoples Park: A Case Study in Value Conflict," depicting the 1969 Berkeley campus confrontation. Each filmstrip is summarized and the narrative is included in the teachers guide, along with questions for review and discussion. Follow-up activities including skits, debates, visual presentations, research projects, essays, further reading, and community action projects are suggested.

According to the publisher, the material was informally tested prior to publication. In addition, a small sample of user feedback was gathered. The results, however, are not available.

DESCRIPTIVE CHARACTERISTICS

Grade Level

___ K-3
___ 4-6
___ 7-8
_X_ 9-10
_X_ 11-12

Materials

___ Student materials
_X_ Teacher guide
_X_ A-V kit
___ Tests
___ Other: ______________

Time

___ Curriculum (2 or more years)
___ Course (one year)
___ Semester (half year)
___ Minicourse (6-9 weeks)
_X_ Units (1-3 weeks)
_X_ Supplementary
___ Other: ______________

Medium Used

___ Readings
___ Worksheets
___ Films
_X_ Filmstrips
_X_ Records or tapes
___ Charts or posters
___ Transparencies
___ Other: ______________

PRECONDITIONS

Amount of Reading

___ Much
_X_ Moderate
___ Very little

Teacher Training

___ Provided in materials
___ Suggested by developers
_X_ Not mentioned
___ Other: ______________

Prejudice/Stereotyping

Much evidence = M
Some evidence = S

___ Racial or Ethnic
___ Sexrole
___ Other: ______________

EVALUATION INFORMATION

Provision for Student Evaluation

___ Instruments specified
___ Procedures specified
___ Guidelines suggested
_X_ Nothing provided
___ Other: ______________

Materials Evaluation

Materials tested = T
Results available = A

_T_ Fieldtested before publication
___ Fieldtested after publication
_T_ User feedback solicited
___ Other: ______________
___ Not evaluated

SUBSTANTIVE CHARACTERISTICS

Values Education Approach

___ Inculcation
___ Moral development
_X_ Analysis
___ Clarification
___ Action learning
___ Other: ______________

Values Education Emphasis

_X_ Major focus
___ One of several concerns
___ A minor concern

Process/Content Emphasis

___ Process of valuing
_X_ Content of valuing

Objectives

___ Stated specifically
___ Stated generally
_X_ Not stated

Student Activities

Used or stressed frequently = F
Used or stressed occasionally = O

_O_ Reading
_O_ Writing
_F_ Class discussion
___ Small-group discussion
___ Games
___ Simulations
_O_ Role playing
_O_ Action projects
_O_ Other: Research

Title: MORAL DILEMMAS OF AMERICAN PRESIDENTS: THE AGONY OF DECISION

Publisher: Pathescope Educational Films, Inc., 71 Weyman Ave., New Rochelle, NY 10802

Date: 1974

Grade Levels: 10-12

Materials and Cost: Audiovisual kit containing 5 sound-filmstrips and teacher's guide (with records—$75.00; with cassettes—$85.00)

Moral Dilemmas of American Presidents: The Agony of Decision is a program intended to place secondary students in a position to understand the "awesome responsibility" a president faces when making crucial decisions affecting the lives of people in the nation and the world. These materials, reflecting the analysis approach to values education, attempt to develop inquiry skills and to give students practice in making decisions by considering facts, alternatives, possible consequences, and value positions.

The program may be used to accompany courses in United States history, political science, international studies, or decision making. Each of the five filmstrips presents a critical social or political issue. Included are the following: (1) Abraham Lincoln's position on slavery and the issue of the Civil War; (2) William H. McKinley and the issue of imperialism versus democratic principles in the case of the annexation of the Philippines; (3) Woodrow Wilson and the League of Nations on the issue of compromise versus sticking to one's principles; (4) Harry S. Truman and the issues of Communism and war in Korea; and (5) John F. Kennedy and the Cuban missile crisis. The issues and alternatives are presented in the filmstrips, as well as the actual decision made. Students must decide which course of action they would have chosen in the same situation. Questions, generalizations, and concepts for discussion are suggested along with written work.

For example, in the case of Lincoln, students must answer the following questions: "Would a "do-nothing" policy have been morally acceptable to you? Why?" "Would a 'giving-in-to-the-Confederacy' position have been morally acceptable to you? Why?" "Is a decision that avoids bloodshed always a good decision?" and "Would you have gone to war to preserve the Union if you were President Lincoln?" Among the generalizations to be tested in this case are: "Abraham Lincoln was indifferent to the continued existence of slavery. His main concern was the preservation of the Union" and "Abraham Lincoln hated slavery and he felt that the Civil War was the only means by which the Union could be scourged of that evil institution." The narration and additional information on each issue are provided for the teacher.

The materials have not been evaluated or fieldtested.

DESCRIPTIVE CHARACTERISTICS

Grade Level

- ___ K-3
- ___ 4-6
- ___ 7-8
- _X_ 9-10
- _X_ 11-12

Materials

- ___ Student materials
- _X_ Teacher guide
- _X_ A-V kit
- ___ Tests
- ___ Other: ______________

Time

- ___ Curriculum (2 or more years)
- ___ Course (one year)
- ___ Semester (half year)
- ___ Minicourse (6-9 weeks)
- _X_ Units (1-3 weeks)
- _X_ Supplementary
- ___ Other: ______________

Medium Used

- ___ Readings
- ___ Worksheets
- ___ Films
- _X_ Filmstrips
- _X_ Records or tapes
- ___ Charts or posters
- ___ Transparencies
- ___ Other: ______________

PRECONDITIONS

Amount of Reading

- ___ Much
- ___ Moderate
- _X_ Very little

Teacher Training

- ___ Provided in materials
- ___ Suggested by developers
- _X_ Not mentioned
- ___ Other: ______________

Prejudice/Stereotyping

Much evidence = M
Some evidence = S

- ___ Racial or Ethnic
- ___ Sexrole
- ___ Other: ______________

EVALUATION INFORMATION

Provision for Student Evaluation

- ___ Instruments specified
- ___ Procedures specified
- ___ Guidelines suggested
- _X_ Nothing provided
- ___ Other: ______________

Materials Evaluation

Materials tested = T
Results available = A

- ___ Fieldtested before publication
- ___ Fieldtested after publication
- ___ User feedback solicited
- ___ Other: ______________
- _X_ Not evaluated

SUBSTANTIVE CHARACTERISTICS

Values Education Approach

- ___ Inculcation
- ___ Moral development
- _X_ Analysis
- _X_ Clarification
- ___ Action learning
- ___ Other: ______________

Values Education Emphasis

- ___ Major focus
- _X_ One of several concerns
- ___ A minor concern

Process/Content Emphasis

- _X_ Process of valuing
- ___ Content of valuing

Objectives

- ___ Stated specifically
- ___ Stated generally
- _X_ Not stated

Student Activities

Used or stressed frequently = F
Used or stressed occasionally = O

- ___ Reading
- _O_ Writing
- _F_ Class discussion
- ___ Small-group discussion
- ___ Games
- ___ Simulations
- ___ Role playing
- ___ Action projects
- ___ Other: ______________

Title: THE MORAL IMPERATIVE

Author: Vincent Ryan Ruggiero

Publisher: Alfred Publishing Company, 74 Channel Dr., Port Washington, NY 11050

Date: 1973

Grade Level: 11-12

Materials and Cost: Student text ($4.95)

Concrete problems faced by students and other people with whom they can relate is a major concern of *The Moral Imperative*. The author states that the moral imperative of our time is "to break the bonds of indecision, move beyond fad and foolishness, and address the dilemmas of modern living, sensitively and sensibly, with regard for their complexity." The text emphasizes principles rather than details and has a two-fold purpose: making ethical issues interesting to read about and discuss and encouraging students to participate in moral inquiry. The book is appropriate with a variety of subject areas, such as speech courses, interdisciplinary studies, or any course aiming at helping students develop sound moral judgment. The book is designed for first-year college students, but could be used with advanced senior high school students.

The Moral Imperative addresses itself to many of the moral questions students have raised or soon will raise. It contains 12 chapters, each exploring avenues by which ethical and moral issues can be analyzed. Students are encouraged to realize that behavior that is acceptable and condoned in one culture might be intolerable and rejected in another. Questions regarding majority action versus one's conscience lead students to a deeper level of thought while considering ethical conduct. "How do we reconcile conflicting obligations?" "How do we handle cases in which the effects are not neatly separable into good and bad?" "How do we determine if people are responsible for their immoral actions?" "Are there degrees of responsibility?" "How can the moral quality of an action be determined?" These are major questions students are asked to consider as they look at contemporary ethical controversies in education, the arts and sciences, media and government, sex, law, and war.

By discussing these and other questions, using concrete conflict situations, the author develops the following moral principles, which he believes should be used to make value judgments: "(1) Obligations should be followed. When two or more obligations are in conflict, we should choose the more important one. (2) Ideals should be served. When they conflict among themselves or with obligations, we should choose the action which does the greater good. (3) Harmful actions should be avoided and beneficial ones achieved. However, harm may be tolerated if it is unavoidable; that is, if it is inseparable from good. Where the effects are mixed, we should choose the action that achieves the greater good or the lesser harm. (4) The person and his action are separate. Our judgments of them should also be separate." Inquiries at the end of each chapter and at the end of the book encompass an even wider range of moral concerns and provide contexts within which to apply these principles.

The Moral Imperative was used by the author in his classroom before publication. No systematic fieldtesting, however, has been done.

DESCRIPTIVE CHARACTERISTICS

Grade Level

___ K-3
___ 4-6
___ 7-8
___ 9-10
_X_ 11-12

Materials

_X_ Student materials
___ Teacher guide
___ A-V kit
___ Tests
___ Other: ________________

Time

___ Curriculum (2 or more years)
___ Course (one year)
___ Semester (half year)
_X_ Minicourse (6-9 weeks)
___ Units (1-3 weeks)
_X_ Supplementary
___ Other: ________________

Medium Used

_X_ Readings
___ Worksheets
___ Films
___ Filmstrips
___ Records or tapes
___ Charts or posters
___ Transparencies
___ Other: ________________

PRECONDITIONS

Amount of Reading

_X_ Much
___ Moderate
___ Very little

Teacher Training

___ Provided in materials
___ Suggested by developers
_X_ Not mentioned
___ Other: ________________

Prejudice/Stereotyping

Much evidence = M
Some evidence = S

___ Racial or Ethnic
___ Sexrole
___ Other: ________________

EVALUATION INFORMATION

Provision for Student Evaluation

___ Instruments specified
___ Procedures specified
_X_ Guidelines suggested
_X_ Nothing provided
___ Other: ________________

Materials Evaluation

Materials tested = T
Results available = A

_T_ Fieldtested before publication
___ Fieldtested after publication
___ User feedback solicited
___ Other: ________________
___ Not evaluated

SUBSTANTIVE CHARACTERISTICS

Values Education Approach

___ Inculcation
___ Moral development
_X_ Analysis
___ Clarification
___ Action learning
___ Other: ________________

Values Education Emphasis

_X_ Major focus
___ One of several concerns
___ A minor concern

Process/Content Emphasis

_X_ Process of valuing
___ Content of valuing

Objectives

_X_ Stated specifically
_X_ Stated generally
___ Not stated

Student Activities

Used or stressed frequently = F
Used or stressed occasionally = O

_F_ Reading
___ Writing
_F_ Class discussion
___ Small-group discussion
___ Games
___ Simulations
___ Role playing
___ Action projects
___ Other: ________________

Curriculum: OPPOSING VIEWPOINTS SERIES

Titles: Volume I—*The Radical Left and the Far Right;* Volume II—*Liberals and Conservatives;* Volume III—*The Ecology Controversy;* Volume IV—*Constructing a Life Philosophy;* Volume V—*America's Prisons;* Volume VI—*American Foreign Policy;* Volume VII—*The Sexual Revolution;* Volume VIII—*Problems of Death. Future Planning Games for Volumes I-VII.*

Editors: David L. Bender and Gary E. McCuen

Publisher: Greenhaven Press, Box 831, Anoka, MN 55303

Dates: 1971-1974

Grade Levels: 8-12

Materials and Cost: 8 student texts ($1.95 each); 7 future planning games ($0.95 each)

The *Opposing Viewpoints Series* consists of eight student texts and accompanying simulation-gaming activities which focus on current issues. The program is designed to develop critical thinking and discussion skills. By using the analysis approach it is hoped that students will learn to distinguish fact from opinion, to determine cause and effect relationships, to evaluate sources of information, and to empathize with others. Throughout the series, a primary goal is to increase students' understanding of the issues and to encourage them to form their own opinions based on the information they gather.

The materials are intended for high school students but could be used successfully in some junior high classes. Readings are short and to the point, and they contain visuals such as pictures, cartoons, and graphs. Each book deals with a different area of controversy and, with its accompanying simulation-gaming sheet, could form the basis of a three- to four-week minicourse. If all of the booklets are used, the course would require at least a full semester. The *Future Planning Games,* which accompany seven of the student texts, suggest three to five small-group activities involving students in conflict situations that call for value analysis. They focus on planning for the future and on considering changes in institutions. These activities may be used to supplement the texts or they may be used independently.

The issues on which the program focuses are varied. *The Radical Left and the Far Right* explores fringe-group opinions on the problem of race. This issue is approached from a political perspective through individual case studies. Viewpoints represented range from those of the Black Panther Party to those of the Imperial Wizard of the Ku Klux Klan. *Liberals and Conservatives* involves the debate over the welfare questions. It presents articles representing conflicting ideas on the subject, such as "The Danger of Welfare" and "Is Welfare a Basic Human Right?" *The Sexual Revolution* explores traditional mores versus new value positions. Included are arguments supporting and contesting such issues as family obsolescence, women's liberation, premarital relations, homosexuality, and sex education in the public schools. Issues in *American Foreign Policy* include self-interest versus idealism, goals of United States foreign policy, and Communism. *America's Prisons* deals with conditions inside correctional institutions, rehabilitation, and the concept of punishment. Environmental issues such as technology, population growth, pollution, and the energy crisis are examined in *The Ecology Crisis*. Values seem to be at issue, along with the question of whether the crisis is real or imagined. *Constructing a Life Philosophy* examines a myriad of alternative life philosophies or value systems from "The Christian's Commandments" and "The Hindu View of Life" to "The New Morality" and "Advice from Ann Landers." Finally, in *The Problems of Death,* such controversial issues as abortion, euthanasia, capital punishment, suicide, and American funeral practices are discussed.

Student activities are dispersed throughout the books. These include suggestions for discussion as well as written exercises that reinforce the development of critical thinking skills. According to the publishers, the materials have been fieldtested. The evaluative data, however, is not available.

DESCRIPTIVE CHARACTERISTICS

Grade Level

___ K-3
___ 4-6
X 7-8
X 9-10
X 11-12

Materials

X Student materials
___ Teacher guide
___ A-V kit
___ Tests
___ Other: ______

Time

___ Curriculum (2 or more years)
___ Course (one year)
X Semester (half year)
___ Minicourse (6-9 weeks)
X Units (1-3 weeks)(each title)
___ Supplementary
___ Other: ______

Medium Used

X Readings
___ Worksheets
___ Films
___ Filmstrips
___ Records or tapes
___ Charts or posters
___ Transparencies
X Other: Activity sheets

PRECONDITIONS

Amount of Reading

X Much
___ Moderate
___ Very little

Teacher Training

___ Provided in materials
___ Suggested by developers
X Not mentioned
___ Other: ______

Prejudice/Stereotyping

Much evidence = M
Some evidence = S

___ Racial or Ethnic
___ Sexrole
___ Other: ______

EVALUATION INFORMATION

Provision for Student Evaluation

___ Instruments specified
___ Procedures specified
___ Guidelines suggested
X Nothing provided
___ Other: ______

Materials Evaluation

Materials tested = T
Results available = A

___ Fieldtested before publication
T Fieldtested after publication
___ User feedback solicited
___ Other: ______
___ Not evaluated

SUBSTANTIVE CHARACTERISTICS

Values Education Approach

___ Inculcation
___ Moral development
X Analysis
___ Clarification
___ Action learning
___ Other: ______

Values Education Emphasis

___ Major focus
X One of several concerns
___ A minor concern

Process/Content Emphasis

X Process of valuing
X Content of valuing

Objectives

___ Stated specifically
___ Stated generally
X Not stated

Student Activities

Used or stressed frequently = F
Used or stressed occasionally = O

F Reading
F Writing
F Class discussion
F Small-group discussion
O Games
O Simulations
___ Role playing
O Action projects
___ Other: ______

Titles: THE ORIGINS OF AMERICAN VALUES: THE PURITAN ETHIC TO THE JESUS FREAKS and HUMAN VALUES IN AN AGE OF TECHNOLOGY

Publisher: The Center for Humanities, Inc., Two Holland Ave., White Plains, NY 10603

Dates: 1972-73

Grade Levels: 9-12

Materials and Cost: For each title: audiovisual kit containing 160 slides in 2 carousel cartridges, 2 tape cassettes or 2 records, and teacher's guide ($104.50)

Human Values in an Age of Technology and *The Origins of American Values* are two sound-slide programs containing color reproductions of art masterpieces and historical and contemporary photography. They are designed to help secondary students understand, respectively, the impact of technological progress on human values and the origins and nature of the American value system. The rationale underlying these two programs emphasizes that the tremendous advances of the machine age and the recent revolution in American values necessitate a systematic examination of past and present values.

Human Values in an Age of Technology outlines humanity's evolution from the age of crude tools to the highly sophisticated machinery of today. Presented in two parts, this series traces technological advances from prehistoric times through the Roman era, Middle Ages, and Renaissance, up to the Industrial Revolution and modern society. The relationship between the positive and negative implications of technology are demonstrated. For example, the materials describe advances in medicine that have prolonged life but have also contributed to the problem of overpopulation. Alvin Toffler's idea of "future shock"—the premature arrival of the future—is also examined.

The *Origins* program deals with the evolution of American values from more than 300 years ago to the present. How values have changed in our brief history can be discerned through various writings, philosophies, and works of art. In the first part of the program, Puritan ideology is presented through the works of Jonathan Edwards and Cotton Mather. Practical values and the work ethic are considered in the works of Benjamin Franklin. Political values are revealed through the writings of John Adams and Thomas Jefferson. Nineteenth-century transcendentalism and the thoughts of Ralph Waldo Emerson and Henry David Thoreau are also described. In Part Two, students see how values and value judgments changed during the last half of the 19th century from the materialism of Russell Conwell to the humanitarianism of Andrew Carnegie. Tracing American value changes through the 1920s and 1930s up to contemporary times, this part concludes by describing how many young Americans are seeking new life styles including new forms of fundamentalist religion.

The teacher's guides for each program contain classroom procedures and discussion questions to help students analyze the values studied. The materials were fieldtested before publication, but the results are not available. According to the publisher, informal feedback from local teachers has been favorable.

DESCRIPTIVE CHARACTERISTICS

Grade Level

___ K-3
___ 4-6
___ 7-8
_X_ 9-10
_X_ 11-12

Materials

___ Student materials
_X_ Teacher guide
_X_ A-V kit
___ Tests
___ Other: ______________

Time

___ Curriculum (2 or more years)
___ Course (one year)
___ Semester (half year)
___ Minicourse (6-9 weeks)
___ Units (1-3 weeks)
_X_ Supplementary
___ Other: ______________

Medium Used

___ Readings
___ Worksheets
___ Films
___ Filmstrips
_X_ Records or tapes
___ Charts or posters
___ Transparencies
_X_ Other: Slides

PRECONDITIONS

Amount of Reading

___ Much
___ Moderate
_X_ Very little

Teacher Training

___ Provided in materials
___ Suggested by developers
_X_ Not mentioned
___ Other: ______________

Prejudice/Stereotyping

Much evidence = M
Some evidence = S

___ Racial or Ethnic
___ Sexrole
___ Other: ______________

EVALUATION INFORMATION

Provision for Student Evaluation

___ Instruments specified
___ Procedures specified
___ Guidelines suggested
_X_ Nothing provided
___ Other: ______________

Materials Evaluation

Materials tested = T
Results available = A

_T_ Fieldtested before publication
___ Fieldtested after publication
_T_ User feedback solicited
___ Other: ______________
___ Not evaluated

SUBSTANTIVE CHARACTERISTICS

Values Education Approach

___ Inculcation
___ Moral development
_X_ Analysis
___ Clarification
___ Action learning
___ Other: ______________

Values Education Emphasis

___ Major focus
_X_ One of several concerns
___ A minor concern

Process/Content Emphasis

___ Process of valuing
_X_ Content of valuing

Objectives

___ Stated specifically
_X_ Stated generally
___ Not stated

Student Activities

Used or stressed frequently = F
Used or stressed occasionally = O

___ Reading
_O_ Writing
_F_ Class discussion
___ Small-group discussion
___ Games
___ Simulations
___ Role playing
___ Action projects
___ Other: ______________

Curriculum: PEOPLE/CHOICES/DECISIONS

Titles: *A Village Family; One City Neighborhood*

Developers: Harold Berlak and Timothy R. Tomlinson

Publisher: Random House, Inc., 201 East 50th St., New York, NY 10022

Date: 1973

Grade Levels: 4-6

Materials and Cost: For each title: student text ($2.73); audiovisual kit including 1 teacher's edition, 1 activity book, 4 filmstrips, and cassettes or records (with cassettes—$62.61, with records—$57.45). Each component may be purchased individually (price information is available from the publisher).

In *People/Choices/Decisions,* upper elementary students become actively involved in examining social and ethical issues faced by changing societies. At present, two units are available, *One City Neighborhood* and *A Village Family;* a number of other units are under development. The program focuses on humanistic case studies that acquaint students with a small group of people who are deeply affected by change. Readings, discussions, and role play are used extensively to develop an increasing awareness of change and an understanding of the tensions and conflicts that result from change. The authors also feel it is important for students to become self-reliant in their thinking abilities and decision-making skills. Specific objectives relating to this goal are stated for each lesson. For example, children are encouraged to take a position on legal and moral dilemmas, to defend their positions, and to explain the reasons for their decisions.

One City Neighborhood is a case study of urban renewal. Conflict arises over a city's decision to uproot residents of a neighborhood proposed for demolition. Students meet members of a family affected by the decision and the city councilmen, and they examine the issue from both points of view. Change versus stability is also the issue in *A Village Family,* in which a Mexican family moves from a rural village to Mexico City. Values analysis skills are stressed in each of the units. For example, in *A Village Family,* when a decision must be made to remain in the village or to move to the city, students participate in an extensive role-playing activity in order to identify more closely with family members. This is followed by a search for specific evidence supporting both positions. Students defend their own points of view in a class discussion.

The program provides no formal evaluation exercises. Rather, teachers are encouraged to evaluate continually and keep anecdotal records of the students' progress through general observation, feedback from written work, class discussion, and role play. It is suggested that this evaluation be consistent with the specific lesson goals.

In the developmental stages, the materials were tested in classes by project directors, by project teachers, and by volunteer teachers. Students showed positive gains in their knowledge of ethnic groups. Through role play, students were able to identify with various characters and life styles. It was also found that student interaction was increased when using these materials. Evaluative data is available through the ERIC system in a report by the authors entitled *The Development of a Model for the Metropolitan St. Louis Social Studies Center. Final Report Project No. Z-004 (ED 012 390).*

DESCRIPTIVE CHARACTERISTICS

Grade Level

___ K-3
_X_ 4-6
___ 7-8
___ 9-10
___ 11-12

Materials

_X_ Student materials
_X_ Teacher guide
_X_ A-V kit
___ Tests
___ Other: ______

Time

___ Curriculum (2 or more years)
___ Course (one year)
_X_ Semester (half year)
_X_ Minicourse (6-9 weeks) (each title)
___ Units (1-3 weeks)
___ Supplementary
___ Other: ______

Medium Used

_X_ Readings
_X_ Worksheets
___ Films
_X_ Filmstrips
_X_ Records or tapes
___ Charts or posters
___ Transparencies
___ Other: ______

PRECONDITIONS

Amount of Reading

_X_ Much
___ Moderate
___ Very little

Teacher Training

___ Provided in materials
___ Suggested by developers
_X_ Not mentioned
___ Other: ______

Prejudice/Stereotyping

Much evidence = M
Some evidence = S

___ Racial or Ethnic
___ Sexrole
___ Other: ______

EVALUATION INFORMATION

Provision for Student Evaluation

___ Instruments specified
___ Procedures specified
_X_ Guidelines suggested
___ Nothing provided
___ Other: ______

Materials Evaluation

Materials tested = T
Results available = A

_A_ Fieldtested before publication
___ Fieldtested after publication
___ User feedback solicited
___ Other: ______
___ Not evaluated

SUBSTANTIVE CHARACTERISTICS

Values Education Approach

___ Inculcation
___ Moral development
_X_ Analysis
___ Clarification
___ Action learning
___ Other: ______

Values Education Emphasis

___ Major focus
_X_ One of several concerns
___ A minor concern

Process/Content Emphasis

_X_ Process of valuing
___ Content of valuing

Objectives

_X_ Stated specifically
___ Stated generally
___ Not stated

Student Activities

Used or stressed frequently = F
Used or stressed occasionally = O

_F_ Reading
_O_ Writing
_F_ Class discussion
_F_ Small-group discussion
_O_ Games
___ Simulations
_F_ Role playing
___ Action projects
___ Other: ______

Curriculum: PUBLIC ISSUES SERIES (Harvard Social Studies Project)

Titles: *Science and Public Policy; Colonial Kenya; The American Revolution; The Railroad Era; Taking a Stand; Religious Freedom; The Rise of Organized Labor; The Immigrant's Experience; Negro Views of America; Municipal Politics; The New Deal; Rights of the Accused; The Lawsuit; Community Change; Communist China; Nazi Germany; 20th Century Russia; The Civil War; Race and Education; Status; Revolution and World Politics; The Limits of War; Organizations Among Nations; Diplomacy and International Law; Privacy; The Progressive Era; Population Control; Jacksonian Democracy; Moral Reasoning; Social Action*

Developers: Donald Oliver and Fred Newmann

Publisher: Xerox Education Publications, Education Center, Columbus, OH 43216

Dates: 1967-74

Grade Levels: 9-12

Materials and Cost: 30 student texts ($0.50 each); teacher's guides (free with purchase of 10 or more student books of the same title)

The *Public Issues Series* consists of 30 separate unit books focusing on controversial public issues. A range of social science disciplines, theories, and concepts are employed in analyzing the issues. The developers (the Harvard Social Studies Project) emphasize that public issues are "problems or value dilemmas persisting throughout history and across cultures." They believe that most important public issues in America today can be clarified by reference to public issues in other places and other times. A special unit book called *Taking a Stand: A Guide to Clear Discussion of Public Issues* has been designed to help students improve their discussion skills.

Since a majority of policy issues can be interpreted and analyzed with reference to social science concepts and theories, the developers make an overt attempt to include many of these in the units. For example, *The Railroad Era* deals with the economic concepts of competition, profit, price determination, and market. *The American Revolution* treats the political science concepts of legitimate authority, power, and sovereignty. *Negro Views of America* focuses on psychological theories of racial difference and self-concept. The material has a heavy orientation toward historical topics, such as the growth of business and industry, the rise of organized labor, Christianity, Puritanism, and immigration.

Various teaching strategies are recommended for successful implementation of the program. These include traditional lecture, Socratic dialogue, reading cases aloud in class, writing analogous cases, and writing proposition papers. Discussion questions often stress analyzing the value issues underlying a specific event or dilemma. In *Communist China,* for example, students are asked, "Was it right for the peasants to seize the landlords' property? Why or why not?" They are urged to consider whether the landlords were guilty of illegal or immoral actions and whether the violence of the peasants was justified. In *Taking a Stand,* students determine the type of value conflict involved in various policy questions, such as, "Should federal aid be given to parochial schools?" They also examine the types of strategies used to support particular value principles. A teacher's guide accompanies each unit, as well as the entire series. These guides provide suggestions for alternative procedures, supplementary activities, teaching aids, and tests to measure concept attainment and application.

The Harvard Social Studies Project, has conducted two major types of evaluation: informal, clinical evaluation of the ongoing teaching and systematic evaluation of the program at its termination. The results of the first are reflected in the revised teaching and testing materials in the series. Results of the second are in the final project report (Newmann and Oliver 1969). The summary of results is rather inconclusive. The degree to which these materials can teach average high school students to carry on intelligent discussions about social issues remains essentially an open one, subject to further examination and testing.

DESCRIPTIVE CHARACTERISTICS

Grade Level

___ K-3
___ 4-6
___ 7-8
_X_ 9-10
_X_ 11-12

Materials

_X_ Student materials
_X_ Teacher guide
___ A-V kit
_X_ Tests
___ Other: ________________

Time

___ Curriculum (2 or more years)
___ Course (one year)
___ Semester (half year)
___ Minicourse (6-9 weeks)
_X_ Units (1-3 weeks) (each title)
___ Supplementary
___ Other: ________________

Medium Used

_X_ Readings
___ Worksheets
___ Films
___ Filmstrips
___ Records or tapes
___ Charts or posters
___ Transparencies
___ Other: ________________

PRECONDITIONS

Amount of Reading

_X_ Much
___ Moderate
___ Very little

Teacher Training

___ Provided in materials
___ Suggested by developers
_X_ Not mentioned
___ Other: ________________

Prejudice/Stereotyping

Much evidence = M
Some evidence = S

___ Racial or Ethnic
___ Sexrole
___ Other: ________________

EVALUATION INFORMATION

Provision for Student Evaluation

_X_ Instruments specified
___ Procedures specified
___ Guidelines suggested
___ Nothing provided
___ Other: ________________

Materials Evaluation

Materials tested = T
Results available = A

_A_ Fieldtested before publication
___ Fieldtested after publication
_T_ User feedback solicited
___ Other: ________________
___ Not evaluated

SUBSTANTIVE CHARACTERISTICS

Values Education Approach

___ Inculcation
___ Moral development
_X_ Analysis
___ Clarification
___ Action learning
___ Other: ________________

Values Education Emphasis

___ Major focus
_X_ One of several concerns
___ A minor concern

Process/Content Emphasis

_X_ Process of valuing
___ Content of valuing

Objectives

_X_ Stated specifically
___ Stated generally
___ Not stated

Student Activities

Used or stressed frequently = F
Used or stressed occasionally = O

_F_ Reading
_O_ Writing
_F_ Class discussion
_O_ Small-group discussion
_O_ Games
___ Simulations
_O_ Role playing
___ Action projects
___ Other: ________________

Curriculum: SOCIAL SCIENCE LABORATORY UNITS

Authors: Ronald Lippitt, Robert Fox, and Lucille Schaible

Publisher: Science Research Associates, 259 East Erie St., Chicago, IL 60611

Date: 1969

Grade Levels: 4-6

Materials and Cost: Student text ($3.88); student project booklets ($0.63 each); set of 5 records ($25.05); teacher's guide ($4.59); teacher's training manual ($3.39)

The seven units in *Social Science Laboratory Units,* a program for intermediate-grade students, use the classroom as a laboratory for guided student inquiries into the causes and effects of human behavior. Believing that social studies often deals too much with the memorization of facts and too little with the social realities students encounter daily, the authors designed this project to allow students to confront social realities in the classroom. Students are taught to use social science methodology and social science concepts to study human behavior. Each lesson includes a statement of specific objectives, such as "to motivate students to explore friendliness with objectivity," "to demonstrate that friendliness is not always appropriate," "and to identify the three parts of the behavior—feelings, intentions, and actions."

Unit 1, *Learning to Use Social Science,* introduces students to the work of social scientists—the methodology and the content of their disciplines. Students learn about techniques of data collection (observing, interviewing, and using questionnaires); distinguishing among observations, inferences, and value judgments; identifying cause-effect relationships; and analyzing multiple and cyclical causation. The remaining six units deal with specific behavioral situations and are entitled *Discovering Differences, Friendly and Unfriendly Behavior, Being and Becoming, Individuals and Groups, Deciding and Doing,* and *Influencing Each Other*. The second unit deals with hereditary and environmental differences, origins of personal preferences, and stereotypes. In the third, students examine the causes of friendly and unfriendly behavior in individuals and groups. Unit 4 focuses on child growth and development and the ways social scientists measure such growth. In the fifth unit, students analyze conflicts between the desires of humans to be alone and to be in groups, group roles and status, group leadership, and group pressures on deviates. Unit 6 explores decision making and the influence of different group members and leaders, while Unit 7 provides studies which show misconceptions about group norms, different kinds of influences on individual and group relationships, and the influence of children and adults on each other. When working with these units, students examine hypothetical cases of social interaction presented as readings, recordings, role-playing episodes, or descriptions and pictures in the project booklets. Using these booklets, students make value analyses of the cases presented and learn to apply social science concepts during class discussion.

Orientation and training for teaching the program are provided in the teacher's manual, *The Teacher's Role in Social Science Investigation,* and a companion record. These resources provide guidance in conducting value inquiry, producing hypothetical cases for study, and organizing groups for laboratory learning. In addition, one chapter identifies various instruments and outlines methods for student evaluation. The materials were fieldtested before publication but results are not available.

DESCRIPTIVE CHARACTERISTICS

Grade Level

__ K-3
X 4-6
__ 7-8
__ 9-10
__ 11-12

Materials

X Student materials
X Teacher guide
__ A-V kit
__ Tests
X Other: Audio component

Time

__ Curriculum (2 or more years)
X Course (one year)
__ Semester (half year)
__ Minicourse (6-9 weeks)
__ Units (1-3 weeks)
__ Supplementary
__ Other: ____

Medium Used

X Readings
X Worksheets
__ Films
__ Filmstrips
X Records or tapes
__ Charts or posters
__ Transparencies
__ Other: ____

PRECONDITIONS

Amount of Reading

X Much
__ Moderate
__ Very little

Teacher Training

X Provided in materials
__ Suggested by developers
__ Not mentioned
__ Other: ____

Prejudice/Stereotyping

Much evidence = M
Some evidence = S

__ Racial or Ethnic
__ Sexrole
__ Other: ____

EVALUATION INFORMATION

Provision for Student Evaluation

X Instruments specified
__ Procedures specified
__ Guidelines suggested
__ Nothing provided
__ Other: ____

Materials Evaluation

Materials tested = T
Results available = A

T Fieldtested before publication
__ Fieldtested after publication
__ User feedback solicited
__ Other: ____
__ Not evaluated

SUBSTANTIVE CHARACTERISTICS

Values Education Approach

__ Inculcation
__ Moral development
X Analysis
__ Clarification
__ Action learning
__ Other: ____

Values Education Emphasis

__ Major focus
X One of several concerns
__ A minor concern

Process/Content Emphasis

X Process of valuing
__ Content of valuing

Objectives

X Stated specifically
__ Stated generally
__ Not stated

Student Activities

Used or stressed frequently = F
Used or stressed occasionally = O

F Reading
O Writing
F Class discussion
__ Small-group discussion
__ Games
__ Simulations
O Role playing
__ Action projects
X Other: Listening

Curriculum: THE SOCIAL SCIENCES: CONCEPTS AND VALUES

Developers: Paul F. Brandwein and The Center for the Study of Instruction

Publisher: Harcourt Brace Jovanovich, Inc., 757 Third Ave., New York, NY 10017

Dates: 1970-75

Grade Levels: K-8

Materials and Cost: Student text for each grade level, 1-6 ($4.20-$7.95); teacher's edition for each level, 1-6 ($5.19-$6.15); teacher's guide, levels 7-8 ($1.75 each); beginning-level posters with teacher's edition (to be announced); activity book, levels 3-6 ($2.94 each); tests, levels 3-6 ($0.60-$0.75 each set); answer key to tests ($0.30 each); audiovisual kit, levels 1-6 (with cassettes—$75.00 each, with records—$69.00 each); teacher's "Handbook of Audio-Visual Aids" ($2.10)

A K-8 curriculum, *The Social Sciences: Concepts and Values* is designed "to facilitate each child's progress by highlighting the recurring patterns of human behavior in physical and cultural environments." The materials emphasize inquiry and analysis and encourage actual student participation in the learning process. Three kinds of objectives, all intended to enhance self-concept and self-esteem, are identified: seeking concepts that help students understand issues and dilemmas they may face, identifying values that guide decisions and are thus reflected in actions, and learning rational thinking skills.

The conceptually structured content focuses on five of the social science disciplines at every grade level: anthropology, sociology, geography, economics, and history/political science. Each concept is dealt with at an increasingly sophisticated level as the students advance from one grade to the next. Students "gather evidence, classify it, label it, compare and contrast it, form hypotheses, test them, form theories [and] test them." They look at a variety of environments and cultures, exploring their own values and those of others. They discover that actions reflect the concerns and values of people. Lessons usually include readings and class discussions in addition to a variety of action activities such as role play and group work. Activity books for grades three through six contain additional activities for individuals or the entire class. Unit tests for grades three through six evaluate how well each child understands the significant concepts of the unit. Suggested guidelines for continuous evaluation at each grade level are included in the teacher's guide.

The kindergarten through sixth-grade materials were fieldtested in classroom situations both before and after publication of the first edition. Problem areas were discovered through these tests and, according to the publisher, have been corrected in the revised editions. The revisions included reducing the reading level, matching evaluation with objectives, and adding more action activities. The seventh- and eighth-grade materials have been fieldtested as part of the Diablo Valley Education Project. An evaluation by six teachers who taught selected units to their junior high school classes determined that the reading level of the materials was appropriate for that age group. The teachers also indicated that five out of the seven or eight units used "held student interest" and "developed concepts clearly." The evaluation of these materials is continuous, with additional data constantly being sought. Results of all tests as well as the results of user feedback, observation, and research are available from The Center for the Study of Instruction, Harcourt Brace Jovanovich Building, Polk and Geary, San Francisco, CA 94109.

DESCRIPTIVE CHARACTERISTICS

Grade Level

X K-3
X 4-6
X 7-8
___ 9-10
___ 11-12

Materials

X Student materials
X Teacher guide
X A-V kit
X Tests
___ Other: ___

Time

X Curriculum (2 or more years)
X Course (one year)(each title)
___ Semester (half year)
___ Minicourse (6-9 weeks)
___ Units (1-3 weeks)
___ Supplementary
___ Other: ___

Medium Used

X Readings
X Worksheets
___ Films
X Filmstrips
X Records or tapes
X Charts or posters
___ Transparencies
___ Other: ___

PRECONDITIONS

Amount of Reading

X Much
___ Moderate
___ Very little

Teacher Training

___ Provided in materials
___ Suggested by developers
X Not mentioned
___ Other: ___

Prejudice/Stereotyping

Much evidence = M
Some evidence = S

___ Racial or Ethnic
___ Sexrole
___ Other: ___

EVALUATION INFORMATION

Provision for Student Evaluation

X Instruments specified
___ Procedures specified
X Guidelines suggested
___ Nothing provided
___ Other: ___

Materials Evaluation

Materials tested = T
Results available = A

A Fieldtested before publication
A Fieldtested after publication
A User feedback solicited
___ Other: ___
___ Not evaluated

SUBSTANTIVE CHARACTERISTICS

Values Education Approach

___ Inculcation
___ Moral development
X Analysis
___ Clarification
___ Action learning
___ Other: ___

Values Education Emphasis

___ Major focus
X One of several concerns
___ A minor concern

Process/Content Emphasis

X Process of valuing
___ Content of valuing

Objectives

X Stated specifically
___ Stated generally
___ Not stated

Student Activities

Used or stressed frequently = F
Used or stressed occasionally = O

F Reading
F Writing
F Class discussion
F Small-group discussion
___ Games
___ Simulations
F Role playing
O Action projects
___ Other: ___

Curriculum: THE TABA PROGRAM IN SOCIAL SCIENCE

Titles: *Anuk's Family of Bali* (grades K-1); *People in Families* (grade 1); *People in Neighborhoods* (2); *People in Communities* (3); *People in States* (4); *People in America* (5); *People in Change* (6 and 7)

Developers: Mary C. Durkin and Anthony H. McNaughton

Publisher: Addison-Wesley Publishing Company, 2725 Sand Hill Rd., Menlo Park, CA 94025

Dates: 1972-74

Grade Levels: K-7

Materials and Cost: Study/Activity posters, 18'' x 24'', with teacher's guide ($39.60); student text for each grade level ($2.31-$6.45); teacher's edition for each grade level ($4.90-$5.70); audio components, levels 1-6 ($38.46 each level); student activity books, levels 3-5 ($1.74 each level); student performance exercises, levels 3-6 ($5.94-$6.93 each level)

The *Taba Program in Social Science* is an elementary program designed to enable students to acquire knowledge, academic and social skills, and selected attitudes. According to the developers, necessity demands that schools teach "durable knowledge," such as powerful generalizations, significant ideas, and concepts, rather than the transmittal and recall of factual information, which today "is too vast, quickly becomes obsolete, and tends to burden the memory without training the mind." Therefore, the *Taba Program* provides student materials that contain a collection of data to be used as the basis for learning activities in which students draw conclusions. In addition, the curriculum helps students examine their own values and understand and respect the values of others, with the ultimate goal of expanding "the student's capacity for citizenship in a participatory democracy." The general instructional goals of the program are stated in specific behavioral objectives which "provide the criteria for continued student evaluation." For example, students completing the Grade Five program are expected to demonstrate 20 skills, including developing concepts (listing, grouping, and labeling), identifying and comparing values, indicating relationships, developing generalizations, and accepting the merits of different ways of living and different points of view.

The materials focus on what the developers define as concepts, main ideas, and facts. The program for each grade level is divided into units, with each unit centering on one or more generalizations, such as "families differ in life style and norms," "the way people choose to live and the knowledge they have influence the use they make of their environment," and "institutions support the life style of a people." Furthermore, each unit also presents information that can be abstracted into key concepts. In total, 11 concepts are developed: causality, conflict, cooperation, cultural change, differences, interdependence, modification, power, society control, tradition, and values. The *Taba Program* also stresses the development of map skills on the grounds that "skill in map use is essential to the process of data collection and interpretation."

Grade One, *People in Families,* is a study of four American families and four families in other cultures. Learning activities encourage students to understand the differences and similarities among these families. Grade Two, *People in Neighborhoods,* studies three contrasting urban neighborhoods. Grade Three, *People in Communities,* investigates four communities in other parts of the world and Grade 4, *People in States,* looks at four foreign states (Mysore, India; Osaka Prefecture in Japan; Serbia, Yugoslavia; and Nova Scotia, Canada). Grade 5, *People in America,* includes information on the life styles of six modern American families and a study of societies in conflict through the American and Mexican Revolutions. Grades Six and Seven, *People in*

Change, is a series focusing on Central Eurasia, Latin America, and the Far East.

Analysis is the dominant approach to values education reflected in the materials. While encouraging students to understand their own values, the Taba Program also provides activities for students to infer and compare the values of others from their reasons and behavior in specific situations. Teacher's guides have been compiled for each grade level in the program. They present step-by-step lesson plans for sequential learning activities. In addition, Addison-Wesley has published a supplementary guide entitled *A Teacher's Handbook to Elementary Social Studies: An Inductive Approach* (2d. ed.), which is preparatory reading for teachers intending to use the program. The handbook costs $5.75 and contains a model for social studies curriculum reform, suggestions for inductive teaching, questions for student evaluation, and student performance exercises for Grades Three to Six.

The *Taba Program* is an outgrowth of the Taba Curriculum Guides. These guides were fieldtested as well as evaluated through interviews with users. Results of the fieldtesting are available from two sources: Addison-Wesley (*Taba Final Report,* order code #7424) and the American Institutes for Research, P.O. Box 1113, Palo Alto, CA 94302 (Project Development Report No. 19). In addition, two of the *Taba Program* student activity books were fieldtested and improved on the basis of the findings *(Getting Together with People in Communities* and *Getting Together with People in States).* The Taba Program has also been evaluated by various school districts throughout the United States. The names of those which have evaluated the materials are available from the publisher.

DESCRIPTIVE CHARACTERISTICS

Grade Level

X K-3
X 4-6
X 7-8
__ 9-10
__ 11-12

Materials

X Student materials
X Teacher guide
X A-V kit
X Tests

Time

X Curriculum (2 or more years)
X Course (one year)
__ Semester (half year)
__ Minicourse (6-9 weeks)
__ Units (1-3 weeks)
__ Supplementary

Medium Used

X Readings
X Worksheets
__ Films
__ Filmstrips
X Records or tapes
X Charts or posters
__ Transparencies
X Other: Activity books

PRECONDITIONS

Amount of Reading

X Much
__ Moderate

Teacher Training

__ Provided in materials
__ Suggested by developers
__ Not mentioned
X Available elsewhere

Prejudice/Stereotyping

Much evidence = M
Some evidence = S

__ Racial or Ethnic
__ Sexrole

EVALUATION INFORMATION

Provision for Student Evaluation

X Instruments specified
__ Procedures specified
__ Guidelines suggested
__ Nothing provided

Materials Evaluation

Materials tested = T
Results available = A

A Fieldtested before publication
T Fieldtested after publication
T User feedback solicited
A Other: See above

SUBSTANTIVE CHARACTERISTICS

Values Education Approach

__ Inculcation
__ Moral development
X Analysis
__ Clarification
__ Action learning

Values Education Emphasis

__ Major focus
X One of several concerns
__ A minor concern

Process/Content Emphasis

X Process of valuing
__ Content of valuing

Objectives

X Stated specifically
__ Stated generally

Student Activities

Used or stressed frequently = F
Used or stressed occasionally = O

F Reading
O Writing
F Class discussion
__ Small-group discussion
__ Games
__ Simulations
__ Role playing
__ Action projects
O Other: Reading maps

Title: TEACHING MORAL VALUES THROUGH BEHAVIOR MODIFICATION: INTERMEDIATE LEVEL

Author: Joan M. Sayre

Publisher: The Interstate Printers & Publishers, Inc., Jackson at Van Buren, Danville, IL 61832

Date: 1972

Grade Levels: 3-5

Materials and Cost: Teacher's guide and 84 poster cards, 8'' x 10'' ($6.95)

Teaching Moral Values Through Behavior Modification: Intermediate Level consists of a teacher's guide that presents 21 value-oriented problem situations with accompanying picture posters. The resource is designed to help students in grades three through five "understand the meaning of moral values." Discussion activities, an important part of the program, are intended to further the development of logical thinking skills. The materials may be used in any intermediate classroom, as well as with exceptional children such as slow learners, the culturally disadvantaged, or children with impaired hearing. A primary-level kit is also available but is not analyzed in this book (Sayre and Mack 1973).

The program consists of units focusing on four general value topics: prejudice (race, religion, economic, handicap, and intelligence), personal ethics (honesty, sportsmanship, and retaliation), responsibility (individual and group), and respect for authority (civil, parental, school, and property). These units contain from three to seven problem stories which the teacher reads to the students. The stories deal with realistic problems that often confront children. For instance, in one story a young boy and his friend are playing catch in the house on a rainy day, although the boy's mother had asked that he not play ball in the house. Accidentally a favorite vase is broken. The boys have to decide what to do. Another situation involves a group of children whispering and laughing about another group of children's customs and beliefs.

Questions are provided after each story in order to stimulate students to offer possible solutions and to discuss what they would do in that situation. At the end of each unit teachers are encouraged to engage students in activities that require them to define the value, discuss different types of the particular value, retell the stories placing the picture cards in sequence, and create and role play similar stories. Most of the activities emphasize the analysis approach to values education (for example, define prejudice, list different types of prejudice) with a few containing clarification questions (for example, "Would you like to be Brad or Richard? Why? Why not?").

The materials have not been systematically evaluated.

DESCRIPTIVE CHARACTERISTICS

Grade Level

X K-3
X 4-6
__ 7-8
__ 9-10
__ 11-12

Materials

__ Student materials
X Teacher guide
__ A-V kit
__ Tests
X Other: Poster cards

Time

__ Curriculum (2 or more years)
__ Course (one year)
__ Semester (half year)
X Minicourse (6-9 weeks)
__ Units (1-3 weeks)
X Supplementary
__ Other: ______

Medium Used

__ Readings
__ Worksheets
__ Films
__ Filmstrips
__ Records or tapes
X Charts or posters
__ Transparencies
__ Other: ______

PRECONDITIONS

Amount of Reading

__ Much
__ Moderate
X Very little

Teacher Training

__ Provided in materials
__ Suggested by developers
X Not mentioned
__ Other: ______

Prejudice/Stereotyping

Much evidence = M
Some evidence = S

__ Racial or Ethnic
__ Sexrole
__ Other: ______

EVALUATION INFORMATION

Provision for Student Evaluation

__ Instruments specified
__ Procedures specified
__ Guidelines suggested
X Nothing provided
__ Other: ______

Materials Evaluation

Materials tested = T
Results available = A

__ Fieldtested before publication
__ Fieldtested after publication
__ User feedback solicited
__ Other: ______
X Not evaluated

SUBSTANTIVE CHARACTERISTICS

Values Education Approach

X Inculcation
__ Moral development
X Analysis
__ Clarification
__ Action learning
__ Other: ______

Values Education Emphasis

X Major focus
__ One of several concerns
__ A minor concern

Process/Content Emphasis

__ Process of valuing
X Content of valuing

Objectives

__ Stated specifically
__ Stated generally
X Not stated

Student Activities

Used or stressed frequently = F
Used or stressed occasionally = O

__ Reading
O Writing
F Class discussion
O Small-group discussion
__ Games
__ Simulations
O Role playing
__ Action projects
X Other: Listening to stories

Curriculum: THE VALUES AND DECISIONS SERIES

Titles: *Union or Secession: The Compromise of 1850; Political Justice: The Haymarket Three; Colonial Defiance: The Boston Tea Party; Impeachment: The Presidency on Trial; Confrontation: The Cuban Missile Crisis; Constitution: One Nation or Thirteen; Neutral Rights: Impressment and the Chesapeake Outrage; Conquest: Manifest Destiny and Mexican Land; Isolation: The U.S. and the League of Nations; Intervention: The Vietnam Buildup*

Developer: Vincent R. Rogers

Publisher: Xerox Education Publications, Education Center, Columbus, OH 43216

Dates: 1972-74

Grade Levels: 7-12

Materials and Cost: Student texts ($.50 each, $4.50 set of 10); teacher guides (free with purchase of 10 or more student books of same title)

The ten booklets composing *The Values and Decisions* series focus on crucial decisions in America's history and the personalities involved in making them. The seventh- through twelfth-grade students using the materials "examine the human and political values that motivated each decision-maker, the values held by the nation as a whole, and the historic focus pushing events to a crisis." Students are exposed to the "personal turmoil of people facing up to the policy decisions" and are encouraged to explore what they might have done given the facts and the contexts of the times. They are asked to consider if the decisions were inevitable and also to consider if similar crises and decisions have occurred at other times in America's history.

Each book contains 48 pages providing students with information and pictures related to a particular theme. A section entitled "Questions and Values" concludes each pamphlet and presents questions for class discussion on the values underlying the issues developed. In *Intervention: The Vietnam Buildup,* for example, students deal with questions such as, "Why do you think that the overwhelming majority of Americans supported President Johnson's decision to bomb North Vietnam?" In *Isolation: The U.S. and the League of Nations,* students are asked, "If the United Nations votes decisions directly contrary to the declared interests of the United States, would this country be justified in cutting down its financial contributions in retaliation? Why or why not?"

Throughout the series, students are exposed to a wide range of values concepts. In *Confrontation: The Cuban Missile Crisis,* for instance, they deal with power and decisions, nationalism versus internationalism, truth versus deception, and national security versus nuclear war. Other pamphlets have students analyze value concepts such as freedom and democracy, national honor and pride, humanitarian values, natural rights, mercantilism, private property, international justice, separation of powers, fair trial, and personal welfare versus public good. These issues are analyzed through classroom discussion, games, and rank ordering of personal responses supplied for various hypothetical situations.

A one-page teacher's guide accompanies each unit. It briefly outlines the value concepts treated in the student materials and provides ten multiple-choice questions teachers can reproduce for classroom review or student evaluation.

In general, the materials reflect ethnic and sex-role stereotyping since the ten crucial issues taken from America's past focus almost entirely on white male personalities. One pamphlet, however, *Political Justice: The Haymarket Three,* presents a brief account of the Black Panthers and the trial of Panther leaders Bobby Seale and Erika Huggins.

DESCRIPTIVE CHARACTERISTICS

Grade Level

___ K-3
___ 4-6
X 7-8
X 9-10
X 11-12

Materials

X Student materials
X Teacher guide
___ A-V kit
X Tests
___ Other: ___________

Time

___ Curriculum (2 or more years)
___ Course (one year)
___ Semester (half year)
___ Minicourse (6-9 weeks)
X Units (1-3 weeks) (each title)
___ Supplementary
___ Other: ___________

Medium Used

X Readings
___ Worksheets
___ Films
___ Filmstrips
___ Records or tapes
___ Charts or posters
___ Transparencies
___ Other: ___________

PRECONDITIONS

Amount of Reading

X Much
___ Moderate
___ Very little

Teacher Training

___ Provided in materials
___ Suggested by developers
X Not mentioned
___ Other: ___________

Prejudice/Stereotyping

Much evidence = M
Some evidence = S

S Racial or Ethnic
S Sexrole
___ Other: ___________

EVALUATION INFORMATION

Provision for Student Evaluation

X Instruments specified
___ Procedures specified
___ Guidelines suggested
___ Nothing provided
___ Other: ___________

Materials Evaluation

Materials tested = T
Results available = A

___ Fieldtested before publication
___ Fieldtested after publication
___ User feedback solicited
___ Other: ___________
X Not evaluated

SUBSTANTIVE CHARACTERISTICS

Values Education Approach

___ Inculcation
___ Moral development
X Analysis
___ Clarification
___ Action learning
___ Other: ___________

Values Education Emphasis

X Major focus
___ One of several concerns
___ A minor concern

Process/Content Emphasis

X Process of valuing
___ Content of valuing

Objectives

___ Stated specifically
___ Stated generally
X Not stated

Student Activities

Used or stressed frequently = F
Used or stressed occasionally = O

F Reading
___ Writing
F Class discussion
___ Small-group discussion
O Games
___ Simulations
___ Role playing
___ Action projects
___ Other: ___________

analysis: teacher materials

Title: INTRODUCTION TO EASTERN PHILOSOPHY, SOCIAL STUDIES: 6416.23

Author: Judy Reeder Payne

Publisher: Division of Instruction, Dade County Public Schools, Miami, FL (available only through ERIC—see Materials and Cost below)

Date: 1971

Grade Levels: 10-12

Materials and Cost: Curriculum guide available only from ERIC Document Reproduction Service, Box 190, Arlington, Virginia 22210 (order ED 071 937: microfiche—$.76, xerography—$1.95 plus postage)

Introduction to Eastern Philosophy, a course of study developed to fit into the quinmester administrative organization of Dade County Public Schools (Miami, Florida), provides a framework for systematically introducing secondary students to five major philosophies/religions of the Eastern World—Hinduism, Buddhism, Confucianism, Taoism, and Shintoism. As stated in the rationale, the influences of Eastern philosophical ideas is beingfelt by American youth as a result of modern transportation and communication and the impact of the Vietnam War. Since the author feels that "young people are searching for a philosophy to guide their lives," she developed this course "to help guide students in the universal search for values and beliefs about the meaning of life."

The course offers opportunities for students to investigate Confucianism, infer its influence upon China, and discover that some of the ideas of today's youth—love, peace, non-competitiveness, anti-materialism, and civil disobedience—can be traced to Eastern philosophies. Seven course goals are listed and each is discussed in terms of focus, objective, and learning activities. For example, the first goal is for students to examine and gather background data on the five major Eastern philosophies. The focus is on *philosophy* and *religion* as terms. Four specific objectives are stated: students will define the two terms, classify them, gather geographical data about the East, and collect population statistics concerning the major countries in the East. A variety of learning activities are suggested for accomplishing each objective. These include having students orally recall the similarities and differences between the two terms and having students identify the square miles contained in each major country in order to grasp the vast expanse of Asia.

The course outline is composed of seven major sections. The first, background of the five major Eastern philosophies, is subdivided into definitions of philosophy and religion, Asian geographical data, Asian population statistics, and population data on Eastern religions. Hinduism, the topic of the second section, lists six items for student investigation: Hinduism as the historical base of all Eastern thought, its beliefs, its vocabulary, its sacred books, Mahatma Ghandi, and the relevance of Hinduism today. The third section deals with Buddhism and focuses on Buddha's life, Buddhist vocabulary, Buddhist beliefs, and the current relevance of Buddhism. Confucianism is the topic of the fourth section and is examined through sacred writings, Confucius' life, comparison of Confucianism and Buddhism, and Confucianism's relevance today. The fifth section looks at Taoism—its mystery, the "chain-argument," the life of Lao-Tse, Taoist beliefs, sacred Taoist writings, the current relevance of Taoism, and the theory and practice of yoga. In the sixth section, Shintoism is studied in relation to Japanese culture. Shintoism's traditions and beliefs, ceremonies, festivals, shrines, temples, and Gods are examined. The final section focuses on various sources fostering the growth of Eastern philosophical beliefs in this country—transportation, communication, the Vietnam War, and drug use.

The objectives and learning activities

focus on student factual learning and analysis of values, ideas, and practices of Eastern philosophic/religious traditions. For example, activities suggested in the seventh section include predicting the growth of Eastern philosophy, critically discussing the implications of the Vietnam War for the spread of Eastern philosophy, comparing today's use of drugs with the Eastern ideal of peace, and discovering and writing about some of today's ideas that may be traced to Eastern philosophical thought.

Title: INTRODUCTION TO VALUE INQUIRY: A STUDENT PROCESS BOOK (American Values Series)

Author: Jack L. Nelson

Publisher: Hayden Book Company, Inc., 50 Essex St., Rochelle Park, NJ 07662

Date: 1974

Grade Levels: 9-12

Materials and Cost: Teacher's guide ($1.56)

Introduction to Value Inquiry was designed as an introductory student unit for the *American Values Series* (see Student Materials section of this chapter for the analysis of the series). It can also serve, however, as a teacher's guide to the series. Stressing the process of examining and questioning value issues, rather than providing solutions, the book offers teachers and students intellectual tools for analyzing "social challenges and choices." "It is intended to make the reader more sensitive to inquiry thinking and value analysis in the consideration of issues."

The first chapter focuses on decision making and the process of value inquiry. The author explains and illustrates through examples and case studies three types of decision (deliberate, thoughtful choice; unconscious, unthoughtful choice; and no choice) and how values are involved in these decisions. Emphasizing the need for rational decision making, the author then outlines a process for value inquiry composed of five steps—issue identification and definition, hypothesis development, evidence gathering and evaluation, hypothesis testing, and drawing tentative conclusions.

The interrelationship between facts and values is described and illustrated in the second chapter. The author stresses the "need to examine social issues in terms of available facts, sources of evidence, quality of verification, and value positions." He also maintains that, just as some facts are unquestionable (such as the earth being a planet in the solar system), some values (such as human dignity), because they are so dominant, are also virtually unquestionable. The chapter concludes with two lengthy case studies (use of mercury and violent crime), complete with facts and figures to which readers are to apply the inquiry process discussed in Chapter 1.

The final chapter attempts to define key terms related to value inquiry. Examples and case studies are again used to amplify the author's points. The terms he attempts to clarify include *values, valuing, ethics, value hierarchy, value conflict,* and *conflict resolution.* Types of values, such as personal and social, terminal and instrumental, are also distinguished. A list of further readings on values in science and social studies is provided at the end of the book.

Title: A METHOD FOR CLARIFYING VALUE STATEMENTS IN THE SOCIAL STUDIES CLASSROOM: A SELF-INSTRUCTIONAL PROGRAM

Authors: Harry G. Miller and Samuel M. Vinocur

Date: 1972

Grade Levels: 9-12

Materials and Cost: Teacher's guide available only from ERIC Document Reproduction Service, Box 190, Arlington, Virginia 22210 (order ED 070 687: microfiche—$0.76, xerography—$1.58 plus postage)

"A Method for Clarifying Value Statements in the Social Studies Classroom: A Self-Instructional Program" is intended to be used in a teacher workshop or small-group situation designed to teach the analysis approach to values education. The authors hope that this program will enable teachers to identify value statements, learn ways to respond in order to clarify student value statements, and become aware of a variety of strategies that will stimulate students to express their values. It is the intention of the authors that these methods be worked into whatever course content is taught by the users. The materials teach a process that teachers could use when dealing with any social issue in the classroom.

The document is divided into three parts, corresponding to the objectives. Activities in each part are to be completed individually by each teacher and then compared and discussed in a small group. In Section I participants distinguish the differences between fact and value statements, as well as between different kinds of value statements. Criteria are given for determining in which category a statement falls. In the second section teachers learn three kinds of responses that help to clarify student value statements. The first response involves asking students to explain, restate, or give examples illustrating their statements. Another teacher response is to ask for evidence or proof—How do you know? Getting students to empathize, to suggest alternatives and to consider social consequences is the third method suggested. The document includes sample dialogues between teachers and students for each of these three types of responses. Participating teachers are given the opportunity to role play their reactions to several student value statements in each of the three ways.

Section III suggests and explains four ways to get students involved: using quotations, cartoons, situations, and simulations. Teachers are asked to suggest four additional techniques. Finally, participants are asked to list at least three value-laden issues that could be explored by the students in their own courses. Teachers evaluate their own responses by comparing and discussing them with those of the other teachers in their group.

A pilot test of this self-instructional program was conducted in Illinois. The names and schools of the participants are given in the document.

Title: RATIONAL VALUE DECISIONS AND VALUE CONFLICT RESOLUTION: A HANDBOOK FOR TEACHERS

Developers: W. Keith Evans, Terry P. Applegate, G. Gary Casper, and Robert W. Tucker

Distributor: Kenneth Lindsay, Coordinator of ESEA Title III, 1400 University Club Building, 136 East South Temple St., Salt Lake City, UT 84111

Materials and Cost: Teacher's guide (approximately $5.00)

Rational Value Decisions and Value Conflict Resolution was developed by the Value Analysis Capability Development Programs of the University of Utah with the cooperation of Granite School District in Salt Lake City. It is an extensive handbook designed to help teachers implement the value analysis model explicated in the 41st Yearbook of the National Council for the Social Studies (Metcalf 1971; see the last entry of this section for an analysis of this work). The handbook is currently available through the ESEA Title III office for Utah, but a commercially published edition is expected to be available within a year.

This handbook seeks to assist teachers and students in developing analytical value skills and making rational value choices. It is divided into three sections. The first, and largest, consists of lessons designed to develop in teachers and students the skills for making sound, rational value judgments. Readers learn and apply key concepts used in the Metcalf value analysis program. Some of these concepts are *simple and comparative value judgments, value terms, value objects, prescriptive statements, value criterion and principle,* and *factual and evaluative claims*. Section 1 is subdivided into six chapters, which generally follow the six basic tasks included in the value analysis model in the 41st Yearbook. Each of the lessons in this section is presented in two alternative ways: the "Program-Student Option"—programmed instructional units for individualized use—and the "Discussion-Handout Option"—handout sheets for leading class discussion. Criterion tests for each unit are included for both options.

Section II, "Strategies and Procedures," presents three procedures for interrelating the units and chapters of Section I with the content of a particular course such as American history or sociology. Illustrations of each procedure, based on actual classroom experimentation, are also provided, along with suggestions for the most effective way to apply procedures. A simulation game, "Muck in the Mock," is also included to demonstrate how value analysis skills and concepts can be applied to that type of activity.

The final section consists of a lesson plan organized into an algorithm (flow chart) which takes students step-by-step through several procedures designed to resolve specific value conflicts. Through use of several worksheets, two students with conflicting positions attempt to agree on the same set of facts, the truth of those facts, the valences associated with those facts (whether they are positive or negative), and, finally, the rank order of the facts.

The lessons embodied in this handbook were fieldtested with four classes receiving instruction in value analysis (experimental group) and four classes that had no values analysis treatment (control group). The results indicated a significant difference in favor of the experimental students in terms of their learning of and predisposition to apply various value analysis skills. No difference existed on measures of self-concept or ego-strength. The experimental students, however, did show a significantly less positive attitude toward value analysis than the students who did not receive the special instruction. It was hypothesized that the repetitive nature of the programmed lessons was probably responsible. This led the developers to create the "Discussion-Handout Option."

For information on the Value Analysis Capability Development Programs, write W. Keith Evans and Terry P. Applegate, co-directors, Bureau of Educational Research, 308 W. Milton Bennion Hall, University of Utah, Salt Lake City, UT 84112.

Title: VALUES AND YOUTH (Teaching Social Studies in an Age of Crisis—No. 2)

Editor: Robert D. Barr

Publisher: National Council for the Social Studies, 1201 Sixteenth St., N.W., Washington, D.C. 20036

Date: 1971

Grade Level: 7-12

Materials and Cost: Teacher's guide ($2.75)

Values and Youth, a book of teacher readings and resources, was compiled with the hope that teachers will give serious consideration to the dilemmas of youth and the urgent social issues of our time in an effort to make social studies education relevant. Barr believes that youth today are different because "the powerful pressures of the contemporary age surround them with a constantly increasing range and variety of cultural alternatives and value choices." Options often conflict with the traditional values of society. Many students are struggling with these choices without really knowing what to consider or how to go about deciding. The editor believes that, in social studies education, students should learn to analyze alternatives, clarify their own values, and make decisions. The book confronts the problem of how value conflicts can be dealt with in the social studies classroom.

"Voice of Youth: Sources for Teachers," one major section of the book, contains articles written by youth from a wide variety of backgrounds. By reading these, teachers may gain insight into values held by young people. Issues presented in this section could also result in some interesting class discussions. Topics discussed range from race relations and poverty, to youth culture, and the generation gap. The second major section discusses the importance of the teacher's role in valuing activities and provides instructional guidelines, teaching models, unit plans, and a number of activities for secondary students that stress the analysis approach to values education. Articles emphasizing this approach are written by such authors as Newmann, Oliver, and Shaver. Values clarification is also discussed and one article by Simon suggests several activities using this approach. Finally, helpful instructional aids, such as music and films, are recommended. A selected bibliography of related materials is also included.

Title: VALUES EDUCATION: RATIONALE, STRATEGIES, AND PROCEDURES

Editor: Lawrence E. Metcalf

Publisher: National Council for the Social Studies, 1201 Sixteenth St., N.W., Washington, D.C. 20036

Date: 1971

Grade Levels: K-12

Materials and Cost: Teacher's guide (paperbound—$5.00, hardbound—$6.50)

Values Education: Rationale, Strategies, and Procedures, the 41st Yearbook of the National Council for the Social Studies, explains the central objectives, techniques, and procedures of a value analysis program developed largely by Jerrold R. Coombs and Milton Meux (Meux 1974). Recent work in expanding and refining that program has been accomplished by the Value Analysis Capability Development Programs in Salt Lake City, Utah, and is reflected in the project's final report (Meux 1974) and teacher's handbook (Evans *et al.* 1974). (See the analysis of *Rational Value Decisions* . . . earlier in this section.)

The first chapter defines *value judgments* ("those judgments which rate things with respect to their worth"), distinguishes the term from *factual judgments* and *attitudes,* outlines the conditions needed for a rational value judgment, and specifies several key objectives of value analysis. Three of these major objectives are "(1) helping students make the most rational value judgment they can about the value issue under consideration, (2) helping students develop the capabilities and dispositions required for making rational value decisions, and (3) teaching students how to resolve value conflict between themselves and other members of a group."

Chapter 2, "Teaching Strategies for Value Analysis," explicates six basic tasks involved in a rational and evaluative decision-making process and discusses techniques that teachers can use to help students with these tasks. The six processes or tasks are identifying and clarifying the value question. assembling purported facts, assessing the truth of purported facts, clarifying relevance of those facts, arriving at a tentative value decision, and testing the value principle implied in the decision. The last section of the chapter discusses how some of the implications of ego development theory apply to the attempt to develop value analysis capabilities in students.

In the third chapter two specific step-by-step procedures for applying the program are explained and illustrated. One is the "Rudimentary Procedure," consisting of eight steps designed to provide the teacher with a flexible structure for helping students through the six value analysis tasks. The other is the "Extended Procedure," consisting of 14 steps that include the use of personal interviews, evidence cards, and group discussions.

The final chapter presents specific methods for resolving value conflicts related to each of the six tasks of value analysis. The primary strategy is to minimize the differences in how the six tasks are applied. For example, the teacher would minimize the differences in how students would interpret the value question or assemble purported facts. Also provided are an illustration of how these methods can be applied to an issue, such as guaranteed annual income, and an enumeration of key logical, procedural, and psychological principles involved in conflict.

An appendix contains a procedure for conducting objective personal interviews and a programmed text for learning the terms and ideas related to this value analysis model.

V

clarification

The clarification approach to values education has emanated primarily from the humanistic education movement and has been popularized through the workshop efforts of Sidney Simon and his associates. The first section of this chapter explains clarification in terms of its rationale, purposes, teaching methods, and instructional model. An illustrative learning activity characteristic of this approach is then provided, followed by a discussion of many of the curriculum materials that use clarification methodology. The chapter concludes with the presentation of analytical summaries of 26 student materials and 13 teacher resources that reflect the clarification approach to values education.

Explanation of the Approach

Rationale and Purpose. The central focus of clarification is helping students use both rational thinking and emotional awareness to examine personal behavior patterns and to clarify and actualize their values. Students are encouraged to identify and become aware of their own values and the interrelationship among values, to uncover and resolve personal value conflicts, to share their values with others, and to act according to their own value choices. Valuing, according to proponents of this approach, is a process of self-actualization involving the subprocesses of choosing freely from among alternatives, reflecting carefully on the consequences of those alternatives, and prizing, affirming, and acting upon one's choices. Values are considered the results of these subprocesses. This specific value conception was developed by Raths *et al.* (1966), although various "humanistic psychologists" have also propounded similar ideas about the nature of values and valuing.* Whereas the inculcation approach relies generally on outside influences and the analysis approach relies on logical and empirical processes, the clarification approach relies on the wisdom of the whole human organism to decide which values are positive and which are negative. Moustakas (1966, p. 11) has described the process of value development from a clarification perspective:

> The individual, being free to be, makes choices and decisions affected by willing, feeling, thinking, and intending. Through self-awareness, the person enters situa-

*The other major clarification theorists are Maslow (1970), Rogers (1969), and Moustakas (1966). Allport (1955), G. Murphy (1958), and Asch (1952) have also expressed views closely related to this conception of valuing.

tions already pointed or set in certain directions. Later the experience of the individual in making choices is often based on conscious, self-determined thought and feeling. The making of choices, as a free being, which can be confirmed or denied in experience, is a preliminary step in the creation of values. Choices which confirm being and lead to enriching and expanding self-awareness, choices which deepen experience and lead to new experience, choices which challenge uniqueness and talent and lead to actualizations, enable the person to establish further his own identity. Ultimately those choices which confirm life and enable the individual to become what he can be are chosen as values. As long as the flow of real life is affirmed, then further life is facilitated. Increasingly, through a process which includes freedom, will, intention, desire, choice, confirmation and responsibility, the individual is growing and expanding in authentic ways; the individual is creating new awarenesses and values; the individual is coming to be what he can be in the light of opportunities and resources outside and potentialities and challenges inside.

Thus, within the clarification framework, a person is an initiator of interaction with society and the environment. Internal rather than external factors are seen as the prime determinants of human behavior. The individual is free to change the environment to meet his or her needs. In order to achieve this, however, a person must use all of his or her resources—including rational and emotional processes, conscious and unconscious feelings, and mind and body functions.*

Teaching Methods. Clarification, more than any other values education approach, utilizes a wide range of methods and techniques. This has occured largely because Simon, the leading advocate of clarification, and his associates have concentrated their efforts on developing and using new valuing strategies. These methods include large- and small-group discussion; individual and group work; hypothetical, contrived, and real dilemmas; rank orders and forced choices; sensitivity and listening techniques; songs and artwork; games and simulations; and personal journals and interviews.

The technique that best exemplifies and is the most characteristic of the clarification approach, however, is the self-analysis reaction worksheet. This usually consists of short readings, questions, drawings, or activities designed to stimulate students to reflect on their own thoughts, feelings, actions, and values.

Instructional Model. The instructional model for clarification is based on the sevenfold process of valuing formulated by Raths *et al.* (1966). This model, unlike the models of other approaches, is not a rigid step-by-step set of procedures; rather, it is a flexible set of guidelines for teachers to use with students. The following procedures are adapted from Raths *et al.* (1966, pp. 38-39):

1) *Choosing from alternatives:* Help students to discover, examine, and choose from among available alternatives.
2) *Choosing thoughtfully:* Help students to weigh alternatives thoughtfully by reflecting on the consequences of each alternative.
3) *Choosing freely:* Encourage students to make choices freely and to determine how past choices were made.
4) *Prizing one's choice:* Encourage students to consider what it is they prize and cherish.
5) *Affirming one's choice:* Provide students opportunities to make public affirmations of their choices.
6) *Acting upon one's choice:* Encourage students to act, behave, and live in accordance with their choices.
7) *Acting repeatedly, over time:* Help students to examine and to establish repeated behaviors or patterns of actions based on their choices.

All of the techniques or strategies designed to clarify values embody one or more aspects of this model. The activity described below is an example of a self-analysis worksheet that operationalizes several procedures outlined in the model.

*The other major clarification theorists are Maslow (1970), Rogers (1969), and Moustakas (1966). Allport (1955), G. Murphy (1958), and Asch (1952) have also expressed views closely related to this conception of valuing.

Illustrative Learning Activity. This activity is an adaptation of the "Twenty Things You Like To Do" strategy devised by Simon *et al.* (1972, pp. 30-34.) It is strongly recommended that the reader actually engage in the activity to gain a clearer understanding of the clarification approach.

First, down the center of the page, the student lists 20 things he or she "loves to do." Then, to the left of each item, the student gives the following information: 1) the date when you last did that activity; 2) "A" if you prefer to do it alone, "P" if you prefer it with people; 3) "$" if it costs more than $3 each time it's done; 4) "N5" if it would not have been on your list 5 years ago; 5) "M" or "F" if it would have been on the list of your mother or father; 6) "*" for your five most important activities; and; 7) "1-5" to rank order those top five.

After this, the student answers the following three questions about the list as a whole: 1) How recently have you done your top five? 2) Which of your 20 do you wish you would do more often? How could you begin to do so? 3) Would you share your top five with the class?

Next, the student chooses one of his or her top five preferences and lists five benefits received from doing it. Finally, the student writes five statements completing the stem, "I learned that I . . ."

Characteristic of the clarification approach is the thoughtful examination of one's personal life which this activity emphasizes. Students begin by recalling the actions they most enjoy (Steps 4 and 7 of the model). The coding phase of the activity also involves these steps. The rank order emphasizes choosing thoughtfully from alternatives (Steps 1 and 2). Affirming one's choices (Step 5) occurs when students are asked to share their top five actions.

Materials and Programs. Clarification is one of the most widespread and controversial approaches to values education. There are nearly as many student and teacher materials using the clarification approach as there are materials embodying all of the other approaches. The original teacher text in values clarification, *Values and Teaching* (Raths *et al.* 1966), is analyzed in this chapter, as well as many of the student and teacher resources that have developed directly or indirectly from the work of Simon, Harmin, and others. The teacher materials directly reflecting Simon's work include *Values Clarification* (Simon *et al.* 1972), *Clarifying Values Through Subject Matter* (Harmin *et al.* 1973), *Composition for Personal Growth* (Hawley 1973), and *Value Exploration Through Role Playing* (Hawley 1975). Student materials that have been developed by various authors who have had some associations with Simon's work include *Search for Values* and *Search for Meaning,* two components of Pflaum's *Dimensions of Personality* program; *Deciding For Myself* (Winston Press); *People Projects* (Addison-Wesley); *Decisions and Outcomes* and *Deciding* (College Entrance Examination Board); and *Making Sense of Our Lives* (Argus).

Many materials, however, have been developed independently of this group of educators and also embody a clarification approach to values education. Among those analyzed in this chapter are *Values in Action* (Winston Press), *Focus on Self-Development* (Science Research Associates), *Developing Understanding of Self and Others–DUSO* (American Guidance Service), and *Toward Affective Development–TAD* (American Guidance Service). Textbook series are also analyzed such as the *Values Education Series* (McDougal, Littell) and *Contact* (Scholastic Magazines). One multimedia program, *Self-Expression and Conduct* (Harcourt Brace Jovanovich) has a humanities focus, while another, *The Valuing Approach to Career Education* (Educational Achievement Corporation), integrates values education with career education. In addition to these resources, many others are analyzed in this chapter, including supplementary filmstrips from Argus Communications and several sound-slide programs from the Center for Humanities.

Although all the materials analyzed in this chapter reflect the clarification approach to values education, some incorporate aspects of other approaches as well. *DUSO,* for example, while using an open-ended approach to questioning in order to clarify students' personal feelings and values, also attempts to inculcate certain values, such as independence, emotion. *Self Expression and Conduct* focuses on five basic values—truth, beauty, justice, love, and faith. The activities, however, attempt to help students clarify their own concepts of these values and to make decisions accordingly. Throughout all these materials there is an implicit or explicit effort to help students value their own individuality, the feelings of others, and purposeful action.

clarification: student materials

Curriculum: ARGUS FILMSTRIPS

Titles: *Lets's Get Organized!; Strike It Rich!; Feelings and Thoughts; The IALAC Story; Truth and Consequences; Fuzzies; Friendly and Hostile; You Have to Want Something; Consumerland: How High the Mountain?; Technology: Master or Slave?; The Wonder of It All; Faces of Man; Roles & Goals; Man the Man; Perception;* and *Why Am I Afraid to Tell You Who I Am?*

Publisher: Argus Communications, 7440 Natchez, Niles, IL 60648

Date: 1974

Grade Levels: 7-12

Materials and Cost: 16 audiovisual kits, each containing filmstrip with record or cassette and teacher's guide ($20.00 each title except last); *Why Am I Afraid to Tell You Who I Am* ($40.00)

This series contains 16 sound-filmstrips intended for junior and senior high students. A few of the filmstrips could also be used with intermediate-grade students. The rationale underlying the materials can be summed up in the motto, "Preparing youth to build a better world." The primary focus of the material is on values clarification and skill development. Objectives for values clarification include building a positive self-concept; understanding the feelings and emotions of self and others; discovering goals; becoming aware and sensitive to self, others, and surroundings; and discovering full human potential. In the area of skill development, it is hoped that students will learn to make decisions based on their values and on a consideration of alternatives and consequences; to organize and plan for the achievement of their goals; to empathize; and to improve their communication skills.

Each filmstrip is made up of either color photographs or cartoons. The content varies from a personal focus, such as "I Am Loveable and Capable" (IALAC), to a social focus, such as exploring technology and the relationship of people to machines. The students examine their values and ask themselves, What's important to me? They take a look at feelings and thoughts, moods and emotions, human likenesses and differences, and differences in perception. Discussion questions and activities for each filmstrip are also included. The activities involve creative writing, games, role play, and other decision-making and clarification exercises. For example, in *Strike It Rich!* students are asked to make a list of times they found it necessary to change their goals. They are then asked, "Why did you change them? Did your values change at the same time? When you change your goals must you also change your values? Why or why not?" These filmstrips may be used in general social studies or English classes, as well as in such classes as sociology, psychology, social issues, human relations, creative writing, communications, and art.

DESCRIPTIVE CHARACTERISTICS

Grade Level

___ K-3
___ 4-6
X 7-8
X 9-10
X 11-12

Materials

___ Student materials
X Teacher guide
X A-V kit
___ Tests
___ Other: ________________

Time

___ Curriculum (2 or more years)
___ Course (one year)
___ Semester (half year)
___ Minicourse (6-9 weeks)
___ Units (1-3 weeks)
X Supplementary
___ Other: ________________

Medium Used

___ Readings
___ Worksheets
___ Films
X Filmstrips
X Records or tapes
___ Charts or posters
___ Transparencies
___ Other: ________________

PRECONDITIONS

Amount of Reading

___ Much
___ Moderate
X Very little

Teacher Training

___ Provided in materials
___ Suggested by developers
X Not mentioned
___ Other: ________________

Prejudice/Stereotyping

Much evidence = M
Some evidence = S

___ Racial or Ethnic
___ Sexrole
___ Other: ________________

EVALUATION INFORMATION

Provision for Student Evaluation

___ Instruments specified
___ Procedures specified
___ Guidelines suggested
X Nothing provided
___ Other: ________________

Materials Evaluation

Materials tested = T
Results available = A

___ Fieldtested before publication
___ Fieldtested after publication
___ User feedback solicited
___ Other: ________________
X Not evaluated

SUBSTANTIVE CHARACTERISTICS

Values Education Approach

___ Inculcation
___ Moral development
___ Analysis
X Clarification
___ Action learning
___ Other: ________________

Values Education Emphasis

X Major focus
___ One of several concerns
___ A minor concern

Process/Content Emphasis

X Process of valuing
___ Content of valuing

Objectives

___ Stated specifically
X Stated generally
___ Not stated

Student Activities

Used or stressed frequently = F
Used or stressed occasionally = O

___ Reading
O Writing
F Class discussion
F Small-group discussion
O Games
___ Simulations
O Role playing
___ Action projects
___ Other: ________________

Curriculum: CONTACT

Titles: *Movies: The Magic of Film; TV: Behind the Tube; Communication: Person to Person; This Land Is Our Land: The American Dream; The Future: Can We Shape It?; Imagination: The World of Inner Space; Environment: Earth in Crises; Prejudice: The Invisible Wall; Drugs: Insights and Illusions; Getting Together: Problems You Face; Law: You, the Police, and Justice; Loyalties: Whose Side Are You On?;* and *Maturity: Growing Up Strong*

Editor: William F. Goodykoontz

Publisher: Scholastic Book Services, 904 Sylvan Ave., Englewood, Cliffs, NJ 07632

Dates: 1968-74

Grade Levels: 7-12

Materials and Cost: Each title, including the following components: 36 reading anthologies, 36 student logbooks, eight 22'' x 32'' posters, teacher's guide, and 1 record ($79.50). (*Communication, This Land Is Our Land, Movies,* and *TV* packages include 1 sound-filmstrip each, which replaces the record. Total package for titles with sound-filmstrips, $89.50.)

The 13 units in the *Contact* program were designed to involve students who have reading difficulties in an informative and personal reading experience. The program's goals are "to help students to read, think, speak, and write better and to help them learn more about a subject of importance to themselves and to society." The anthologies provide opportunities for students to express and clarify their thoughts and feelings. In the teacher's guide that accompanies each unit, specific lesson objectives are stated. For example, in the unit dealing with loyalties, one objective is "to stimulate students to think about the importance—and some of the problems—of loyalty among friends; . . . to give . . . examples of conflicts of loyalties among friends; and to tell how they would resolve each conflict—and why."

The anthology of readings, which is the major component of each unit, contains short stories, plays, letters, poetry, and questions that focus on topics reflecting individual interests—personal loyalty, maturation, imagination—as well as social issues—prejudice, environment, the law. For example, the unit that deals with maturity encourages students to look at the topics of self-knowledge, family behavior, responsibility, and individual behavior. *Law* explores the legal rights and responsibilities of citizens, the relationships between police and citizens, and the values underlying our legal system. Exercises in the Student Logbook that accompanies each unit ask students to analyze statements, express their feelings about the characters in a story, and react to the people or action in an illustration. The units also include records that are intended to encourage students to express their thoughts and feelings.

In addition to learning objectives, the teacher's guide outlines the readings and contains lesson plans, suggestions for motivating student interest in the anthology, and a variety of follow-through activities such as debates, TV-style interviews, story telling, drawing, and library research.

The anthologies were evaluated and revised before publication. User feedback was solicited through classroom visits, workshops, informal interviews, and questionnaires requesting specific reactions and general recommendations for improvement. In addition, *Loyalties, Law, Environment,* and *Future* were extensively tested by the Diablo Valley Education Project, Orinda, California. *Law: You, the Police and Justice,* for example, was evaluated by eight teachers in grades seven through ten. A summary of their individual reports indicates that the text "developed the concepts clearly," "held very high student interest," and was useful in individualized and group settings.

DESCRIPTIVE CHARACTERISTICS

Grade Level

__ K-3
__ 4-6
X 7-8
X 9-10
X 11-12

Materials

X Student materials
X Teacher guide
__ A-V kit
__ Tests
__ Other: ______

Time

__ Curriculum (2 or more years)
__ Course (one year)
__ Semester (half year)
__ Minicourse (6-9 weeks)
X Units (1-3 weeks)
X Supplementary
__ Other: ______

Medium Used

X Readings
__ Worksheets
__ Films
X Filmstrips
X Records or tapes
X Charts or posters
__ Transparencies
X Other: Logbooks

PRECONDITIONS

Amount of Reading

X Much
__ Moderate
__ Very little

Teacher Training

__ Provided in materials
__ Suggested by developers
X Not mentioned
__ Other: ______

Prejudice/Stereotyping

Much evidence = M
Some evidence = S

__ Racial or Ethnic
__ Sexrole
__ Other: ______

EVALUATION INFORMATION

Provision for Student Evaluation

__ Instruments specified
__ Procedures specified
X Guidelines suggested
__ Nothing provided
__ Other: ______

Materials Evaluation

Materials tested = T
Results available = A

A Fieldtested before publication
__ Fieldtested after publication
A User feedback solicited
A Other: 4 units tested elsewhere
__ Not evaluated

SUBSTANTIVE CHARACTERISTICS

Values Education Approach

__ Inculcation
__ Moral development
__ Analysis
X Clarification
__ Action learning
__ Other: ______

Values Education Emphasis

__ Major focus
X One of several concerns
__ A minor concern

Process/Content Emphasis

__ Process of valuing
__ Content of valuing

Objectives

X Stated specifically
__ Stated generally
__ Not stated

Student Activities

Used or stressed frequently = F
Used or stressed occasionally = O

F Reading
F Writing
O Class discussion
__ Small-group discussion
__ Games
O Simulations
O Role playing
__ Action projects
O Other: Attitude surveys

Titles: DECIDING and DECISIONS AND OUTCOMES

Authors: H. B. Gelatt, Barbara Varenhorst, Richard Carey, and Gordon P. Miller

Publisher: College Entrance Examination Board, 888 Seventh Ave., New York, NY 10019

Dates: 1972, 1973

Grade Levels: 7-9, 10-12

Materials and Cost: For each title: student text ($2.50); teacher's guide (for *Deciding*—$2.00; for *Decisions and Outcomes*—$3.00); teacher's guides free with set of 20 or more student books

Deciding, a junior high school program, and *Decisions and Outcomes,* a program for senior high school students, both focus on developing students' decision-making skills, especially in regard to educational and career opportunities. Objectives include the examination and clarification of personal values and goals, the ability to identify and create new alternatives, and the ability to make decisions based on the consideration of alternatives and values. According to the authors, the overall goal of the program is for students to be able to apply the decision-making skills acquired in the course to their own lives.

There are six interrelated content areas covered in each course: "identifying critical decision points; recognizing and clarifying personal values; identifying alternatives and creating new ones; seeking, evaluating, and utilizing information; risk-taking; and developing strategies for decision making." Self-discovery and awareness of personal values are emphasized continuously. One lesson, for example, asks students to list their three most important values and a recent action in which they demonstrated each value. A variety of activities, including simulations, role play, written exercises, and discussion, are employed to give the students practice in making decisions. These activities are usually part of a worksheet that includes drawings and charts. The materials can be used as the basis of a minicourse in decision making, as supplementary materials for a year-long course in social studies, English, or health, or as the basis for a guidance program.

The College Entrance Examination Board conducts training sessions for teachers and leaders who are using these materials. They also provide a training film, which is available on a free loan basis. Student feedback forms are provided with the materials and it is suggested that teachers continuously be aware of informal student input during the lessons.

The programs have been fieldtested. Several extensive questionnaires were developed and used for this purpose. One study used *Deciding* with 200 students in grades seven, eight, and ten for 12 to 15 class sessions. Although no significant behavioral changes were reported in the experimental students, "there was some indication that students who had *Deciding* were more inclined to think about making decisions" and "felt surer about the things that interested them most" than those in the control group.

DESCRIPTIVE CHARACTERISTICS

Grade Level

__ K-3
__ 4-6
X 7-8
X 9-10
X 11-12

Materials

X Student materials
X Teacher guide
__ A-V kit
__ Tests
__ Other: ________

Time

__ Curriculum (2 or more years)
__ Course (one year)
__ Semester (half year)
X Minicourse (6-9 weeks)
__ Units (1-3 weeks)
X Supplementary
__ Other: ________

Medium Used

X Readings
X Worksheets
__ Films
__ Filmstrips
__ Records or tapes
__ Charts or posters
__ Transparencies
__ Other: ________

PRECONDITIONS

Amount of Reading

__ Much
X Moderate
__ Very little

Teacher Training

__ Provided in materials
__ Suggested by developers
__ Not mentioned
X Other: Available from publisher

Prejudice/Stereotyping

Much evidence = M
Some evidence = S

__ Racial or Ethnic
__ Sexrole
__ Other: ________

EVALUATION INFORMATION

Provision for Student Evaluation

X Instruments specified
__ Procedures specified
__ Guidelines suggested
__ Nothing provided
__ Other: ________

Materials Evaluation

Materials tested = T
Results available = A

A Fieldtested before publication
A Fieldtested after publication
A User feedback solicited
__ Other: ________
__ Not evaluated

SUBSTANTIVE CHARACTERISTICS

Values Education Approach

__ Inculcation
__ Moral development
__ Analysis
X Clarification
__ Action learning
__ Other: ________

Values Education Emphasis

X Major focus
__ One of several concerns
__ A minor concern

Process/Content Emphasis

X Process of valuing
__ Content of valuing

Objectives

__ Stated specifically
X Stated generally
__ Not stated

Student Activities

Used or stressed frequently = F
Used or stressed occasionally = O

O Reading
O Writing
F Class discussion
F Small-group discussion
__ Games
O Simulations
O Role playing
__ Action projects
__ Other: ________

Curriculum: DECIDING FOR MYSELF: A VALUES-CLARIFICATION SERIES

Titles: *Set A: Clarifying My Values; Set B: My Everyday Choices; Set C: Where Do I Stand?*

Developer: Wayne Paulson

Publisher: Winston Press, Inc., 25 Groveland Terrace, Minneapolis, MN 55403

Date: 1974

Grade Levels: 6-12

Materials and Cost: Student materials ($2.40 each set of 10 eight-page units; 3 sets—$7.20); teacher's guide ($3.96)

Deciding for Myself: A Values Clarification Series is intended for students in grades six through 12, as well as for adults. According to the author, the purpose of values clarification, and the goal of the series, is to create an environment in which students learn the processes of values development. The valuing process involves certain basic elements with which students become familiar while using these materials. These include exploring the meaning of personal freedom, considering alternatives and consequences, learning to prioritize, learning communication skills, and, finally, being able to integrate behavior with thoughts and feelings. Objectives involving the student's thoughts, feelings, and actions are stated at the beginning of each unit and lesson. In one lesson, entitled "Roles (What Are We Doing Here?)," students examine their current roles in life, what it is about these roles that they like or do not like, and how they would like their roles to change in the future.

The topics covered in these materials include clarifying personal values, making everyday choices, and expressing feelings about important social issues. The leader's guide presents a model for providing valuing experiences. The model includes a values issue, a basic strategy, a working structure, and a sharing structure. For example, if students are thinking about the issue of roles, the basic strategy might be a simulation or an activity in which students express their feelings through dialogue, drawing, or writing. The working structure could involve just the individual, a small group, or the total group. The sharing structure might involve the group's focusing on one student at a time or having individual participants briefly share their responses with one other. This model can be applied to each lesson in the materials and may be used to extend the course after the three sets of materials have been covered.

The materials can be used as the basis for a weekend seminar; as a minicourse; in a guidance program; or over a period of one to three years supplementing courses such as social studies, career education, home economics, environmental education, and religion. The effectiveness of the course relies on a classroom climate in which participants feel free to express their ideas and share their feelings. Therefore, the author urges that students must not be forced to participate, must have the right to pass on a response if they so desire, and must have all responses accepted as right answers. No positive or negative evaluations should be made either by the leader or by other participants. Further, the leader must also be a participant. The leader's guide provides detailed suggestions for conducting the course and creating an open atmosphere. The author recommends that any teacher using the materials first become familiar with the guide.

Many of the activities in this series were fieldtested by the author in classrooms and workshops, but no formal results or data were gathered. User feedback indicates that these materials are well organized and that the leader's guide "offers the kind of instructions any teacher can use." The materials were also favorably reviewed in two religious educational journals—*SCAN* and *Probe*. The October 1974 issue of *Probe* states that it is an "excellent stimulus for rethinking values." *SCAN* (vol. 3, no. 5, 1974) states that the teacher's guide "summarizes well the basics of values clarification."

DESCRIPTIVE CHARACTERISTICS

Grade Level

___ K-3
X 4-6
X 7-8
X 9-10
X 11-12

Materials

X Student materials
X Teacher guide
___ A-V kit
___ Tests
___ Other: ________________

Time

___ Curriculum (2 or more years)
___ Course (one year)
___ Semester (half year)
X Minicourse (6-9 weeks)
___ Units (1-3 weeks)
X Supplementary
___ Other: ________________

Medium Used

___ Readings
X Worksheets
___ Films
___ Filmstrips
___ Records or tapes
___ Charts or posters
___ Transparencies
___ Other: ________________

PRECONDITIONS

Amount of Reading

___ Much
X Moderate
___ Very little

Teacher Training

___ Provided in materials
___ Suggested by developers
X Not mentioned
___ Other: ________________

Prejudice/Stereotyping

Much evidence = M
Some evidence = S

___ Racial or Ethnic
___ Sexrole
___ Other: ________________

EVALUATION INFORMATION

Provision for Student Evaluation

___ Instruments specified
___ Procedures specified
___ Guidelines suggested
X Nothing provided
___ Other: ________________

Materials Evaluation

Materials tested = T
Results available = A

T Fieldtested before publication
___ Fieldtested after publication
___ User feedback solicited
A Other: ________________
___ Not evaluated

SUBSTANTIVE CHARACTERISTICS

Values Education Approach

___ Inculcation
___ Moral development
___ Analysis
X Clarification
___ Action learning
___ Other: ________________

Values Education Emphasis

X Major focus
___ One of several concerns
___ A minor concern

Process/Content Emphasis

X Process of valuing
___ Content of valuing

Objectives

X Stated specifically
___ Stated generally
___ Not stated

Student Activities

Used or stressed frequently = F
Used or stressed occasionally = O

O Reading
F Writing
F Class discussion
F Small-group discussion
___ Games
___ Simulations
O Role playing
O Action projects
O Other: ________________

Titles: DECISION-MAKING: DEALING WITH CRISES and DECIDING RIGHT FROM WRONG: THE DILEMMA OF MORALITY TODAY

Publisher: The Center for Humanities, Inc., Two Holland Ave., White Plains, NY 10603

Date: 1974

Grade Levels: 9-12

Materials and Cost: For each title: audiovisual kit containing 160 slides in 2 carousel cartridges, 2 tape cassettes or 2 records, and teacher's guide *(Decision-Making*–$99.85; *Deciding Right from Wrong*–$104.50)

Decision-Making and *Deciding Right from Wrong* are two sound/slide programs that present various value crises and moral dilemmas in order to teach students certain decision-making and judgment-forming skills. *Decision-Making* is intended to "help students learn four skills of crisis-management: recognizing that the crisis exists, becoming aware of emotional reactions to the crisis, moving beyond emotional reactions to a rational consideration of the crisis, and analyzing the alternative methods of dealing with the crisis." The purpose of *Deciding Right from Wrong* is to encourage students to examine the origins of their own and society's moral standards. These sound slides can be used in a variety of curriculum areas such as English, social studies, humanities, guidance, and art.

Decision-Making deals with some of the personal problems young people encounter while growing up—drinking, pregnancy, school, and problems at home. An example is that of 17-year-old Jennifer Denton, who is pregnant. She seeks her sister's advice about what to do. After discussing and analyzing every alternative, she must make the final decision. *Deciding Right from Wrong* examines the circumstances under which some crucial historical and literary decisions have been made and the personal and social consequences that followed. For instance, one personality treated in the slides is Senator Edmund Ross of Kansas, who cast the deciding vote against convicting President Andrew Johnson. As a result, his political career abruptly came to an end. The program also points out that the concept of right and wrong varies according to time, place, and culture. An example is the case of Kitty Genovese, who was murdered in New York City. No one came to her aid even though more than 30 people heard her screams for help.

The teacher's guide contains warm-up activities, discussion questions, and research activities for additional inquiry and discussion.

The materials were fieldtested before publication but the results are not available. According to the publisher, informal feedback from local teachers was favorable.

DESCRIPTIVE CHARACTERISTICS

Grade Level

___ K-3
___ 4-6
___ 7-8
X 9-10
X 11-12

Materials

___ Student materials
X Teacher guide
X A-V kit
___ Tests
___ Other: ___

Time

___ Curriculum (2 or more years)
___ Course (one year)
___ Semester (half year)
___ Minicourse (6-9 weeks)
___ Units (1-3 weeks)
X Supplementary
___ Other: ___

Medium Used

___ Readings
___ Worksheets
___ Films
___ Filmstrips
X Records or tapes
___ Charts or posters
___ Transparencies
X Other: Slides

PRECONDITIONS

Amount of Reading

___ Much
___ Moderate
X Very little

Teacher Training

___ Provided in materials
___ Suggested by developers
X Not mentioned
___ Other: ___

Prejudice/Stereotyping

Much evidence = M
Some evidence = S

___ Racial or Ethnic
___ Sexrole
___ Other: ___

EVALUATION INFORMATION

Provision for Student Evaluation

___ Instruments specified
___ Procedures specified
___ Guidelines suggested
X Nothing provided
___ Other: ___

Materials Evaluation

Materials tested = T
Results available = A

T Fieldtested before publication
___ Fieldtested after publication
T User feedback solicited
___ Other: ___
___ Not evaluated

SUBSTANTIVE CHARACTERISTICS

Values Education Approach

___ Inculcation
___ Moral development
___ Analysis
X Clarification
___ Action learning
___ Other: ___

Values Education Emphasis

X Major focus
___ One of several concerns
___ A minor concern

Process/Content Emphasis

X Process of valuing
___ Content of valuing

Objectives

X Stated specifically
___ Stated generally
___ Not stated

Student Activities

Used or stressed frequently = F
Used or stressed occasionally = O

___ Reading
O Writing
F Class discussion
___ Small-group discussion
___ Games
___ Simulations
___ Role playing
___ Action projects
___ Other: ___

Curriculum: DEVELOPING UNDERSTANDING OF SELF AND OTHERS (DUSO), D-1, D-2

Author: Don Dinkmeyer

Publisher: American Guidance Service, Publisher's Bldg., Circle Pines, MN 55014

Dates: 1970, 1973

Grade Levels: K-1, 2-4

Materials and Cost: 2 multimedia kits, each including records or cassettes, discussion cards, posters with display easel, hand puppets, activity cards, story books or records, discussion pictures, and teacher's guide: DUSO D-1 (total package—$95.00); DUSO D-2 (total package—$98.00).

An experiential learning package, *Developing Understanding of Self and Others* (DUSO) is designed to help students in the primary grades better understand their own thoughts, feelings, and actions, as well as those of others. The author believes it is necessary to satisfy a child's emotional and social needs before cognitive learning can take place. Concerned with personalizing and humanizing education, he feels it is imperative for learning experiences to strengthen a child's self-esteem, rather than diminish it, as is often the case. DUSO therefore primarily focuses on affective and social development. Objectives include understanding and accepting oneself as a unique and worthy human being; understanding, respecting, and empathizing with others; and becoming aware of one's own feelings and values. For each activity a more specific objective is given, such as "to see how positive and negative criticism can influence a person's involvement" or "to develop in children an appreciation of individual differences and to help them understand that individuality enables each person to make a unique contribution to the total effort."

Students begin all lessons by listening to a story. The stories depict real life situations such as losing a bike, learning how to swim, and competing for the first drink at the water fountain. The theme and objectives in the story are then stressed in the accompanying activities. These include discussion of problem situations, role plays, puppet activities, and career awareness exercises. Each of the lesson themes represents what the author feels is an important developmental task for the child. Among the themes examined are awareness of feelings, understanding of values, personal abilities, and emotional maturity. The two materials packages may each be used on a daily basis for an entire school year, or a teacher or guidance counselor may choose only certain parts of the program to meet the particular needs and interests of students.

For the materials to be used successfully, the learning climate is most important. The guide suggests that it is crucial for children to feel free to express and act out their ideas and feelings. To establish such an open, trusting atmosphere, the teacher and other students must accept all responses from each child without positive or negative evaluation.

Some evidence of sex-role sterotyping does exist in these materials. One tendency is to reinforce the image of the helpless girl assisted by the strong boy. Duso the Dolphin (a male), for instance, helps Flopsy Flounder (a female) become less floundering and more decisive. In another story Duso and Lefty (an octopus) save the life of Clarissa Clam.

Classroom fieldtests of these materials were conducted over a period of three years with students from a wide variety of backgrounds. A list of the participating schools and coordinators is included in each of the leader's manuals. In addition, all of the fieldtest results, as well as forms used to gather user feedback results, are available. A list of research studies, articles, and reviews about DUSO may also be obtained from the publisher. One study used a "randomized post-test only" design to determine how effective DUSO was in achieving goals such as helping students to understand feelings, others, self, choices, and consequences. Although the experimental classroom means on these dimensions were slightly higher than those of the control classrooms, these differences were not statistically significant.

DESCRIPTIVE CHARACTERISTICS

Grade Level

X K-3
X 4-6
___ 7-8
___ 9-10
___ 11-12

Materials

X Student materials
X Teacher guide
X A-V kit
___ Tests
___ Other: ___

Time

X Curriculum (2 or more years)
___ Course (one year)
___ Semester (half year)
___ Minicourse (6-9 weeks)
___ Units (1-3 weeks)
X Supplementary
___ Other: ___

Medium Used

X Readings
___ Worksheets
___ Films
___ Filmstrips
X Records or tapes
X Charts or posters
___ Transparencies
X Other: Puppets Activity Cards

PRECONDITIONS

Amount of Reading

___ Much
___ Moderate
X Very little

Teacher Training

___ Provided in materials
___ Suggested by developers
X Not mentioned
___ Other: ___

Prejudice/Stereotyping

Much evidence = M
Some evidence = S

___ Racial or Ethnic
S Sexrole
___ Other: ___

EVALUATION INFORMATION

Provision for Student Evaluation

___ Instruments specified
___ Procedures specified
___ Guidelines suggested
X Nothing provided
___ Other: ___

Materials Evaluation

Materials tested = T
Results available = A

A Fieldtested before publication
A Fieldtested after publication
A User feedback solicited
A Other: Research studies
___ Not evaluated

SUBSTANTIVE CHARACTERISTICS

Values Education Approach

___ Inculcation
___ Moral development
___ Analysis
X Clarification
___ Action learning
___ Other: ___

Values Education Emphasis

X Major focus
___ One of several concerns
___ A minor concern

Process/Content Emphasis

___ Process of valuing
X Content of valuing

Objectives

X Stated specifically
___ Stated generally
___ Not stated

Student Activities

Used or stressed frequently = F
Used or stressed occasionally = O

___ Reading
___ Writing
F Class discussion
F Small-group discussion
___ Games
___ Simulations
F Role playing
___ Action projects
O Other: Listening, Puppets Singing

Curriculum: DIMENSIONS OF PERSONALITY

Titles: *Let's Begin* (grade K); *Now I'm Ready* (1); *I Can Do It* (2); *What About Me* (3); *Here I Am* (4); *I'm Not Alone* (5); *Becoming Myself* (6)

Authors: Carl Fischer and Walter Limbacher

Publisher: Pflaum Publishing, 2285 Arbor Blvd., Dayton, OH 45439

Dates: 1969-70, 1972

Grade Levels: K-6

Materials and Cost: Kindergarten picture cards or filmstrips and teacher's guide ($39.95); student text, grades 1-3 ($1.75 each grade); group activity sheets ($3.75 each set for 4 students); student text, grades 4-6 ($2.25-$3.25 paperbound, $3.75-$4.75 hardbound each grade); spirit masters ($2.00-$3.10 each set); teacher's editions ($4.45-$5.75 each)

The authors of *Dimensions of Personality* believe that too often schools tend to educate only students' intellect, ignoring their affective development. These materials are based on the belief that a child's feelings and emotions affect all other aspects of learning. It is the intent of this program to provide structured learning experiences for fostering affective development in elementary children. The overall objective for the primary materials is to make possible a smooth social and emotional adjustment to school. Realizing that upper elementary students are going through important social and emotional changes in their lives, the authors intend the intermediate materials to help students understand and accept these changes. Objectives of the curriculum include increasing self-awareness, understanding feelings and emotions, clarifying values, developing a positive self-concept, becoming aware of human likenesses and differences, learning how to get along with others, learning to empathize, understanding reasons for human behavior, and learning how to make satisfying decisions.

The curriculum program at each level focuses on five areas of development related to the affective domain: self-image development, emotional development, intellectual development, physical development, and social development. Competencies and relationships related to these areas are stressed. Each course can be completed in a semester, but the program will be strengthened if taught over an entire school year. This longer time offers additional opportunity for reinforcing the concepts presented in the lessons. Though some students may find the reading too difficult, this problem can be solved easily by having a student or the teacher read aloud. In the kindergarten program there is no reading for the students; rather there are picture stories for which students supply their own dialogue.

The lessons in the program tend to be experience oriented. Teacher's editions suggest a variety of involvement activities to accompany the lessons. In the third-grade material, for example, there is a lesson on fear in which the class is divided into "clubs" of four members each. Each group proceeds to color its clubhouse poster. Soon the rules are changed and clubs are limited to three members. The child from each group who happens to choose the red crayon twice is left out and ignored. This is immediately followed by a class discussion of the fear of being left out, the feelings of those who had to leave their clubs, and the feelings of the remaining members who had to turn out a friend. Subsequent activities deal with other kinds of fears in order to give students a realistic view of this emotion.

The program encourages parental involvement and support by suggesting that parents be given the opportunity to read the book and asked to increase communications with their child.

Evaluation of students by both teachers and parents is encouraged through observation and discussion, in and out of the classroom. Questionnaires are sent to all who use this program in their classes in order to obtain feedback. Interviews, observations, and workshops with users have also been carried out, and the California State Textbook Adoption Committee conducted a readability analysis of the materials. The evaluation results, however, are not available to the public.

DESCRIPTIVE CHARACTERISTICS

Grade Level

X K-3
X 4-6
___ 7-8
___ 9-10
___ 11-12

Materials

X Student materials
X Teacher guide
___ A-V kit
___ Tests
___ Other: ___

Time

X Curriculum (2 or more years)
X Course (one year) each title
___ Semester (half year)
___ Minicourse (6-9 weeks)
___ Units (1-3 weeks)
X Supplementary
___ Other: ___

Medium Used

X Readings
X Worksheets
___ Films
X Filmstrips
___ Records or tapes
___ Charts or posters
___ Transparencies
X Other: Picture cards

PRECONDITIONS

Amount of Reading

X Much
___ Moderate
___ Very little

Teacher Training

___ Provided in materials
___ Suggested by developers
X Not mentioned
___ Other: ___

Prejudice/Stereotyping

Much evidence = M
Some evidence = S

___ Racial or Ethnic
___ Sexrole
___ Other: ___

EVALUATION INFORMATION

Provision for Student Evaluation

___ Instruments specified
___ Procedures specified
X Guidelines suggested
___ Nothing provided
___ Other: ___

Materials Evaluation

Materials tested = T
Results available = A

___ Fieldtested before publication
T Fieldtested after publication
T User feedback solicited
___ Other: ___
___ Not evaluated

SUBSTANTIVE CHARACTERISTICS

Values Education Approach

___ Inculcation
___ Moral development
___ Analysis
X Clarification
___ Action learning
___ Other: ___

Values Education Emphasis

X Major focus
___ One of several concerns
___ A minor concern

Process/Content Emphasis

X Process of valuing
X Content of valuing

Objectives

X Stated specifically
___ Stated generally
___ Not stated

Student Activities

Used or stressed frequently = F
Used or stressed occasionally = O

F Reading
O Writing
F Class discussion
F Small-group discussion
O Games
___ Simulations
___ Role playing
F Action projects
___ Other: ___

Curriculum: DIMENSIONS OF PERSONALITY: SEARCH FOR MEANING

Authors: Ronald Klein, Rose Marie Kramer, Romaine Owens, Mary Jane Simmons, and Karen Walsch

Publisher: Pflaum Publishing, 2285 Arbor Blvd., Dayton, OH 45439

Date: 1974

Grade Levels: 7-8

Materials and Cost: Teacher's multimedia kit containing teacher's guide, book of 71 spirit masters, and 12 posters, 17" x 11" ($44.95)

Search for Meaning is the junior high school component of the *Dimensions of Personality* curriculum. Considering this period of adolescence as "the time of deepest probing," the developers have provided experiences designed to help students examine their lives and clarify their personal values in regard to certain external and internal forces and to their relationships with family and peers. Specific objectives are provided for each of the 36 lessons in the program. The objective of Lesson 2 of the unit on organizations, for example, is "to provide an experience through which the student is able to consider and evaluate the effectiveness of organizations in achieving desirable goals."

Search for Meaning focuses on the personal values and behaviors of students in three areas: external forces, internal forces, and relationships with others. Each of these areas contains from nine to 15 lessons printed on spirit masters and organized into units. "Internal Drives," for example, contains units on capability, flexibility, growth, and responsibility. "Encounter" deals with family, friends, and boy-girl relationships. The typical lesson as detailed in the teacher's guide begins with a brief warm-up discussion, followed by a self-analysis worksheet that usually involves some writing in which students critically examine an aspect of their lives related to the topic under consideration. Sometimes this activity involves the use of role play or simulation, as in the exercise in which students assume the roles of members of a family who are meeting to discuss concerns such as vacation plans or smoking regulations. In this lesson students react to questions such as, "Would you like to live in this family?" and "Which person in the family would you most like to be?" The exercise concludes with a small-group or class debriefing session, after which students are encouraged to file their worksheets as a personal record of their value choices.

Fragmentary responses to a questionnaire administered to users of this program have been mixed and inconclusive. Eleven of 12 respondents indicated that the lessons were relevant for their students. Generally the teachers reported that students were interested and enjoyed the discussions. Because of the predominance of dittoed handouts, teachers did state that "sometimes students groaned, 'Not another worksheet'." The results of this survey may be obtained from the publisher.

DESCRIPTIVE CHARACTERISTICS

Grade Level

___ K-3
___ 4-6
X 7-8
___ 9-10
___ 11-12

Materials

X Student materials
X Teacher guide
___ A-V kit
___ Tests
X Other: Spirit masters, posters

Time

X Curriculum (2 or more years)
X Course (one year)
___ Semester (half year)
___ Minicourse (6-9 weeks)
___ Units (1-3 weeks)
X Supplementary
___ Other: ________

Medium Used

___ Readings
X Worksheets
___ Films
___ Filmstrips
___ Records or tapes
X Charts or posters
___ Transparencies
___ Other: ________

PRECONDITIONS

Amount of Reading

___ Much
X Moderate
___ Very little

Teacher Training

___ Provided in materials
___ Suggested by developers
X Not mentioned
___ Other: ________

Prejudice/Stereotyping

Much evidence = M
Some evidence = S

___ Racial or Ethnic
___ Sexrole
___ Other: ________

EVALUATION INFORMATION

Provision for Student Evaluation

___ Instruments specified
___ Procedures specified
___ Guidelines suggested
X Nothing provided
___ Other: ________

Materials Evaluation

Materials tested = T
Results available = A

___ Fieldtested before publication
___ Fieldtested after publication
A User feedback solicited
___ Other: ________
___ Not evaluated

SUBSTANTIVE CHARACTERISTICS

Values Education Approach

___ Inculcation
___ Moral development
___ Analysis
X Clarification
___ Action learning
___ Other: ________

Values Education Emphasis

X Major focus
___ One of several concerns
___ A minor concern

Process/Content Emphasis

X Process of valuing
X Content of valuing

Objectives

X Stated specifically
___ Stated generally
___ Not stated

Student Activities

Used or stressed frequently = F
Used or stressed occasionally = O

O Reading
F Writing
F Class discussion
O Small-group discussion
___ Games
O Simulations
O Role playing
___ Action projects
___ Other: ________

Curriculum: DIMENSIONS OF PERSONALITY: SEARCH FOR VALUES

Developers: Gerri Curwin, Rick Curwin, Rose Marie Kramer, Mary Jane Simmons, and Karen Walsch

Publisher: Pflaum Publishing, 2285 Arbor Blvd., Dayton, OH 45439

Date: 1972

Grade Levels: 9-12

Materials and Cost: Teacher's guide and 77 spirit masters ($44.95)

Search for Values is part of the *Dimensions of Personality* curriculum. The program contains 44 lessons designed to help secondary students clarify their personal values in relation to seven topics—time, competition, authority, personal space, commitment, relationships, and images. *Search for Values* is "a tool kit of strategies and techniques which, if taken seriously, can help [persons] see more clearly the directions [their] day-to-day life choices are taking." The developers feel that teenagers can be helped "to sort out their actions and feelings about the world within and around them" and thereby be more able to cope with value conflicts as adults. Specific objectives are given for each lesson. For example, lessons in the unit on competition focus on the following student objectives: to consider the cost of winning, to explore whether competition is an inherent condition of life, and to weigh the degree of one's commitment to learning.

Each unit treats one of the seven topics identified above. Within each there are from five to seven lessons that confront students with important value questions. In the unit dealing with relationships, for instance, students seek personal answers to the following questions: "How do I relate, what do I relate, and with whom?" "How important is the process of sharing, and is the process more than the sum of its parts?" "What are my expectations regarding relationships? Are they real, or ideal?" By answering such questions and completing various reaction worksheets for each of the topics, students discuss and examine their personal value commitments and the strength of such commitments. The teaching procedures are specifically outlined in the teacher's guide and clearly reflect the values clarification approach.

Some evaluative data has been gathered from a questionnaire sent by the publisher to users of the program. The fragmentary results of this poll were mixed but generally favorable. Fifteen of 17 respondents indictated that "the lessons were relevant" to their students. However, some lessons were rated by some teachers as too difficult and others too juvenile for their high school students. All respondents agreed that the instructions in the teacher's guide were "adequate" or "more than sufficient." Results of this survey may be obtained from the publisher.

DESCRIPTIVE CHARACTERISTICS

Grade Level

__ K-3
__ 4-6
__ 7-8
X 9-10
X 11-12

Materials

X Student materials
X Teacher guide
__ A-V kit
__ Tests
X Other: Spirit masters

Time

X Curriculum (2 or more years)
X Course (one year)
__ Semester (half year)
__ Minicourse (6-9 weeks)
__ Units (1-3 weeks)
X Supplementary
__ Other: ____

Medium Used

__ Readings
X Worksheets
__ Films
__ Filmstrips
__ Records or tapes
__ Charts or posters
__ Transparencies
__ Other: ____

PRECONDITIONS

Amount of Reading

__ Much
X Moderate
__ Very little

Teacher Training

__ Provided in materials
__ Suggested by developers
X Not mentioned
__ Other: ____

Prejudice/Stereotyping

Much evidence = M
Some evidence = S

__ Racial or Ethnic
__ Sexrole
__ Other: ____

EVALUATION INFORMATION

Provision for Student Evaluation

__ Instruments specified
__ Procedures specified
__ Guidelines suggested
X Nothing provided
__ Other: ____

Materials Evaluation

Materials tested = T
Results available = A

__ Fieldtested before publication
__ Fieldtested after publication
A User feedback solicited
__ Other: ____
__ Not evaluated

SUBSTANTIVE CHARACTERISTICS

Values Education Approach

__ Inculcation
__ Moral development
__ Analysis
X Clarification
__ Action learning
__ Other: ____

Values Education Emphasis

__ Major focus
__ One of several concerns
__ A minor concern

Process/Content Emphasis

X Process of valuing
X Content of valuing

Objectives

X Stated specifically
__ Stated generally
__ Not stated

Student Activities

Used or stressed frequently = F
Used or stressed occasionally = O

O Reading
F Writing
O Class discussion
F Small-group discussion
__ Games
__ Simulations
O Role playing
__ Action projects
__ Other: ____

Title: DYNAMIC CONSUMER DECISION MAKING

Publisher: Educational and Consumer Relations Department, J. C. Penney Company, Inc., 1301 Avenue of the Americas, New York, NY 10019

Date: 1972

Grade Levels: 9-12

Materials and Cost: Multimedia kit containing teacher's guide, slides, cassettes, overhead transparencies, worksheets, and 8½'' x 11'' flip chart ($11.50). Note: There was only one printing of this program. When the current supply is depleted, there is no plan to publish more copies.

This unit provides activities that focus on consumer decision making. According to the rationale, the activities are to help consumers see the importance of obtaining information before making decisions; make decisions that are more consistent with what is important to them; better understand their own decisions; recognize that there is a reward or payoff for making conscious, deliberate, informed decisions; and know that the quality of life and the environment is affected by consumer decisions. Three general types of decision-making activities are presented: probing, processing information, and clarifying values. Probing or questioning activities are provided so that students can determine what information they need to sort out, use, and evaluate. Processing activities focus on the way people collect, sort, select, organize, store, and use information. Activities in clarifying values are provided to ''determine what is important to a person.'' Objectives are specified for each lesson. For example, the first activity presented in each of the three sections is intended to accomplish the following: ''From this motivational activity it is hoped that participants will notice that consumers make decisions in personal, unique ways; appreciate the role questioning can play in decision making; observe that consumers reflect their values in using information and making decisions; and recognize that decision-making is a dynamic, ongoing process.''

The activities were developed in response to the pressures experienced by today's consumers who ''must make more choices than ever before. . . For example, as a consumer shopping for food today you must be able to sort through, evaluate, and decide from among over 6,000 food items in a typical supermarket!'' The developers feel that consumer behavior has also changed in the following ways: (1) More education has produced more knowledgeable consumers who now demand product performance and will likely voice dissent if their expectations are not met. (2) Consumers have more discretionary income and are buying more products than ever before. (3) The number and sophistication of products have contributed to expanding consumer consciousness. (4) Media has made consumers more aware of many new services and products. (5) Consumers have more time away from work and often have the resources to become involved in improving the quality of their lives.

The multimedia unit is divided into four sections: ''Educator's Core,'' ''Extension,'' ''Secondary School,'' and ''Limited Resources.'' The core provides educators with introductory information about the consumer in today's society and states reasons for being concerned with consumer decisions. In addition, it elaborates on the processes used during decision making. ''Extension'' presents three activities through a variety of formats—cassettes, slides, simulations, and class discussions. Learners work with various topics, such as voting and vacations, to gain awareness of consumer decision making. Four activities compose the section for secondary schools. Working with open-ended worksheets and overhead transparencies, students are encouraged to complete open-ended sentences, such as, ''I spend too much money . . .,'' ''If I'm in a depressed mood I may spend my money . . . '' and ''I usually postpone buying when . . ." The three activities in the section "Limited Resources" provide role-playing situations and a flip-chart activity in order to help participants determine whether or not consumers reflect what is important to them in using information and making decisions, appreciate the variety of ways in which they get information, and look at and evaluate alternatives.

DESCRIPTIVE CHARACTERISTICS

Grade Level

___ K-3
___ 4-6
___ 7-8
_X_ 9-10
_X_ 11-12

Materials

_X_ Student materials
_X_ Teacher guide
_X_ A-V kit
___ Tests
___ Other: ______________

Time

___ Curriculum (2 or more years)
___ Course (one year)
___ Semester (half year)
___ Minicourse (6-9 weeks)
_X_ Units (1-3 weeks)
___ Supplementary
___ Other: ______________

Medium Used

___ Readings
_X_ Worksheets
___ Films
___ Filmstrips
_X_ Records or tapes
_X_ Charts or posters
_X_ Transparencies
_X_ Other: Slides

PRECONDITIONS

Amount of Reading

___ Much
_X_ Moderate
___ Very little

Teacher Training

___ Provided in materials
___ Suggested by developers
_X_ Not mentioned
___ Other: ______________

Prejudice/Stereotyping

Much evidence = M
Some evidence = S

___ Racial or Ethnic
___ Sexrole
___ Other: ______________

EVALUATION INFORMATION

Provision for Student Evaluation

___ Instruments specified
___ Procedures specified
___ Guidelines suggested
_X_ Nothing provided
___ Other: ______________

Materials Evaluation

Materials tested = T
Results available = A

___ Fieldtested before publication
___ Fieldtested after publication
___ User feedback solicited
___ Other: ______________
_X_ Not evaluated

SUBSTANTIVE CHARACTERISTICS

Values Education Approach

___ Inculcation
___ Moral development
___ Analysis
_X_ Clarification
___ Action learning
___ Other: ______________

Values Education Emphasis

___ Major focus
_X_ One of several concerns
___ A minor concern

Process/Content Emphasis

_X_ Process of valuing
___ Content of valuing

Objectives

_X_ Stated specifically
___ Stated generally
___ Not stated

Student Activities

Used or stressed frequently = F
Used or stressed occasionally = O

_O_ Reading
_F_ Writing
_F_ Class discussion
___ Small-group discussion
___ Games
___ Simulations
_F_ Role playing
___ Action projects
___ Other: ______________

Title: ENVIRONMENTAL VALUES ACTION CARDS

Publisher: Minnesota State Department of Education, 642 Capitol Square Bldg., St. Paul, MN 55101 (Attn: Mr. Dick Clark)

Date: 1974

Grade Levels: 1-6

Materials and Cost: 50 cards, 7'' x 7'' (free while limited supply lasts; afterward, price will be determined)

Intended as idea banks for teachers, the *Environmental Values Action Cards* (EVA) were developed with a three-fold objective: ''to make children aware of themselves and of others''; ''to encourage children to explore values, both intrinsic and extrinsic''; and to give them the opportunity ''to explore means of expression that are significantly different from those normally used in the classroom.''

Appropriate for elementary students, the EVA cards ''consist of an initial metaphor usually depicted on the front side of [a] card and one or more actions that extend the metaphor.'' A card entitled ''Same,'' for example, encourages students to find some things that are the same and to answer several questions, ''How are they the same?'' and ''How did they get to be the same?'' The card then suggests related actions and questions including, ''Find two leaves from a tree. Are they the same? . . .Are you and your friends the same? How are all people the same?''

The cards suggest 49 separate actions that expose children to a wide range of concepts, human experiences, and physical phenomena. These include time, dreams, mistakes, sadness, winning and losing, fear, touch, likes and dislikes, wind, clouds, similarity, circles, trust, and monsters. Students working with the cards are engaged in many different types of activities such as role playing, testing food, listening, pantomiming, drawing pictures, writing stories, singing, dancing, and story telling. All cards have a similar format. On the front is a glossy black and white picture with a large word or phrase. The reverse side then suggests an action related to the idea depicted on the front and provides questions and more actions to help develop the student's understanding of the concept or experience. For example, one card shows two sets of children's hands holding a hamster and has the label ''Touchy.'' The action accompanying the picture invites students to ''pick something you want to touch and get to know it by touching. Touch it all over. How did it feel?'' More activities and questions related to touch are also listed.

No teacher's guide accompanies the cards. Rather, teachers are encouraged to explore and create their own ways for introducing them to their students. Since the cards presently are available only in a preliminary trial edition little is known about their classroom effectiveness and fieldtesting is not complete. The principal means for evaluation will be the information teachers provide on questionnaires after working with the experimental edition.

DESCRIPTIVE CHARACTERISTICS

Grade Level

X K-3
X 4-6
___ 7-8
___ 9-10
___ 11-12

Materials

X Student materials
___ Teacher guide
___ A-V kit
___ Tests
___ Other: ______

Time

___ Curriculum (2 or more years)
___ Course (one year)
___ Semester (half year)
___ Minicourse (6-9 weeks)
___ Units (1-3 weeks)
X Supplementary
___ Other: ______

Medium Used

___ Readings
___ Worksheets
___ Films
___ Filmstrips
___ Records or tapes
___ Charts or posters
___ Transparencies
X Other: Photo cards

PRECONDITIONS

Amount of Reading

___ Much
___ Moderate
X Very little

Teacher Training

___ Provided in materials
___ Suggested by developers
X Not mentioned
___ Other: ______

Prejudice/Stereotyping

Much evidence = M
Some evidence = S

___ Racial or Ethnic
___ Sexrole
___ Other: ______

EVALUATION INFORMATION

Provision for Student Evaluation

___ Instruments specified
___ Procedures specified
___ Guidelines suggested
X Nothing provided
___ Other: ______

Materials Evaluation

Materials tested = T
Results available = A

T Fieldtested before publication
___ Fieldtested after publication
T User feedback solicited
___ Other: ______
___ Not evaluated

SUBSTANTIVE CHARACTERISTICS

Values Education Approach

___ Inculcation
___ Moral development
___ Analysis
X Clarification
___ Action learning
___ Other: ______

Values Education Emphasis

___ Major focus
X One of several concerns
___ A minor concern

Process/Content Emphasis

___ Process of valuing
___ Content of valuing

Objectives

___ Stated specifically
X Stated generally
___ Not stated

Student Activities

Used or stressed frequently = F
Used or stressed occasionally = O

___ Reading
O Writing
___ Class discussion
O Small-group discussion
O Games
___ Simulations
O Role playing
F Action projects
O Other: Singing, dancing, drawing, story telling, testing, listening

Title: EXPLORING MORAL VALUES

Author: Louis E. Raths

Publisher: Warren Schloat Productions, Inc., 150 White Plains Rd., Tarrytown, NY 10591

Date: 1969

Grade Levels: 2-6

Materials and Cost: Audiovisual kit containing 15 filmstrips, 1 introductory record, and teacher's guide ($90.00).

Exploring Moral Values consists primarily of 15 silent filmstrips that dramatize a variety of situations involving moral and ethical judgments. The main purpose of the program is to allow young students to explore and clarify response patterns creatively, in ways satisfying to them. It is hoped that students will be able to "learn more about themselves, gain confidence in their own judgment, and define their own values."

The filmstrips cover four distinct areas: prejudice, personal values, authority, and honesty. In the area of prejudice, situations relating to race, religion, nationality, wealth, intellectual ability, and physical disability are highlighted. The personal value stories deal with kindness, courtesy, and the golden rule (behaving responsibly toward one's family, community, and friends). Revolving around the authority theme are issues related to being the oldest child; peers with delegated authority, such as in family, school, or recreational activities; and adults with authority, such as teachers, parents, police, and park officials. The honesty filmstrips focus on incidents that involve the individual in the prevention of others' deviant social activity while managing his or her own conduct prudently. In one such case a boy sees another boy about his age taking candy away from a younger child. Students must decide what they would do if they had witnessed the situation: ignore it, comfort the child, get the candy back from the bully, or take some kind of alternative action. After each dilemma students are asked to identify the feelings of those involved in the situation and react to such statements as, "Don't talk to strangers" and "Is might right?"

To enhance freedom in class discussion, the author recommends that the teacher assume an open-ended and noncommittal posture while commenting or asking questions. The teacher's guide offers a format including discussion topics and related activities such as role play, field trips, written exercises, research projects, and discussion activities. The grade level and ability of the student will dictate which activities are appropriate. Ideas for student evaluation can be obtained from the "related activities" section of the teacher's guide, although no formal evaluation procedures are provided.

DESCRIPTIVE CHARACTERISTICS

Grade Level

X K-3
X 4-6
___ 7-8
___ 9-10
___ 11-12

Materials

___ Student materials
X Teacher guide
X A-V kit
___ Tests
___ Other: ________________

Time

___ Curriculum (2 or more years)
___ Course (one year)
___ Semester (half year)
___ Minicourse (6-9 weeks)
___ Units (1-3 weeks)
X Supplementary
___ Other: ________________

Medium Used

___ Readings
___ Worksheets
___ Films
X Filmstrips
___ Records or tapes
___ Charts or posters
___ Transparencies
___ Other: ________________

PRECONDITIONS

Amount of Reading

___ Much
X Moderate
___ Very little

Teacher Training

___ Provided in materials
___ Suggested by developers
X Not mentioned
___ Other: ________________

Prejudice/Stereotyping

Much evidence = M
Some evidence = S

___ Racial or Ethnic
___ Sexrole
___ Other: ________________

EVALUATION INFORMATION

Provision for Student Evaluation

___ Instruments specified
___ Procedures specified
___ Guidelines suggested
X Nothing provided
___ Other: ________________

Materials Evaluation

Materials tested = T
Results available = A

___ Fieldtested before publication
___ Fieldtested after publication
___ User feedback solicited
___ Other: ________________
X Not evaluated

SUBSTANTIVE CHARACTERISTICS

Values Education Approach

___ Inculcation
___ Moral development
___ Analysis
X Clarification
___ Action learning
___ Other: ________________

Values Education Emphasis

X Major focus
___ One of several concerns
___ A minor concern

Process/Content Emphasis

X Process of valuing
X Content of valuing

Objectives

___ Stated specifically
X Stated generally
___ Not stated

Student Activities

Used or stressed frequently = F
Used or stressed occasionally = O

O Reading
O Writing
F Class discussion
___ Small-group discussion
___ Games
___ Simulations
O Role playing
___ Action projects
___ Other: ________________

Curriculum: FOCUS ON SELF-DEVELOPMENT

Titles: *Stage One: Awareness; Stage Two: Responding; Stage Three: Involvement*

Developers: Judith L. Anderson, Carole J. Lang, Melody Henner, Patricia Miner, and Virginia R. Scott

Publisher: Science Research Associates, 259 East Erie St., Chicago, IL 60611

Dates: 1970, 1971, 1972

Grade Levels: K-6

Materials and Cost: Three multimedia kits: *Stage One,* containing pupil activity book, teacher's guide, 5 color filmstrips with records or cassettes, 4 story records or cassettes, 20 black-and-white photoboards, and an easel (complete kit with records— $108, with cassettes—$121); *Stage Two* and *Stage Three,* each containing pupil activity book, teacher's guide, 6 color filmstrips with records or cassettes, 20 black-and-white photoboards, and easel (each complete kit with records—$121, with cassettes—$135); 25 copies of *Stage One* activity books or set of spirit masters ($11.40); 25 copies of *Stage Two* or *Stage Three* activity books or set of spirit masters ($13.75); specimen set of each stage, including teacher's guide ($15.00); guidance counselor handbook for *Stage One* separate ($2.85). Individual components may be purchased separately.

Focus on Self-Development is an audiovisual program designed for use in kindergarten through sixth-grade classrooms. The "overall objectives are to lead the child toward an understanding of self, an understanding of others, and an understanding of the environment and its effects." The goal of the program is to bring out the child's feelings and ideas in order that he or she may think about and act on them. Focusing on guidance, the materials assist students in examining values and behavior. It is the authors' belief that a flexible guidance program that allows free expression without fear of disapproval should be started as soon as a child enters school. Unit objectives are included for each part of the program. For example, the goal of the unit on awareness is "to help the child identify problems and to determine and weigh the consequences of possible solutions, particularly in terms of how certain solutions will affect others."

The concepts presented in the program are built around three stages found in Krathwohl's *Taxonomy of Educational Objectives, Handbook II: Affective Domain* (Krathwohl *et al.* 1964). *Stage One: Awareness* emphasizes awareness of self, others, and evironment and is directed toward the first level of the taxonomy, receiving. The topics include self-concept development, awareness of self, others, and environment through the senses, socialization, sharing, and problem solving. *Stage Two: Responding* is based on the second level of the taxonomy, which is aimed at stimulating active reponses to the concepts presented. The topics in this unit include self-concept, abilities, limitations, interests, concerns, communications, companionship, acceptance, and rejection. *Stage Three: Involvement* is based on valuing, the third category of Krathwohl's taxonomy. This involves students with self, others, and environment as they discover what they value.

Detailed lesson plans are provided in the teacher's guides for each level. The plans include statements of major focus and purpose, transcripts of records, questions for discussion, suggested follow-up activities, and a list of supplementary materials. The activities include obtaining guest speakers, role playing, small-group discussion, and completing open-ended sentences, such as, "I make my family very happy when I . . ." and "I feel responsible when . . ." The developers suggest that any attempt at evaluating learning outcomes should be done in terms of observable personal growth on the part of each student.

Results of fieldtesting preliminary units indicated that teachers and students were both interested and enthusiastic about the materials. In the *Stage Two* study "teachers unanimously reported that the students rarely, if ever, found the materials upsetting or threatening.'' Several inner-city teachers, however, "expressed difficulty in getting some of the less mature students to understand such concepts as goals, self-concept, and responsibility.'' The published version of the program was revised based on these studies. Fieldtest results are reported in the teacher's guides.

DESCRIPTIVE CHARACTERISTICS

Grade Level

- X K-3
- X 4-6
- ___ 7-8
- ___ 9-10
- ___ 11-12

Materials

- X Student materials
- X Teacher guide
- X A-V kit
- ___ Tests
- ___ Other: ________________

Time

- ___ Curriculum (2 or more years)
- ___ Course (one year)
- ___ Semester (half year)
- ___ Minicourse (6-9 weeks)
- ___ Units (1-3 weeks)
- X Supplementary
- ___ Other: ________________

Medium Used

- ___ Readings
- X Worksheets
- ___ Films
- X Filmstrips
- X Records or tapes
- ___ Charts or posters
- ___ Transparencies
- X Other: ________________

PRECONDITIONS

Amount of Reading

- ___ Much
- X Moderate
- ___ Very little

Teacher Training

- ___ Provided in materials
- ___ Suggested by developers
- X Not mentioned
- ___ Other: ________________

Prejudice/Stereotyping

Much evidence = M
Some evidence = S

- ___ Racial or Ethnic
- ___ Sexrole
- ___ Other: ________________

EVALUATION INFORMATION

Provision for Student Evaluation

- ___ Instruments specified
- ___ Procedures specified
- ___ Guidelines suggested
- X Nothing provided
- ___ Other: ________________

Materials Evaluation

Materials tested = T
Results available = A

- A Fieldtested before publication
- ___ Fieldtested after publication
- A User feedback solicited
- ___ Other: ________________
- ___ Not evaluated

SUBSTANTIVE CHARACTERISTICS

Values Education Approach

- ___ Inculcation
- ___ Moral development
- ___ Analysis
- X Clarification
- ___ Action learning
- ___ Other: ________________

Values Education Emphasis

- ___ Major focus
- X One of several concerns
- ___ A minor concern

Process/Content Emphasis

- X Process of valuing
- ___ Content of valuing

Objectives

- ___ Stated specifically
- X Stated generally
- ___ Not stated

Student Activities

Used or stressed frequently = F
Used or stressed occasionally = O

- O Reading
- O Writing
- F Class discussion
- O Small-group discussion
- ___ Games
- ___ Simulations
- O Role playing
- ___ Action projects
- ___ Other: ________________

Titles: HARD CHOICES: STRATEGIES FOR DECISION-MAKING and CLARIFYING YOUR VALUES: GUIDELINES FOR LIVING

Publisher: The Center for Humanities, Inc., Two Holland Ave., White Plains, NY 10603

Dates: 1974-75

Grade Levels: 9-12

Materials and Cost: For each title: audiovisual kit containing 160 slides in 2 carousel cartridges, 2 tape cassettes or 2 records, and teacher's guide ($99.85)

Hard Choices and *Clarifying Your Values* are two sound-slide series that depict through photographs, movie frames, and works of art various value conflict situations dramatized in literature and motion pictures. The developer believes that making choices about goals and values in our society can be a very tedious and difficult process. These two programs therefore are designed to teach students certain skills with which to make decisions, to evaluate the risks involved, and to analyze and define their value systems as they routinely relate to people and events.

Hard Choices emphasizes the importance of defining a decision, establishing values, recognizing alternatives, gathering information, and applying decision-making strategies based on risks and probabilities. Students are presented with examples describing how various contemporary persons such as Dick Gregory and Shirley MacLaine and several literary characters such as Conrack and Siddartha reacted to conflict. Students are frequently asked how they would have handled an identical situation. This program ends with a discussion about how students can learn to evaluate a decision once it has been made.

Clarifying Your Values describes specific situations involving the risks and advantages of action in accordance with one's own values. For example, from excerpts of *To Kill a Mockingbird,* students see the possible consequences when Atticus Finch decides to defend a black man in small Southern town. Another example shows a high school student committing herself to the goal of becoming a professional ice skater. Students can readily see the demands and sacrifices as well as the rewards resulting from pursuing such a goal.

For each of these programs discussion suggestions, research questions, and related activities are provided in the teacher's guide.

The materials were fieldtested before publication, but the results are not available. According to the publisher, informal feedback from local teachers has been favorable.

DESCRIPTIVE CHARACTERISTICS

Grade Level

__ K-3
__ 4-6
__ 7-8
X 9-10
X 11-12

Materials

X Student materials
X Teacher guide
__ A-V kit
__ Tests
__ Other: ________

Time

__ Curriculum (2 or more years)
__ Course (one year)
__ Semester (half year)
__ Minicourse (6-9 weeks)
__ Units (1-3 weeks)
X Supplementary
__ Other: ________

Medium Used

__ Readings
__ Worksheets
__ Films
__ Filmstrips
X Records or tapes
__ Charts or posters
__ Transparencies
X Other: Slides

PRECONDITIONS

Amount of Reading

__ Much
__ Moderate
X Very little

Teacher Training

__ Provided in materials
__ Suggested by developers
X Not mentioned
__ Other: ________

Prejudice/Stereotyping

Much evidence = M
Some evidence = S

__ Racial or Ethnic
__ Sexrole
__ Other: ________

EVALUATION INFORMATION

Provision for Student Evaluation

__ Instruments specified
__ Procedures specified
__ Guidelines suggested
X Nothing provided
__ Other: ________

Materials Evaluation

Materials tested = T
Results available = A

T Fieldtested before publication
__ Fieldtested after publication
T User feedback solicited
__ Other: ________
__ Not evaluated

SUBSTANTIVE CHARACTERISTICS

Values Education Approach

__ Inculcation
__ Moral development
__ Analysis
X Clarification
__ Action learning
__ Other: ________

Values Education Emphasis

X Major focus
__ One of several concerns
__ A minor concern

Process/Content Emphasis

X Process of valuing
__ Content of valuing

Objectives

__ Stated specifically
X Stated generally
__ Not stated

Student Activities

Used or stressed frequently = F
Used or stressed occasionally = O

__ Reading
O Writing
F Class discussion
__ Small-group discussion
__ Games
__ Simulations
__ Role playing
__ Action projects
__ Other: ________

Curriculum: LIFELINE

Titles: *In Other People's Shoes: Sensitivity; In Other People's Shoes: Consequences; In Other People's Shoes: Points of View; Proving the Rule?; What Would You Have Done?; Learning to Care: Rationale and Methods of the Lifeline Program*

Developers: Peter McPhail, Hilary Chapman, J. R. Ungoed-Thomas, and Lillian Teeman

Publisher: Argus Communications, 7440 Natchez Ave., Niles, Il 60658

Date: 1975

Grade Levels: 7-12

Materials and Cost: Student situation cards (each of the three *In Other People's Shoes* sets—$10.00); student situation booklets (*Proving the Rule?,* set of five booklets—$7.50; *What Would You Do?,* set of six booklets—$6.50); teacher's guide ($10.00). Introductory package including 1 copy of each of the cards and booklets and 1 teacher's guide ($47.50). Quantity discounts are available for all student materials.

Lifeline is a series designed to help secondary students learn to care and to choose. Caring involves considering and being sensitive to the needs, feelings, and interests of others; learning to understand different points of view and to empathize with them; and, finally, being able to get along with others. Learning to choose involves the students in examining alternatives, weighing consequences, and making decisions consistent with what they value. An extensive survey of secondary school pupils determined that the specific situations dealt with in the materials were the main areas of adolescent concern in relation to personal, interpersonal, and moral problems. It is hoped that *Lifeline* will provide a link between the school and the lives of the students by focusing on such needs. The approach taken is one of values clarification. The author feels it is important for students to develop a strong sense of identity in order to deal successfully with personal and social dilemmas.

It is suggested that *Lifeline* be taught not as a separate course but in conjunction with other subjects, such as social studies, humanities, health education, sex education, race relations, and community service courses. There are basically three parts to the series, each of which focuses on situation analysis and involves increasingly complex situations. These situations put students in a position to decide what their own values are and to understand those of others better.

In Other People's Shoes deals with open-ended, person-to-person situations in familiar contexts. Students must decide what they would do, consider what the consequences might be, and learn to understand a conflict from another person's point of view. The conflict situations in this part concern sex, age, class, race, culture, religion, politics, and psychology. In *Proving the Rule?* students are encouraged to identify rules, expectations, and pressures with the idea of learning to cope with, alter, or eliminate them in accordance with their needs and values. The content of this part centers on young people—their families, friends, and neighbors—and how the pressures and demands of society may be faced in a variety of situations. These situations involve personal and social identity, relationships within groups, and conflicts between different groups. *What Would You Have Done?* presents six actual case studies occurring during the 20th century in different cultures around the world. The situations are complex and deal with such concepts as commitment, racial conflict, disaster, compassion, persecution, and drug addiction.

A variety of techniques are suggested for teaching each *Lifeline* dilemma in order to meet both student and teacher needs. Role play and dramatic action are encouraged prior to discussion; the author feels these techniques are likely to promote both emotional and rational involvement and thus provide a realistic understanding of the situations and personalities involved. A section of the teacher's guide is devoted to the crucial role the teacher must assume in implementing the materials. Teacher education is suggested, emphasizing improved teacher communication skills, personal development, and well-being. The *Lifeline* approach and materials may be used for such inservice training. A sample collection of dilemmas from the series has been suggested for the purpose of educating teachers who will be using the materials in their classes. In addition, a teacher training film is available from the publisher on a free-loan basis.

The program was developed by the British Schools Council Project as a result of five years of research and testing with over 20,000 British students from a wide variety of backgrounds. The materials have also been tested in the United States. Based on the results, the program has been revised particularly for use in American classrooms. The results of this project are reported and discussed in *Moral Education in the Secondary School* (McPhail *et al.* 1972).

DESCRIPTIVE CHARACTERISTICS

Grade Level

___ K-3
___ 4-6
X 7-8
X 9-10
X 11-12

Materials

X Student materials
X Teacher guide
___ A-V kit
___ Tests
___ Other: ______

Time

X Curriculum (2 or more years)
___ Course (one year)
___ Semester (half year)
___ Minicourse (6-9 weeks)
___ Units (1-3 weeks)
X Supplementary
___ Other: ______

Medium Used

X Readings
___ Worksheets
___ Films
___ Filmstrips
___ Records or tapes
___ Charts or posters
___ Transparencies
X Other: ______

PRECONDITIONS

Amount of Reading

___ Much
X Moderate
___ Very little

Teacher Training

X Provided in materials
X Suggested by developers
___ Not mentioned
___ Other: ______

Prejudice/Stereotyping

Much evidence = M
Some evidence = S

___ Racial or Ethnic
___ Sexrole
___ Other: ______

EVALUATION INFORMATION

Provision for Student Evaluation

___ Instruments specified
___ Procedures specified
___ Guidelines suggested
X Nothing provided
___ Other: ______

Materials Evaluation

Materials tested = T
Results available = A

A Fieldtested before publication
T Fieldtested after publication
___ User feedback solicited
___ Other: ______
___ Not evaluated

SUBSTANTIVE CHARACTERISTICS

Values Education Approach

___ Inculcation
___ Moral development
___ Analysis
X Clarification
___ Action learning
___ Other: ______

Values Education Emphasis

X Major focus
___ One of several concerns
___ A minor concern

Process/Content Emphasis

X Process of valuing
___ Content of valuing

Objectives

___ Stated specifically
X Stated generally
___ Not stated

Student Activities

Used or stressed frequently = F
Used or stressed occasionally = O

O Reading
O Writing
F Class discussion
F Small-group discussion
___ Games
___ Simulations
F Role playing
___ Action projects
O Other: ______

Title: MAKING SENSE OF OUR LIVES

Author: Merrill Harmin

Publisher: Argus Communications, 7440 Natchez Ave., Niles, IL 60648

Date: 1974

Grade Levels: 7-12

Materials and Cost: 74 Value Sheets: Option I-1 spirit master of 1 Value Sheet, 1 poster, and 1 Teacher Suggestion Sheet ($1.00); Option II-1 pad of 35 copies of 1 Value Sheet, 1 poster, and 1 Teacher Suggestion Sheet ($1.50); 10 percent discount available with purchase of 50 or more Value Sheet sets, either option. 3 Value Cassettes, each accompanied by spirit master of student activity and Teacher Suggestion Sheet ($8.00 each; $22.00 for all 3). 15 color Process Posters, 22" x 34" ($15.00 per set).

Making Sense of Our Lives is a collection of value clarification lessons intended to help students discover meaning and direction in their own lives. Objectives include helping students become "more aware of their strengths and respectful of the strengths of others"; "more understanding of the complexities of real life problems"; "more ready to speak up and take initiative for what they believe in"; and "more able to listen to each other." The value sheets and cassette programs can be used to enrich other subject matter or, by themselves, to develop value clarification skills. The materials are intended for use in small groups as well as with individuals or an entire class.

There are 74 value sheets, all of which follow a similar format. First, a problem is stated. This is followed by an individual activity, a small-group activity, and a follow-up activity. The teacher's suggestion sheet includes the concepts to be clarified in the particular lesson, related subjects, a suggested sequence for the lesson, and guides for discussion.

The subjects of the value sheets include problems dealing with prisons, race, old age, the future, careers, women's studies, political science, feelings, friendship, self-confidence, and values. The several cassette programs deal with dilemmas ranging from hunger to personal relations and conflict resolution. One lesson, entitled "Parents' High Hopes," poses the problem of parental expectations. The student begins the lesson by reading the story of how John is constantly reminded by his father of the high hopes he has for him. Then students are asked to complete four activities in which they compare their own parents' expectations to those of John's father and their own feelings to John's feelings. After sharing thoughts with a small group, students join in a full-class discussion. As a follow-up activity, the student is asked to write a serious or funny play about parents who pressure a child to become a doctor.

The materials were not systematically fieldtested but Harmin did use many of the activities in workshops prior to publication. Results from those efforts are not available.

DESCRIPTIVE CHARACTERISTICS

Grade Level

___ K-3
___ 4-6
_X_ 7-8
_X_ 9-10
_X_ 11-12

Materials

_X_ Student materials
_X_ Teacher guide
___ A-V kit
___ Tests
___ Other: ______________

Time

___ Curriculum (2 or more years)
___ Course (one year)
___ Semester (half year)
___ Minicourse (6-9 weeks)
___ Units (1-3 weeks)
_X_ Supplementary
___ Other: ______________

Medium Used

___ Readings
_X_ Worksheets
___ Films
___ Filmstrips
_X_ Records or tapes
_X_ Charts or posters
___ Transparencies
___ Other: ______________

PRECONDITIONS

Amount of Reading

_X_ Much
___ Moderate
___ Very little

Teacher Training

___ Provided in materials
___ Suggested by developers
_X_ Not mentioned
___ Other: ______________

Prejudice/Stereotyping

Much evidence = M
Some evidence = S

___ Racial or Ethnic
___ Sexrole
___ Other: ______________

EVALUATION INFORMATION

Provision for Student Evaluation

___ Instruments specified
___ Procedures specified
___ Guidelines suggested
_X_ Nothing provided
___ Other: ______________

Materials Evaluation

Materials tested = T
Results available = A

_T_ Fieldtested before publication
___ Fieldtested after publication
___ User feedback solicited
___ Other: ______________
___ Not evaluated

SUBSTANTIVE CHARACTERISTICS

Values Education Approach

___ Inculcation
___ Moral development
___ Analysis
_X_ Clarification
___ Action learning
___ Other: ______________

Values Education Emphasis

_X_ Major focus
___ One of several concerns
___ A minor concern

Process/Content Emphasis

_X_ Process of valuing
___ Content of valuing

Objectives

___ Stated specifically
_X_ Stated generally
___ Not stated

Student Activities

Used or stressed frequently = F
Used or stressed occasionally = O

_F_ Reading
_F_ Writing
_F_ Class discussion
_F_ Small-group discussion
___ Games
___ Simulations
___ Role playing
___ Action projects
_O_ Other: Listening

Title: MAKING VALUE JUDGMENTS: DECISIONS FOR TODAY

Author: Carl Elder

Publisher: Charles E. Merrill Publishing Company, 1300 Alum Creek Dr., Columbus, OH 43216

Date: 1972

Grade Levels: 7-12

Materials and Cost: Student text ($3.96); teacher's guide ($1.00)

Making Value Judgments contains a student text and teacher's manual that are designed to stimulate classroom discussion and student inquiry into the critical issues facing today's young people—drugs, crime, prejudice, careers, alcohol, goals, pollution, and personal relationships. According to the teacher's guide, the purpose of the materials is "to help young people make sound value judgments by providing them with guidelines to help them clarify their values and to make decisions."

The 14 chapters composing the student booklet encourage secondary students to investigate social issues, such as drugs and pollution, from a personal viewpoint. In the sixth chapter, for example, students work with the question, "Do I want to use drugs?" The issue they deal with in Chapter 11 is, "What should I do about pollution?" Such issues are posed to the students in a variety of ways—through value dilemma episodes, case studies, and stories.

The teacher's guide presents teaching suggestions, student activities, and a list of audiovisual aids. In addition, it provides general guidelines for student evaluation. Written responses in the form of short-answer, completion, and true-false tests are the modes suggested for evaluation. A "Values Attitude Response Questionnaire" is also provided.

The materials were classroom tested by Elder before publication and results are available from the publisher. In addition, user feedback was solicited through workshops and questionnaires.

DESCRIPTIVE CHARACTERISTICS

Grade Level

- ___ K-3
- ___ 4-6
- X 7-8
- X 9-10
- X 11-12

Materials

- X Student materials
- X Teacher guide
- ___ A-V kit
- ___ Tests
- ___ Other: ___

Time

- ___ Curriculum (2 or more years)
- ___ Course (one year)
- X Semester (half year)
- ___ Minicourse (6-9 weeks)
- X Units (1-3 weeks)
- ___ Supplementary
- ___ Other: ___

Medium Used

- X Readings
- ___ Worksheets
- ___ Films
- ___ Filmstrips
- ___ Records or tapes
- ___ Charts or posters
- ___ Transparencies
- ___ Other: ___

PRECONDITIONS

Amount of Reading

- X Much
- ___ Moderate
- ___ Very little

Teacher Training

- X Provided in materials
- ___ Suggested by developers
- ___ Not mentioned
- ___ Other: ___

Prejudice/Stereotyping

Much evidence = M
Some evidence = S

- ___ Racial or Ethnic
- ___ Sexrole
- ___ Other: ___

EVALUATION INFORMATION

Provision for Student Evaluation

- ___ Instruments specified
- ___ Procedures specified
- X Guidelines suggested
- ___ Nothing provided
- ___ Other: ___

Materials Evaluation

Materials tested = T
Results available = A

- A Fieldtested before publication
- ___ Fieldtested after publication
- T User feedback solicited
- ___ Other: ___
- ___ Not evaluated

SUBSTANTIVE CHARACTERISTICS

Values Education Approach

- ___ Inculcation
- ___ Moral development
- ___ Analysis
- X Clarification
- ___ Action learning
- ___ Other: ___

Values Education Emphasis

- X Major focus
- ___ One of several concerns
- ___ A minor concern

Process/Content Emphasis

- X Process of valuing
- X Content of valuing

Objectives

- ___ Stated specifically
- ___ Stated generally
- X Not stated

Student Activities

Used or stressed frequently = F
Used or stressed occasionally = O

- F Reading
- F Writing
- F Class discussion
- ___ Small-group discussion
- ___ Games
- ___ Simulations
- O Role playing
- O Action projects
- ___ Other: ___

Title: MEETING YOURSELF HALFWAY: 31 VALUE CLARIFICATION STRATEGIES FOR DAILY LIVING

Author: Sidney B. Simon

Publisher: Argus Communications, 7440 Natchez Ave., Niles, IL 60648

Date: 1974

Grade Levels: 7-12

Materials and Cost: Student/teacher book ($4.95); student/teacher book with spirit masters ($18.50)

Meeting Yourself Halfway is a book of value-clarification strategies for secondary students and adults. The author believes that because of the many conflicting values present in society, it is necessary for individuals to learn to decide which values are most important to them. The overall objective is self-discovery. To be able to answer the questions "Who am I?" and "What do I value?" is essential if a person is to learn to choose freely and to live a full, meaningful life with direction. The suggested strategies help students "locate, sort out, and build a set of values." Students hopefully will learn to make their thoughts and feelings consistent with their behavior.

There are 31 strategies suggested, each of which focuses on the processes involved in choosing, prizing, and acting—three integral parts of the value-clarification process. The strategies are group oriented and encourage dialogue. They are self-explanatory and may be used independently by a small group or possibly by an individual. The approach taken is a positive, personally affirming one, focusing on individuals. Activities include "taking inventory" of different aspects of the students' lives; learning and practicing decision-making skills; considering priorities, risks, and consequences; and taking action. Students are encouraged to commit themselves by writing down (for their own reference) their answers, decisions, and reactions to the strategies.

Evaluation is left to the individual. The rationale implies that you will be successful in using this book if you increase the extent to which you "do what you value" and "value what you do." Some general guidelines for determining such behavior are provided.

DESCRIPTIVE CHARACTERISTICS

Grade Level

___ K-3
___ 4-6
_X_ 7-8
_X_ 9-10
_X_ 11-12

Materials

_X_ Student materials
_X_ Teacher guide
___ A-V kit
___ Tests
___ Other: ______________

Time

___ Curriculum (2 or more years)
___ Course (one year)
___ Semester (half year)
_X_ Minicourse (6-9 weeks)
___ Units (1-3 weeks)
_X_ Supplementary
___ Other: ______________

Medium Used

_X_ Readings
_X_ Worksheets
___ Films
___ Filmstrips
___ Records or tapes
___ Charts or posters
___ Transparencies
___ Other: ______________

PRECONDITIONS

Amount of Reading

___ Much
_X_ Moderate
___ Very little

Teacher Training

___ Provided in materials
___ Suggested by developers
_X_ Not mentioned
___ Other: ______________

Prejudice/Stereotyping

Much evidence = M
Some evidence = S

___ Racial or Ethnic
___ Sexrole
___ Other: ______________

EVALUATION INFORMATION

Provision for Student Evaluation

___ Instruments specified
___ Procedures specified
_X_ Guidelines suggested
___ Nothing provided
___ Other: ______________

Materials Evaluation

Materials tested = T
Results available = A

___ Fieldtested before publication
___ Fieldtested after publication
___ User feedback solicited
___ Other: ______________
_X_ Not evaluated

SUBSTANTIVE CHARACTERISTICS

Values Education Approach

___ Inculcation
___ Moral development
___ Analysis
_X_ Clarification
___ Action learning
___ Other: ______________

Values Education Emphasis

_X_ Major focus
___ One of several concerns
___ A minor concern

Process/Content Emphasis

_X_ Process of valuing
___ Content of valuing

Objectives

___ Stated specifically
_X_ Stated generally
___ Not stated

Student Activities

Used or stressed frequently = F
Used or stressed occasionally = O

_O_ Reading
_F_ Writing
___ Class discussion
_F_ Small-group discussion
_F_ Games
___ Simulations
___ Role playing
___ Action projects
___ Other: ______________

Title: PEOPLE PROJECTS

Author: Merill Harmin

Publisher: Addison-Wesley Publishing Company, 2725 Sand Hill Rd., Menlo Park, CA 94025

Date: 1973

Grade Levels: 4-8

Materials and Cost: Student materials (teacher's guide included in each set)—set A, grades 4-6; set B, grades 4-7; set C, grades 6-8 (each set—$19.92)

People Projects consists of three sets of activity cards and a teacher's guide designed to provide students in intermediate and junior high grades with structured, self-directed projects which teach thinking, valuing, and human relations skills. The activity cards may be used to supplement a basal language arts or social studies program, contributing to both cognitive and affective growth. One of the author's chief concerns is to help the student move away from patterns of apathy, conformity, and blind impulsivity, toward a more thoughtful and responsible commitment to life. Seven objectives for the program are listed: encourage students to learn how to think about personal events; find satisfaction in thinking about personal events; learn how to sort out and clarify confusions and inconsistencies; appreciate what others are experiencing; develop small-group skills, especially listening skills; develop abilities for responsible self-direction; and become mature in value thinking.

A wide variety of personal value topics are dealt with in the 120 activities. These topics relate to parents and family, school, friends, animals, and other situations of interest to young students. One activity card, for example, encourages students to react to an incident in which a teacher hit a student so hard he had to go to the hospital. Students think about and discuss their first reactions, their attitudes toward teachers' hitting students, and any similar experiences they have had.

In implementing the materials, the author suggests that the teacher either divide the class randomly into groups of three or four to work briefly on different activities or conduct a whole-class session using one project. After the program is under way, students can be encouraged to work alone or in small groups, whichever is more comfortable for them. They can engage in the activities in their free time or at prearranged times. A six-page chart in the teacher's guide summarizes the title, focus, and key activities of each project card.

The teacher's guide specifies several student self-evaluation procedures. For example, students might grade themselves using this scheme: "A . . . I did this project well. I am proud of my work. B . . . I did fine, but, not as well as I would have liked. C . . . Fair work. D . . . I don't feel good about my work." Subjective evaluative data on use of these materials is available from the author at the Department of Secondary Education, University of Southern Illinois, Edwardsville, Illinois. In addition, suggestions for evaluating the effectiveness of the program are provided in the teacher's guide.

DESCRIPTIVE CHARACTERISTICS

Grade Level

___ K-3
X 4-6
X 7-8
___ 9-10
___ 11-12

Materials

X Student materials
X Teacher guide
___ A-V kit
___ Tests
___ Other: ________

Time

___ Curriculum (2 or more years)
___ Course (one year)
___ Semester (half year)
___ Minicourse (6-9 weeks)
___ Units (1-3 weeks)
X Supplementary
___ Other: ________

Medium Used

___ Readings
___ Worksheets
___ Films
___ Filmstrips
___ Records or tapes
___ Charts or posters
___ Transparencies
X Other: Poject cards

PRECONDITIONS

Amount of Reading

___ Much
X Moderate
___ Very little

Teacher Training

___ Provided in materials
___ Suggested by developers
X Not mentioned
___ Other: ________

Prejudice/Stereotyping

Much evidence = M
Some evidence = S

___ Racial or Ethnic
___ Sexrole
___ Other: ________

EVALUATION INFORMATION

Provision for Student Evaluation

___ Instruments specified
___ Procedures specified
X Guidelines suggested
___ Nothing provided
___ Other: ________

Materials Evaluation

Materials tested = T
Results available = A

A Fieldtested before publication
___ Fieldtested after publication
___ User feedback solicited
___ Other: ________
___ Not evaluated

SUBSTANTIVE CHARACTERISTICS

Values Education Approach

___ Inculcation
___ Moral development
___ Analysis
X Clarification
___ Action learning
___ Other: ________

Values Education Emphasis

___ Major focus
X One of several concerns
___ A minor concern

Process/Content Emphasis

X Process of valuing
___ Content of valuing

Objectives

___ Stated specifically
X Stated generally
___ Not stated

Student Activities

Used or stressed frequently = F
Used or stressed occasionally = O

O Reading
F Writing
O Class discussion
F Small-group discussion
O Games
___ Simulations
O Role playing
O Action projects
___ Other: ________

Title: A PROBE INTO VALUES

Author: John G. Church

Publisher: Harcourt Brace Jovanovich, Inc., 757 Third Ave., New York, NY 10017

Date: 1973

Grade Levels: 4-6

Materials and Cost: 40 pamphlets (four sets—$24.00)

A Probe into Values is part of the curriculum, *The Social Sciences: Concepts and Values* (see the Student Materials section of Chapter IV, ANALYSIS, for a description of the curriculum). *Probe* includes 40 different problem situations students might encounter from day to day. Through the rational examination of alternatives, each child decides what he or she would do in the given situation. These activities are intended to increase the child's personal awareness of the values at issue. The materials focus on the process of valuing, teaching students to deal with value conflicts in everyday life.

Each dilemma is presented in a pamphlet in story form. After reading the story, students in small groups list possible alternative courses of action that could be taken in the situation. When these are determined, each child decides what his or her own course of action would be. The group then discusses the situation and how different persons affected might feel. Finally, students re-evaluate their positions and are given the opportunity to change their points of view. There is no teacher's guide, but each activity is self-explanatory. In one case a boy sees a beautiful blanket knitted for a friend's grandfather and he decides he would like to learn to knit so he could make a blanket for his grandfather. His friends think that knitting is "sissy." The students then decide what they would do if they were the boy. In another case a little girl wonders if she should do something she feels is wrong just because "everybody else is doing it." A wide variety of value issues are dealt with, including truth, roles, promises, and individuality. The author emphasizes that there are no right and wrong solutions to the dilemmas. The important factor is that students are considering alternatives and making personal decisions.

The materials were fieldtested in classroom situations before publication. Results are available from the Center for the Study of Instruction, Harcourt Brace Jovanovich Building, Polk and Geary, San Francisco, CA 94109. The results indicate that the reading level of the stories is difficult for students with lesser abilities. If used with poor readers, it may be advantageous for the teacher or another student to read the pamphlet to the group.

DESCRIPTIVE CHARACTERISTICS

Grade Level

___ K-3
X 4-6
___ 7-8
___ 9-10
___ 11-12

Materials

X Student materials
___ Teacher guide
___ A-V kit
___ Tests
___ Other: ________

Time

___ Curriculum (2 or more years)
___ Course (one year)
___ Semester (half year)
X Minicourse (6-9 weeks)
___ Units (1-3 weeks)
X Supplementary
___ Other: ________

Medium Used

___ Readings
___ Worksheets
___ Films
___ Filmstrips
___ Records or tapes
___ Charts or posters
___ Transparencies
X Other: Pamphlets

PRECONDITIONS

Amount of Reading

___ Much
X Moderate
___ Very little

Teacher Training

___ Provided in materials
___ Suggested by developers
X Not mentioned
___ Other: ________

Prejudice/Stereotyping

Much evidence = M
Some evidence = S

___ Racial or Ethnic
___ Sexrole
___ Other: ________

EVALUATION INFORMATION

Provision for Student Evaluation

___ Instruments specified
___ Procedures specified
___ Guidelines suggested
X Nothing provided
___ Other: ________

Materials Evaluation

Materials tested = T
Results available = A

A Fieldtested before publication
___ Fieldtested after publication
___ User feedback solicited
___ Other: ________
___ Not evaluated

SUBSTANTIVE CHARACTERISTICS

Values Education Approach

___ Inculcation
___ Moral development
___ Analysis
X Clarification
___ Action learning
___ Other: ________

Values Education Emphasis

X Major focus
___ One of several concerns
___ A minor concern

Process/Content Emphasis

X Process of valuing
___ Content of valuing

Objectives

___ Stated specifically
___ Stated generally
X Not stated

Student Activities

Used or stressed frequently = F
Used or stressed occasionally = O

O Reading
O Writing
O Class discussion
F Small-group discussion
___ Games
___ Simulations
___ Role playing
___ Action projects
___ Other: ________

Title: SEARCHING FOR VALUES: A FILM ANTHOLOGY

Developers: Jim Hanley and Don Thompson

Publisher: Learning Corporation of America, 711 Fifth Ave., New York, NY 10022

Date: 1972

Grade Levels: 9-12

Materials and Cost: 15 films, averaging 16 minutes showing time each (rental fee per film—$25; purchase price per film—$250; purchase price for entire set—$3000); teacher's guide for each film and teacher's manual, containing exercises and questions for every film, are provided free of charge.

Searching for Values: A Film Anthology is a series of 15 films that have been adapted and edited from major motion pictures for classroom use. Each film deals with a particular value problem—loneliness (excerpt taken from the film *Five Easy Pieces),* killing (from *Bless the Beasts and Children),* truth (from *On the Waterfront),* and so on. Reflecting a clarification approach to values education, the materials provide narratives to "excite students to discuss the values, conflicts, and decision of the characters, as well as broader themes and issues"; to provoke student recognition and questioning of individual and societal values, attitudes, and goals; to "engage students in a deeper search for self awareness"; and to provide teachers with vivid case studies for their classes. Specific objectives for each film are implied in the developers' discussion of the main theme and basic values treated in each film. For example, the study guide for the film "Loneliness...and Loving" encourages students to look at various human experiences: alienation, loneliness, escapism, lack of commitment, the inability to love, and the substitution of sex for love.

These materials explore various social issues and community problems. Aggression, violence, political power and the public good, law, and war are some of the issues students are asked to discuss from a personal, as well as a societal point of view. For example, in the film "My Country Right or Wrong?" students confront themselves, their peers, and their teachers on issues related to patriotism. Looking at the dimensions of patriotism, they discuss the draft, the conflict within family and society over traditional norms, and the strength needed for and the consequences of creating an independent, personal lifestyle.

The teacher's manual describes procedures and activities for using all the films in the classroom. It includes a synopsis of each film; classroom exercises; questions for discussion; and a selected list of additional information, exercises, and questions related to each film's basic theme. One exercise used in the unit "I Who Am, Who Am I?" (based on *The Swimmer*) includes an autobiographical questionnaire that asks students questions such as, "Is there one person you love above all others?" and "When you are alone, do you always feel lonely? Only sometimes?"

In a subtle fashion the materials reflect sex-role and ethnic stereotyping: all 15 films feature male heroes and in 14 these heroes are white. Fieldtesting during the formative stages was done informally by getting feedback from teachers, students, and other users. The results were printed in the February 1973 issue of *Film News.* A copy of this report is available from Learning Corporation of America. Although generally favorable, the results did vary depending upon the particular film and how it was used.

DESCRIPTIVE CHARACTERISTICS

Grade Level

___ K-3
___ 4-6
___ 7-8
X 9-10
X 11-12

Materials

___ Student materials
X Teacher guide
X A-V kit
___ Tests
___ Other: ___

Time

___ Curriculum (2 or more years)
___ Course (one year)
___ Semester (half year)
___ Minicourse (6-9 weeks)
___ Units (1-3 weeks)
X Supplementary
X Other: 1 class period per film

Medium Used

___ Readings
___ Worksheets
X Films
___ Filmstrips
___ Records or tapes
___ Charts or posters
___ Transparencies
___ Other: ___

PRECONDITIONS

Amount of Reading

___ Much
___ Moderate
X Very little

Teacher Training

___ Provided in materials
___ Suggested by developers
___ Not mentioned
___ Other: ___

Prejudice/Stereotyping

Much evidence = M
Some evidence = S

S Racial or Ethnic
S Sexrole
___ Other: ___

EVALUATION INFORMATION

Provision for Student Evaluation

___ Instruments specified
___ Procedures specified
___ Guidelines suggested
X Nothing provided
___ Other: ___

Materials Evaluation

Materials tested = T
Results available = A

___ Fieldtested before publication
___ Fieldtested after publication
A User feedback solicited
___ Other: ___
___ Not evaluated

SUBSTANTIVE CHARACTERISTICS

Values Education Approach

___ Inculcation
___ Moral development
___ Analysis
X Clarification
___ Action learning
___ Other: ___

Values Education Emphasis

X Major focus
___ One of several concerns
___ A minor concern

Process/Content Emphasis

X Process of valuing
___ Content of valuing

Objectives

___ Stated specifically
X Stated generally
___ Not stated

Student Activities

Used or stressed frequently = F
Used or stressed occasionally = O

___ Reading
O Writing
F Class discussion
___ Small-group discussion
___ Games
___ Simulations
___ Role playing
___ Action projects
F Other: Viewing films

Curriculum: SELF-EXPRESSION AND CONDUCT: THE HUMANITIES

Titles: *Blue, Level 1; Red, Level 2; Green, Level 3*

Developer: Paul F. Brandwein

Publisher: Harcourt Brace Jovanovich, Inc., 757 Third Ave., New York, NY 10017

Dates: 1974-75

Grade Levels: 1-3

Materials and Cost: Student text (*Levels 1* and *2*—$3.90; *Level 3*—$4.50); teacher's guide (*Levels 1* and *2*— $3.90; *Level 3*—$4.50); other components include records, color sound-filmstrips (6-8 for each grade level, available with records or cassettes) and *Level 3* pupil learning activities (PLAs); individual components may be purchased separately; total package excluding student books (*Level 1* with records—$157.80, with cassettes—$169.80; *Level 2* with records—$121.80, with cassettes—$130.80, *Level 3* with records—$167.40, with cassettes—$176.40); *Level 1* activity kits are also available (art—$198.00, dance/drama—$177.00, music—$240.00). Activity kits for *Levels 2* and *3* are forthcoming.

Self-Expression and Conduct: The Humanities is a multimedia program for grades K-6. The materials include activity books, records, sound-filmstrips, and other media to help children develop and understand their feelings about themselves and the world through five modes of expression: art, movement and dance, play and drama, music, and language. According to the developers, the components in each level will "lead children to an understanding of humanity's basic values: truth, beauty, justice, love, and faith." Instruction for each level is organized around a major theme, with some aspect of the theme developed through one of the five modes of expression. As these major themes are developed, children encounter the basic values presented in each level. It is intended that "slowly, experience by experience, their understanding of these values grows as they progress through the program." The developers anticipate that the increasing awareness of these values will begin to affect the choices children make for themselves.

The textbook lessons provide the central core of each program. Instructional objectives are listed for each lesson. For example, a lesson in the *Level 1* program has the following objectives: "Children draw, paint, and model to express their thoughts and feelings. They focus on an aspect of beauty as they use color to make pictures and objects that they consider beautiful." Each lesson begins with an activity intended to motivate learning. The content of the lesson is presented next, followed by a "Transfer to Values" section. The textbooks are supplemented by other learning aids such as records, activity kits, and filmstrips. All of these help develop the basic theme presented in each level: seeking/perception (*Level 1*), sharing/communication (*Level 2*), and caring/craftsmanship (*Level 3*). *Level 1* offers students experiences in perception. These are developed first by stressing children's perceptions of the world around them—their outer environment—and then by focusing on their perceptions of personal feelings—their inner environment. *Level 2* emphasizes communication. It first stresses the ways in which children communicate or share their responses to their environment and their feelings toward others, and then focuses on the "imaginative ways in which children seek to explain and integrate their ideas and feelings." In *Level 3* children learn about craftsmanship, which is defined on the child's level as caring. They are encouraged to learn about "what they do in all aspects of their lives . . ., about doing the best they can do in the arts . . . and about being the best person they can be in their relationships with other people." The "Transfer to Values" activities accompanying each lesson include group projects such as a give-away celebration, an age-grade ceremony, a guild meeting, and a knightsof-the-round-table service project. "Transfer to Values" activities also include the answering of such questions as, "Is it fair?" "Why do you like it?" and "How do you know that it is true?"

A separate teacher's resource book accompanies each level. It introduces the lesson clusters with an overview and background information, explains each lesson and identifies the behavioral objectives, modes of expression, time period, and materials needed. Specific suggestions are also given for introducing the activity, for teaching the content, and for the "Transfer to Values" activities. Procedures for evaluating pupil progress in the arts and in their expression of the basic values are explicit in the program. The emphasis is on continuous observation of students by the teachers.

Two units, one from *Level 1* and one from *Level 2,* were fieldtested prior to publication by 72 teachers in 50 school districts throughout the nation. Forty-one teachers completed the evaluation form. The results indicated that the materials were appropriate for students in grades 1, 2, and 3, and "effective in introducing children to the stated objectives in the arts and values." Revisions were made based on the field studies and the published version is now being tested. That data will be available from the Center for the Study of Instruction, Harcourt Brace Jovanovich Building, Polk and Geary, San Francisco, CA 94109.

DESCRIPTIVE CHARACTERISTICS

Grade Level

X K-3
__ 4-6
__ 7-8
__ 9-10
__ 11-12

Materials

X Student materials
X Teacher guide
X A-V kit
__ Tests
X Other: Activity cards and foldouts

Time

X Curriculum (2 or more years)
X Course (one year) Each title.
__ Semester (half year)
__ Minicourse (6-9 weeks)
__ Units (1-3 weeks)
__ Supplementary
__ Other: ______

Medium Used

X Readings
__ Worksheets
__ Films
X Filmstrips
X Records or tapes
__ Charts or posters
__ Transparencies
X Other: Activity cards Activity kits

PRECONDITIONS

Amount of Reading

X Much
__ Moderate
__ Very little

Teacher Training

__ Provided in materials
__ Suggested by developers
X Not mentioned
__ Other: ______

Prejudice/Stereotyping

Much evidence = M
Some evidence = S

__ Racial or Ethnic
__ Sexrole
__ Other: ______

EVALUATION INFORMATION

Provision for Student Evaluation

__ Instruments specified
X Procedures specified
__ Guidelines suggested
__ Nothing provided
__ Other: ______

Materials Evaluation

Materials tested = T
Results available = A

A Fieldtested before publication
T Fieldtested after publication
__ User feedback solicited
__ Other: ______
__ Not evaluated

SUBSTANTIVE CHARACTERISTICS

Values Education Approach

__ Inculcation
__ Moral development
__ Analysis
X Clarification
__ Action learning
__ Other: ______

Values Education Emphasis

__ Major focus
X One of several concerns
__ A minor concern

Process/Content Emphasis

X Process of valuing
X Content of valuing

Objectives

X Stated specifically
__ Stated generally
__ Not stated

Student Activities

Used or stressed frequently = F
Used or stressed occasionally = O

F Reading
O Writing
__ Class discussion
F Small-group discussion
O Games
__ Simulations
O Role playing
O Action projects
O Other: Dancing, drawing, making things, singing, listening

Title: TOWARD AFFECTIVE DEVELOPMENT (TAD)

Authors: Henry Dupont, Ovitta Sue Gardner, and David S. Brody

Publisher: American Guidance Service, Inc., Publishers' Bldg., Circle Pines, MN 55014

Date: 1974

Grade Levels: 3-6

Materials and Cost: Multimedia kit including 44 illustrations, 93 discussion pictures, 1 filmstrip, 1 cassette, 36 exercise cards, 2 posters, 16 student activity sheets, 40 feeling wheels, a box of colored chips, 2 sets of 37 illustrated career folders, and a teacher's guide ($90.00)

Toward Affective Development (TAD) is an activity-oriented program for students in grades three through six. The authors believe that children's self-concept and social relations influence their behavior and classroom achievement. Therefore, emphasis is placed on educating the whole child. TAD has been designed to develop in students a positive self-image and to increase their understanding of human behavior. The goals of the program reflect the values clarification approach. They include becoming open to new experiences; understanding feelings and emotions; understanding the relationship between thoughts, feelings, and behavior; recognizing individual needs and differences; learning to understand and get along with others; and identifying long-range goals through self-discovery. The program also hopes to develop communication skills such as self-expression and the ability to listen and empathize; social skills, such as cooperation; and decision-making skills.

The goals and objectives of the program have been adapted from child development theory. The focus on development reflects the moral development approach to values education and, although this approach is not the major one, it has been applied to some extent. The materials show an awareness of different levels or stages of development. In some cases different teaching methods are suggested for use with students at different stages of development. In addition, several of the lessons mention different types of responses that may be expected from students of different levels of maturity.

TAD may be used effectively as a one-year course or as a coordinated third-through sixth-grade program. It is recommended that these materials be integrated into the regular curriculum. They may be used with guidance or remedial programs as well. The program is divided into five sections: "Reaching In and Reaching Out," "Your Feelings and Mine," "Working Together," "Me: Today and Tomorrow," and "Feeling, Thinking, Doing." These, in turn, are divided into units. Objectives are specified for each section, unit, and lesson. Each lesson contains the following information: purpose, space requirement, approximate time, materials needed, vocabulary, an activity, and possible learning outcomes. Many units also contain follow-up activities that apply the lesson to other subjects. The content focuses on situations similar to those children might encounter in their own lives. Teaching techniques include large- and small-group discussion, role play, brainstorming, and a variety of other involvement activities.

Although no teacher training is mentioned, the teacher's manual offers guidelines for teaching the materials and explains the authors' concept of the teacher's role. Students are evaluated primarily through teacher observation. The outcomes for each lesson reflect the objective and are to be used as evaluation guides. For example, in one lesson, the purpose is "to encourage students to share and cooperate in a group effort." The outcome is, "Students will grumble some about the need for more scissors, paste, and paper, but then they will discover several different ways to share and cooperate."

TAD was tested over a period of three

years with more than 2000 students from a wide variety of social and ethnic backgrounds. From the 400 original lessons, 191 were selected in which the outcome was observed to be consistent with the objective. The evaluative data from the fieldtesting is now being compiled and will be available shortly from the publisher. According to the authors, continued long-term evaluation is being conducted as well, and user feedback is encouraged. A master's degree study at the University of Wisconsin concluded that "selected *TAD* lessons were effective in creating awareness of alternatives to psycho-social situations in a sample of sixth grade children." This study also found "that the participants reported overwhelming, positive views about the program" (John E. LeCapitaine, School of Psychology, University of Wisconsin—Eau Claire, May 1975).

DESCRIPTIVE CHARACTERISTICS

Grade Level

X K-3
X 4-6
__ 7-8
__ 9-10
__ 11-12

Materials

X Student materials
X Teacher guide
X A-V kit
__ Tests
__ Other: ______

Time

X Curriculum (2 or more years)
X Course (one year)
__ Semester (half year)
__ Minicourse (6-9 weeks)
__ Units (1-3 weeks)
X Supplementary
__ Other: ______

Medium Used

X Readings
X Worksheets
__ Films
X Filmstrips
X Records or tapes
X Charts or posters
__ Transparencies
X Other: Cards

PRECONDITIONS

Amount of Reading

__ Much
X Moderate
__ Very little

Teacher Training

__ Provided in materials
__ Suggested by developers
X Not mentioned
__ Other: ______

Prejudice/Stereotyping

Much evidence = M
Some evidence = S

__ Racial or Ethnic
__ Sexrole
__ Other: ______

EVALUATION INFORMATION

Provision for Student Evaluation

__ Instruments specified
__ Procedures specified
X Guidelines suggested
__ Nothing provided
__ Other: ______

Materials Evaluation

Materials tested = T
Results available = A

A Fieldtested before publication
__ Fieldtested after publication
A User feedback solicited
A Other: Research study
__ Not evaluated

SUBSTANTIVE CHARACTERISTICS

Values Education Approach

__ Inculcation
X Moral development
__ Analysis
X Clarification (Major approach)
__ Action learning
__ Other: ______

Values Education Emphasis

X Major focus
__ One of several concerns
__ A minor concern

Process/Content Emphasis

X Process of valuing
__ Content of valuing

Objectives

X Stated specifically
__ Stated generally
__ Not stated

Student Activities

Used or stressed frequently = F
Used or stressed occasionally = O

O Reading
O Writing
F Class discussion
F Small-group discussion
O Games
O Simulations
F Role playing
O Action projects
__ Other: Brainstorming

Curriculum: VALUES EDUCATION SERIES

Titles: *Deciding How to Live on Spaceship Earth: The Ethics of Environmental Concern; Deciding How to Live as Society's Children: Individuals' Needs and Institutional Expectations; Deciding on the Human Use of Power: The Exercise and Control of Power in an Age of Crisis*

Authors: Rodney F. Allen, Carmelo P. Foti, Daniel M. Ulrich, and Steven H. Woolard; Sheila O'Fahey, Pamela Carey Batz, Frances Gelsone, and Ronald W. Petrich; Mauren Carey, Paul Chapman, Robert Cunnane, Antony Mullaney, and Anne Walsh

Publisher: McDougal, Littell and Company, Box 1667-B, Evanston, IL 60204

Dates: 1973, 1974

Grade Levels: 9-12

Materials and Cost: Student text ($3.24); teacher's guide ($1.50)

The Values Education Series (formerly Plover Books) is currently composed of three student texts and a separate teacher's guide (see the Teacher Materials section of Chapter VI for an analysis of the guide) designed to involve students personally, thoughtfully, and emotionally in three major social issues—the environment, society, and power. A fourth student text, which will deal with politics, is forthcoming. The developers believe that active involvement in crucial contemporary problems should embrace humanistic as well as rational processes. The series therefore stresses the general objectives of helping students to become aware of their values, to develop moral reasoning skills, to strive for personal meaning and ultimate commitments, and to choose "a responsible, satisfying life style."

Each chapter of the student texts focuses on a specific aspect of the individual social issue under consideration. *Spaceship Earth* deals with the use of natural resources, noise pollution, the energy crisis, and other environmental concerns. *Society's Children* is organized into chapters on femininity/masculinity, education, work, and the family. *The Human Use of Power* focuses on various types of power—individual, group, economic, political, and international. These issues are presented through short case studies that depict real-life dilemmas. Students are encouraged to choose from among alternative solutions, to justify their reasons, to infer the values underlying conflict, and to make decisions based on their value choices. Other activities include "sensitivity modules" designed to encourage students to observe and gather data in the community. In one module, students are asked to observe the front yards in their neighborhood and to think of several ways the yards might be improved in beauty and variety. They are then asked if they would be willing to try one of the suggested improvements on their own yards.

Suggestions for assessing student growth in value development are presented in the teacher's guide. These include analysis of videotaped discussions, self-analysis of student work, teacher observation, and written tests patterned after the exercises in the texts. Sections of two of the texts, *Spaceship Earth* and *Society's Children,* were fieldtested by their authors in several classrooms before publication. Informal evaluation data from teachers who have used the materials have also been obtained for each text. According to the publisher, the results of this effort and a more formal evaluation on portions of *Society's Children* were very favorable. These results are not published or generally available.

DESCRIPTIVE CHARACTERISTICS

Grade Level

- ___ K-3
- ___ 4-6
- ___ 7-8
- X 9-10
- X 11-12

Materials

- X Student materials
- X Teacher guide
- ___ A-V kit
- ___ Tests
- ___ Other: ______

Time

- ___ Curriculum (2 or more years)
- X Course (one year)
- ___ Semester (half year)
- X Minicourse (6-9 weeks) Each title
- ___ Units (1-3 weeks)
- ___ Supplementary
- ___ Other: ______

Medium Used

- X Readings
- ___ Worksheets
- ___ Films
- ___ Filmstrips
- ___ Records or tapes
- ___ Charts or posters
- ___ Transparencies
- ___ Other: ______

PRECONDITIONS

Amount of Reading

- X Much
- ___ Moderate
- ___ Very little

Teacher Training

- ___ Provided in materials
- ___ Suggested by developers
- X Not mentioned
- ___ Other: ______

Prejudice/Stereotyping

Much evidence = M
Some evidence = S

- ___ Racial or Ethnic
- ___ Sexrole
- ___ Other: ______

EVALUATION INFORMATION

Provision for Student Evaluation

- ___ Instruments specified
- ___ Procedures specified
- X Guidelines suggested
- ___ Nothing provided
- ___ Other: ______

Materials Evaluation

Materials tested = T
Results available = A

- T Fieldtested before publication
- ___ Fieldtested after publication
- T User feedback solicited
- ___ Other: ______
- ___ Not evaluated

SUBSTANTIVE CHARACTERISTICS

Values Education Approach

- ___ Inculcation
- X Moral development
- X Analysis
- X Clarification
- ___ Action learning
- ___ Other: ______

Values Education Emphasis

- X Major focus
- ___ One of several concerns
- ___ A minor concern

Process/Content Emphasis

- ___ Process of valuing
- X Content of valuing

Objectives

- ___ Stated specifically
- X Stated generally
- ___ Not stated

Student Activities

Used or stressed frequently = F
Used or stressed occasionally = O

- F Reading
- O Writing
- F Class discussion
- O Small-group discussion
- ___ Games
- ___ Simulations
- O Role playing
- O Action projects
- ___ Other: ______

Title: VALUES IN ACTION

Developers: Fannie Shaftel and George Shaftel

Publisher: Winston Press, 25 Groveland Terrace, Minneapolis, MN 55403

Date: 1970

Grade Levels: 4-6

Materials and Cost: Audiovisual kit containing 10 filmstrips (9 in color), 3 records, and teacher's guide ($99.00)

Values in Action encourages students through discussion, problem solving, and role playing, to "examine their values and to realize that there are varied ways of solving their problems." The rationale explains that "children need help in confronting the many dilemmas in their lives"—dilemmas involving their values. According to the developers, role playing is an effective tool for helping students work with such confrontations. The objectives for the materials are specifically stated and intend for the discussion and role playing-experiences to provide children with such things as opportunities to see universal problems and situations in a familiar setting, chances for defining and exploring alternative ways of solving a problem and seeing the probable consequences of such solutions, and opportunities for dialogue with a sympathetic adult.

Students examine nine problem situations which are presented through a filmstrip, a recording, discussion, and role-play activities. The problem situations treated involve group and peer pressure, honesty, rules, friendship, helping others, pride, and responsibility. For example, in the story "Benefit of the Doubt" students investigate the following dilemma: "Can you have the courage to see—and to admit to others—that your actions have been cruel, even though this admission may cost you the approval of others?"

An accompanying teacher's guide provides an introduction to the program, an overview of each filmstrip, a transcript of the recording, and guidelines for presenting each of the student sections. A short explanation of the role-playing and discussion techniques used and a demonstration lesson provide the teacher with some training for using these materials.

DESCRIPTIVE CHARACTERISTICS

Grade Level

___ K-3
_X_ 4-6
___ 7-8
___ 9-10
___ 11-12

Materials

___ Student materials
_X_ Teacher guide
_X_ A-V kit
___ Tests
___ Other: ______________

Time

___ Curriculum (2 or more years)
___ Course (one year)
___ Semester (half year)
___ Minicourse (6-9 weeks)
_X_ Units (1-3 weeks)
___ Supplementary
___ Other: ______________

Medium Used

___ Readings
___ Worksheets
___ Films
_X_ Filmstrips
_X_ Records or tapes
___ Charts or posters
___ Transparencies
___ Other: ______________

PRECONDITIONS

Amount of Reading

___ Much
___ Moderate
_X_ Very little

Teacher Training

_X_ Provided in materials
___ Suggested by developers
___ Not mentioned
___ Other: ______________

Prejudice/Stereotyping

Much evidence = M
Some evidence = S

___ Racial or Ethnic
___ Sexrole
___ Other: ______________

EVALUATION INFORMATION

Provision for Student Evaluation

___ Instruments specified
___ Procedures specified
___ Guidelines suggested
_X_ Nothing provided
___ Other: ______________

Materials Evaluation

Materials tested = T
Results available = A

___ Fieldtested before publication
___ Fieldtested after publication
___ User feedback solicited
___ Other: ______________
_X_ Not evaluated

SUBSTANTIVE CHARACTERISTICS

Values Education Approach

___ Inculcation
___ Moral development
___ Analysis
_X_ Clarification
___ Action learning
___ Other: ______________

Values Education Emphasis

_X_ Major focus
___ One of several concerns
___ A minor concern

Process/Content Emphasis

_X_ Process of valuing
___ Content of valuing

Objectives

_X_ Stated specifically
___ Stated generally
___ Not stated

Student Activities

Used or stressed frequently = F
Used or stressed occasionally = O

___ Reading
___ Writing
_F_ Class discussion
___ Small-group discussion
___ Games
___ Simulations
_F_ Role playing
___ Action projects
___ Other: ______________

Curriculum: THE VALUING APPROACH TO CAREER EDUCATION

Titles: *K-2 Series, 3-5 Series,* and *6-8 Series*

Developer: M. F. Smith

Publisher: Education Achievement Corporation, P. O. Box 7310, Waco, TX 76710

Dates: 1973-74

Grade Levels: K-8

Materials and Cost: *K-2 Series* (total package—$347.50); *3-5 Series* (total package—$453.95); *6-8 Series* (total package $271.29). Components may be purchased separately and include teacher's guides, story books, reading sheets, audiovisual kits, games, hand puppets, file boxes with folders, spirit masters, activity cards, posters, charts, and pre- and post-tests.

The Valuing Approach to Career Education is a multimedia instructional system containing three series—K-2, 3-5, and 6-8. Each series is divided into 12 to 15 learning sequences, each of which includes from eight to 15 lessons. The developers have defined career as a "life path rather than as a job or series of jobs." They view career development as "a primary facet of general development" and as a continuous, dynamic process. The program integrates four valuing skills and instructional activities with ten career education concepts and 12 thinking skills. The four valuing skills are identifying values, clarifying values, managing conflicting values, and developing empathy. The career education concepts emphasized include "career developing is a life-long process," "everyone makes career decisions," "people work to satisfy many needs," "worker roles are interdependent," and "technology brings about change in our society." Included in the 12 thinking skills are observing and reporting, summarizing, interpreting, generalizing, and imagining. Within the framework of these three components, each series focuses on three general objectives: to clarify the students' personal values, to teach career concepts, and to develop thinking skills.

The content of the series is presented through a wide range of instructional aids, including color sound-filmstrips, games, audio cassettes with read-along storybooks, spirit master work sheets, activity cards, posters and charts, puppets, and file boxes containing various lesson activities. In the *K-2 Series* characters such as Hannibal Hippo and Dwendy and the Seven Dworks stress the importance of feelings and values. The materials engage children in a variety of activities that can clarify their personal values in relation to work. For example, in one lesson Hannibal Hippo gets lost. He is helped by many persons who work in the neighborhood and explain to him why they like their jobs. In a discussion activity children then look at such questions as, "What happened in the story?" and "How do you feel when you help someone?"

In the *3-5 Series* children encounter new characters, including Benjamin Beadstringer and Cowslip Pollen, who help to teach various career-education concepts and develop valuing and thinking skills. In one lesson, for instance, students listen to a story about Factoryville and Carnival Land; it is designed to demonstrate that work for some people may be play for others. The *6-8 Series* focuses on the personal dimensions of the world of work, society, and the process of decision making. For example in one of the learning sequences students explore the relationships between an individual's work role and the other facets of his or her life, examine the roles of management and labor, and hypothesize about ways in which work roles affect people's leisure plans.

Extensive facilitator's guides for each series integrate "all components into a criterion-referenced, performance-based design containing valuing rationale, development and management data, measurement with evaluation data, synopses of learning sequences, and detailed lesson plans.'' In addition, the guides contain suggestions for using values clarification strategies. Student evaluation is provided in the program through pre- and post-tests that consist of yes/no items indicating cognitive and affective growth. The publisher offers a one-day inservice training workshop in values clarification with purchase of a series. Depending upon the extent of the purchase, this workshop may be provided free.

The entire program has been fieldtested in Florida and results, favorable though not statistically significant, are available from the publisher in the *Final Research Report* of the project (Smith 1974). The 3-5 program was also evaluated in another study, which produced results showing that ''a career oriented curriculum is effective in significantly reducing female stereotyping at higher grade levels'' (Parks, School of Education, University of Northern Colorado, Greeley, Colorado, 1974).

DESCRIPTIVE CHARACTERISTICS

Grade Level

X K-3
X 4-6
X 7-8
__ 9-10
__ 11-12

Materials

X Student materials
X Teacher guide
X A-V kit
X Tests
__ Other: ______

Time

X Curriculum (2 or more years)
__ Course (one year)
__ Semester (half year)
__ Minicourse (6-9 weeks)
__ Units (1-3 weeks)
__ Supplementary
__ Other: ______

Medium Used

X Readings
X Worksheets
__ Films
X Filmstrips
X Records or tapes
X Charts or posters
__ Transparencies
X Other: Puppet, activity cards, games

PRECONDITIONS

Amount of Reading

X Much
__ Moderate
__ Very little

Teacher Training

__ Provided in materials
X Suggested by developers
__ Not mentioned
__ Other: ______

Prejudice/Stereotyping

Much evidence = M
Some evidence = S

__ Racial or Ethnic
__ Sexrole
__ Other: ______

EVALUATION INFORMATION

Provision for Student Evaluation

X Instruments specified
__ Procedures specified
__ Guidelines suggested
__ Nothing provided
__ Other: ______

Materials Evaluation

Materials tested = T
Results available = A

A Fieldtested before publication
__ Fieldtested after publication
__ User feedback solicited
A Other: Research study
__ Not evaluated

SUBSTANTIVE CHARACTERISTICS

Values Education Approach

__ Inculcation
__ Moral development
__ Analysis
X Clarification
__ Action learning
__ Other: ______

Values Education Emphasis

__ Major focus
X One of several concerns
__ A minor concern

Process/Content Emphasis

X Process of valuing
__ Content of valuing

Objectives

X Stated specifically
__ Stated generally
__ Not stated

Student Activities

Used or stressed frequently = F
Used or stressed occasionally = O

F Reading
O Writing
__ Class discussion
F Small-group discussion
F Games
__ Simulations
__ Role playing
__ Action projects
F Other: Listening

clarification: teacher materials

Title: CLARIFYING VALUES THROUGH SUBJECT MATTER: APPLICATIONS FOR THE CLASSROOM

Authors: Merrill Harmin, Howard Kirschenbaum, and Sidney B. Simon

Publisher: Winston Press, Inc., 25 Groveland Terrace, Minneapolis, MN 55403

Date: 1973

Grade Levels: 6-12

Materials and Cost: Teacher's guide ($2.95)

Clarifying Values Through Subject Matter is a sourcebook of suggestions, questions, and examples that a teacher can use to incorporate values clarification into the teaching of various subject areas. The authors generally believe that education should be more relevant to students; their approach to accomplishing that goal is to help teachers focus on the values of the students within the context of regular course work.

The introductory sections of the book briefly describe the rationale and goals of values clarification and identify various guidelines teachers should use to implement this approach. Also included is an explanation and illustration of three levels of teaching a subject area—facts, concepts, and values.

The next major section illustrates these three levels with sets of questions related to a variety of subject areas including literature, history, math, physics, foreign languages, home economics, art, music, and bookkeeping. In relation to the Civil War, for example, the teacher might ask, at the facts level, "Who was Robert E. Lee?" On the concept level, a teacher might ask, "What qualities or events make a hero or a villain?" In order to probe into the values level, one might ask, "Under what circumstances would you kill a person?"

The last major section of the book illustrates the application of 15 value clarifying strategies or activities with environmental education content. The strategies include value sheets (short readings and a set of questions), rank orders (three or four alternatives ordered according to personal preference), unfinished sentences ("I would rather live with a little pollution than . . ."), and a time diary (chart recording what the student did during the week). The author urges that these strategies be used as models to be adapted to other subject areas.

Title: COMPOSITION FOR PERSONAL GROWTH: VALUES CLARIFICATION THROUGH WRITING

Authors: Robert C. Hawley, Sidney B. Simon, and D. D. Britton

Publisher: Hart Publishing Company, Inc., 719 Broadway, New York, NY 10002

Date: 1973

Grade Levels: 7-12

Materials and Cost: Teacher's guide ($4.95)

Composition for Personal Growth is a guide designed for teaching writing with a focus on values. It has also been used in drug education programs; by group counselors, social studies teachers, foreign language teachers, religious educators; and in scouting and YMCA programs. The objective of this book is to take the boredom out of written assignments and make them relevant, interesting, and rewarding to the writer. Through the techniques outlined, students are expected to gain ability in clarifying who they are, how they are perceived by others, and what they value. It is the authors' belief that "through composition, students can become more aware of the congruence or disparity between their values and their actions; more aware of the forces causing disparity and the skills needed to effect congruence."

The guide consists of nine chapters with the first one devoted to an explanation of the personal growth approach to basic composition. This approach contrasts with the traditional approach in various ways, including motivation, content, and tasks. The personal growth approach requires that the subject be meaningful to the student and that feedback be descriptive and come from peers. Chapters 2 through 5 contain self-analysis and clarification activities designed to elicit personal information that students can use in their compositions. The topics deal with indentity, interpersonal relations, values, and personal growth. Chapters 6 and 7 give both general and specific methods for implementing the personal growth approach to composition. For example, the teacher may label corners of the room with words characterizing certain behavior, such as *wall flower, joker,* and *dominator,* and allow students to join the group they think best describes them. Another method is to use a force-field analysis to decide whether to adopt a certain course of action. The last two chapters offer suggestions and procedures for ongoing activities that stimulate reflective thinking.

The authors offer a word of caution with regard to student evaluation. If grades must be given, it should be done on an individual basis and all parties need to understand what work is to be graded and what criteria are to be used.

Title: MORE VALUES CLARIFICATION: A GUIDEBOOK FOR THE USE OF VALUES CLARIFICATION IN THE CLASSROOM

Authors: Sidney B. Simon and Jay Clark

Publisher: Pennant Educational Materials, 4680 Alvarado Canyon Rd., San Diego, CA 92120

Date: 1975

Grade Levels: 7-12

Materials and Cost: Teacher's guide ($3.95)

More Values Clarification provides teachers and students with tools for recognizing, developing, and strengthening values. According to the authors, "values clarification is a way of examining our lives and determining values that are important to us. [It] is a process which can help us become more aware of our values—those fixed, and those changing or emerging." The writers feel that people who clarify their own values become more purposeful and more productive human beings. Values clarification is seen as the process that "tries to change apathy to purposefulness and productiveness."

Of the 11 chapters composing the book, the first five provide an introduction to and overview of values clarification, in addition to a conversation between the two authors. In these opening chapters, information is given on a variety of topics, including working with groups, working with students on probation, building values, and building a climate of trust. The authors' division of values clarification into three processes (choosing values, prizing values, and acting on values) is explained. In Chapters 6 through 9, values clarification strategies are divided into three categories: "starter," "advanced," and "probing" strategies. The authors warn that it is important to begin with the starter strategies, since moving into advanced strategies too soon or probing deeply before the individual or group is ready may produce disastrous consequences. Thirty-three strategies are presented, ranging from nonthreatening, trust-building activities, such as preparing one-minute biographies and identifying the kinds of "people I need," to more sensitive and probing activities, such as discussing human sexuality and planning action for personal growth. In the tenth chapter, value-action and ways to measure such action are discussed, along with measures for evaluating a values clarification program. The authors conclude the book with a brief discussion of the things participants in values clarification workshops have learned and shared.

Title: A NEW ROLE FOR GEOGRAPHIC EDUCATION: VALUES AND ENVIRONMENTAL CONCERNS

Author: Richard Cole

Publisher: National Council for Geographic Education, 115 North Marion St., Oak Park, IL 60301

Date: 1974

Grade Levels: 3-12

Materials and Cost: Teacher's guide ($3.00)

A New Role for Geographic Education is a monograph for teachers interested in applying values clarification techniques to the study of geography. The author attempts to merge two educational trends that he feels are important. He states that "geography has contributed to a revised concern over environmental awareness, while education has provided a new focus on human values and sensitivity." Since blind obedience is no longer acceptable, especially by young citizens, and since teacher influence has previously been either value neutral or inculcation oriented, the purpose of this monograph is to offer an alternative. The alternative is for teachers to help students clarify and develop their own sets of values. The author's purpose in developing this is "to present instructional techniques for bringing students at all levels to an awareness of their own values and value conflict; for guiding student exploration of values related to geographic problems; and for helping students to develop a set of values that is consistent with both personal and social needs."

The author begins by explaining that the new role of geographic education involves "the direct examination of personal and social values in geographic and environmental phenomena surrounding each individual." Next, values and valuing are defined and discussed using the conceptions of Rokeach (1970) and Raths (Raths *et al.* 1966). The next section offers guidelines and strategies for fostering the valuing process in the geography classroom. Three steps involved in value-clarifying activities are identified: "(1) The student recognizes and understands a value-laden issue or situation. (2) The student makes a value statement regarding the situation or issue. (3) The teacher responds to the student's statement in such a way that the student will think further about the values involved."

A variety of teaching techniques are explained, such as idea building, personal preference analysis, peer persuasion, and affirmative action. Each technique is explained in terms of purpose, classroom organization, ground rules, teacher and student roles, and procedures. A model lesson integrating the above guidelines, steps, and techniques is then elaborated and illustrated. Finally, the appendix includes a section by O. Fred Donaldson called "Exploring Values Through Examining Human Use of Space." In it he shows how his students examined and described places of their own choosing with regard to urban geographical phenomena and how they perceived individuals were using each space.

According to the author, certain components of this monograph were used in adult inservice training and with students before and after publication. No results, however, are available.

Title: ROLE-PLAYING FOR SOCIAL VALUES: DESICION-MAKING IN THE SOCIAL STUDIES

Authors: Fannie R. Shaftel and George Shaftel

Publisher: Prentice-Hall, Inc., Englewood Cliffs, NJ 07632

Date: 1967

Grade Levels: K-8

Materials and Cost: Teacher's guide ($9.50)

Role-Playing for Social Values, a book of role-playing theory and applications, emphasizes the clarification approach to values education. Its purpose is to familiarize teachers with the strategy of role playing and to suggest ways of using this strategy in classrooms. The authors see role play as an effective technique for citizenship education and group counseling and for helping students to understand and live with themselves and to understand and live with others. In role-playing activities, students are involved in realistic problem situations. Working out these problems in the classroom helps prepare the children for similar dilemmas that may arise in their own lives. Objectives for students include the clarification of their own values, the development of a sensitivity to the feelings and welfare of others, the development of a positive self-concept, and the development of decision-making skills. The authors feel strongly that the place for learning about self and others, about personal and social relationships, values, and decisions is in the social studies classroom.

The book is divided into two sections. The first explains what role play is and how to implement it. This section answers the question, "Why role play?" and deals with the guidance functions of this kind of activity, such as diagnosing tensions and sources of strain. The importance of the teacher's being nonevaluative yet supportive is stressed. A variety of ways to use role play—for example, with disadvantaged students or with the mentally retarded—are suggested, as are thematic sequences that can be used effectively with students. Finally, this section contains a checklist for guiding role play and a bibliography for further reading.

The second part of the book is a series of problem stories posing dilemmas typical of those often faced by children and young adolescents. These fall into four categories: Individual Integrity, Group Responsibility, Self-Acceptance, and Managing One's Feelings. One story in the first category, for instance, dramatizes the dilemma of Marty, a young boy who lent money to Bryan but was not paid back despite repeated requests. Marty has an opportunity to get the money back by stealing it in a way that will cause Bryan much trouble. Students discuss and role play possible solutions. Each story is introduced with a statement of the problem and suggestions for presenting the material to the students. A typical role-play activity would involve the warm-up or introduction, selection of roles, preparation of the audience, setting the stage, the first enactment, discussion and evaluation, further enactments, further discussion and evaluation, and generalizations.

Title: TEACHING FOR SOCIAL VALUES IN THE SOCIAL STUDIES

Authors: Maxine Dunfee and Claudia Crump

Publisher: Association for Childhood Education International, 3615 Wisconsin Ave., NW, Washington, D.C. 20016

Date: 1974

Grade Levels: K-6

Materials and Cost: Teacher's guide ($2.75)

Teaching for Social Values in the Social Studies is a book of teacher readings and suggested activities intended to help elementary children clarify their values and better understand those of others. Values clarification, according to the authors, is not to be studied as an academic subject by itself, but rather should be a part of social studies instruction. In studying real people, their relationships, interactions, and problems, it is hoped children will be able to see how people's values affect their actions. The authors believe that many of the personal and social problems of our society result from value conflicts that go unresolved. They contend that we must begin by teaching our children how to value, and thus prepare them for dealing effectively with future societal and global dilemmas. The primary objective is to develop a positive self-concept in children so that they are secure in their feelings about themselves and see themselves as useful, competent, and accepted human beings. The authors believe that "as pupils become more adept in resolving value questions that confront them on a personal level, they are practicing skills indispensable to dealing with problems of the larger social environment."

The content of the book centers on teaching children not what, but how to value. The general formula used for all of the activities involves each child in identifying the issue, examining alternatives and consequences, and deciding upon a course of action. After the students have worked through a number of personal value clarification activities, social issues are introduced. The topics covered include "building self-concept, widening the friendship circle, overcoming bias and prejudice, making democracy a reality, and renewing the environment." Each chapter suggests a variety of activities such as role playing, simulations, case studies, and discussions that relate to one of the issues studied. One open-ended questioning activity, for instance, asks students to complete the following sentence: "When I look at my friends and then look at myself I feel . . ."

Although most of the activities reflect a clarification approach to values education, some are analysis oriented. Moreover, since the authors believe that students should adopt certain values, such as a positive self-concept, a desire to renew the environment, and a willingness to participate in democracy, the materials also manifest the inculcation approach.

No tests accompany the suggested activities. However, the book gives the teacher an idea of what kinds of behavior and action to look for, as well as questions to keep in mind while observing the children. There are, in addition, suggestions for involving parents in the evaluation process.

Title: VALUE CLARIFICATION IN THE CLASSROOM: A PRIMER

Authors: J. Doyle Casteel and Robert J. Stahl

Publisher: Goodyear Publishing Company, Inc., 15115 Sunset Blvd , Pacific Palisades, CA 90272

Date: 1975

Grade Levels: 9-12

Materials and Cost: Teacher's guide ($7.95)

Value Clarification in the Classroom: A Primer was designed to be used in undergraduate, graduate, and inservice teacher education courses. The authors strongly believe that value clarification should be included in such courses as social studies, English, and science as a part of the ongoing instructional program. They reason that the valuing process is integrally involved in knowing and thinking, in personal and social activities, and in decision making. Also, they believe that values are learned and can be taught. The book is intended "to help teachers organize and guide instruction in the area of values clarification." It is hoped that teachers will come to understand what students actually do when they are involved in values clarification, what they as teachers can do to facilitate this behavior, and what kinds of materials and activities are most likely to stimulate this type of behavior in students. Casteel and Stahl emphasize that values clarification is one of the most important responsibilities of the classroom teacher since it increases students' ability to analyze personal and social values, to express themselves, to empathize, to solve problems, and to make decisions.

Four phases of value clarification are identified. In the comprehension phase students develop an understanding of a learning resource as it relates to the concept, idea, or theme that is the object of valuation. The relational phase stresses interrelationships among data, the learning resource, and the object of valuation. Value preferences and feelings are expressed in the valuation phase. These three phases can be experienced through the use of value sheets—items that embody the teaching strategy recommended by the authors. During the fourth, or reflective, phase students reflect on the values and the feelings they have experienced and publicly revealed. This phase is possible to experience only after students have participated in several value clarification activities related to a common theme. The importance of the teacher's role in guiding students through these phases is stressed. Four types of questions are suggested in order to help teachers elicit student responses at the varying value clarification phases. They are empirical, relational, valuing, and feeling questions.

The major part of the book is devoted to a particular strategy: the value sheet. Six formats for value sheets are suggested and several samples that can be used at the secondary level are given for each. The following are the formats that have been identified, along with the major components of each: (1) the *standard format* is simply a learning resource such as a narrative, a cartoon, a filmstrip or a record, or a set of discussion questions; (2) the *forced-choice format* presents a problematic situation and contains a limited list of alternatives or choices, a decision sheet, and a set of discussion questions; (3) the *affirmative format* presents a problematic situation with space for students to invent their own alternative solutions, and a set of discussion questions; (4) the *rank-order format* presents a situation with a number of options, accompanied by a list of the options, a set of concise directions for rank-ordering the options, and a set of discussion questions; (5) the *classification format* presents a situation in which the student must select from a list the most highly valued options at the expense of other highly valued options and contains a set of discussion questions; (6) the *criterion format* presents problematic situation along with explicit directions, decision sheets, a set of discussion questions, a "universe of policies" (a complete list of possible solutions to the problem), a "universe of data" (a list of statements related to the problem presumed to be true), and a "universe of criteria" (a group of end values upon which preferences or decisions are based).

For each format there are explicit directions for developing new or modified value sheets, as well as checklists to review in order to make certain nothing of significance has been omitted. Activities include reading, class discussion, small-group discussion, writing, and some role play. The sample value sheets deal with the clarification of values related to such areas as government, human relations, the population explosion, history, anthropology, euthanasia, legal education, policy making, feminism, racial conflict, career education, church-state relations, and economics.

Title: VALUE EDUCATION IN THE SCIENCES: THE STEP BEYOND CONCEPTS AND PROCESSES

Author: David J. Kuhn

Date: 1973

Grade Levels: 7-12

Materials and Cost: Paper available from ERIC Document Reproduction Service, Box 190, Arlington, Virginia 22210 (order ED 080 317: microfiche—$.76, xerography—$1.58 plus postage). Also available from David J. Kuhn, University of Wisconsin—Parkside, Kenosha, WI 53140.

"Value Education in the Sciences" is a paper concerned with the question of how individual value systems may be clarified and applied to the study of science and to the world in general. The author feels that, traditionally, science has been studied on the factual and the conceptual levels without allowing attitudes and feelings to enter into that study. One important objective of this paper is to make teachers, curriculum planners, and other educational personnel aware that students need to explore the social implications of science. Facts and concepts, according to the author, are not to be discarded but used to emphasize the social implications of science.

The content of this paper centers around the introduction of a values approach to science instruction. The author offers several definitions of values given by such individuals as Rogers (1964) and Raths (Raths *et al.* 1966). Through the values continuum and rank-order technique, the author stresses that value clarification can become an important component of science education. Believing that science teaching can occur on three levels—facts, concept-process, and values—the author gives examples of how the topic "Life in Pond Water" could be presented at each level. On the knowledge level, a student might be asked to name the environmental factors that might affect the number of organisms living in pond water. On the concept level, various things might be considered—food chain, biological community, and aquatic ecosystem. A question such as "How does water pollution affect your family?" would elicit value-laden responses. The author discusses and illustrates teaching strategies that bring a values dimension to science instruction. These include role playing, simulations, sensitivity modules, values continua and attitude surveys.

Title: VALUE EXPLORATION THROUGH ROLE PLAYING: PRACTICAL STRATEGIES FOR USE IN THE CLASSROOM

Author: Robert C. Hawley

Publisher: Hart Publishing Company, Inc., 15 West 4th St., New York, N.Y. 10012

Date: 1975

Grade Levels: 7-12

Materials and Cost: Teacher's guide ($3.95)

Value Exploration Through Role Playing is designed to give "teachers the specific know-how they need to incorporate role-playing into their repertoire of teaching techniques. For role-playing is not an end in itself; it is just one means in the service of good teaching, teaching which promotes the growth of each learner." The author believes that role playing is a critical technique since it meets a variety of individual needs simultaneously and thereby reaches many students. Role playing is viewed as an appropriate learning activity because it is "one teaching method that involves students actively in the learning process, both in simulated interactions and in determining what path to take in the discussions that follow roleplay. Further, "roleplaying is a common and natural human activity, not just another artificial structure limited to the classroom."

Six chapters and a recommended reading list compose the book. The content reflects the clarification approach to values education. The first chapter, "Decisions: An Open-Chair Role Play," describes the open-chair technique for role play and three elaborations of this format, including the alter-ego voice and role reversal. The teaching procedures involve the following steps: the teacher orients the students to the subject matter, elicits topics of concern from the class by using the open-chair technique to reduce the risk, sets up the role play situation, and arranges the class for the activity.

"Formats," the second chapter, provides an overview of the various forms for role playing. By presenting a variety of formats, the author encourages teachers to "choose the ones that seem most appropriate to their teaching styles and to the particular needs of their classes." The methods discussed include Blackboard Role Play, Blackboard Press Conference, Historical and Literary Impersonations, Six Characters in Search of a Novel, Secrets, Possessions, and Decision-Agent Role Play. In "Chapter Three: Teaching with Role Playing," the pedagogical structures and concerns of role play are discussed. A seven-part sequence of teaching concerns is examined along with critical thinking skills, brainstorming, a six-part valuing process, and the evaluation of role-playing sessions.

The fourth chapter discusses five categories of benefit that can be derived from role playing: problem solving, rehearsing, reporting, developing empathy, and managing the class. "What to Do When Things Go Wrong," the fifth chapter, identifies some typical classroom problems, including unconventional views, discussion "killers," and horsing around, and suggests general ways for dealing with such situations. In the last chapter, "Role Playing and the Development of Moral Judgment," the author summarizes Kohlberg's scheme (as a method for holding vivid, intensive discussions on moral issues and for providing a kind of vicarious role taking that develops the ability to empathize with persons in similar positions).

Suggestions for both teacher and student evaluation are given in Chapter Three. It contains two forms to assist in the evaluation of role-playing sessions, the "Teacher Self-Evaluation Form" and the "Student Feedback Form."

Title: VALUES AND TEACHING: WORKING WITH VALUES IN THE CLASSROOM

Authors: Louis E. Raths, Merrill Harmin, and Sidney B. Simon

Publisher: Charles E. Merrill Publishing Co., 1300 Alum Creek Dr., Columbus, OH 43216

Date: 1966

Materials and Cost: Teacher's guide ($7.50)

Values and Teaching is the original teacher resource on the clarification approach to values education. The authors explain their theory of values, review the research, discuss their methodology for values clarification, illustrate the use of several strategies to help students clarify their values, and discuss guidelines and problems in applying this approach. When developing this resource, authors were motivated by the following assumption: if children are helped to use the valuing process [clarification], they will behave in ways that are less apathetic, confused, and irrational and in ways that are more positive, purposeful, and enthusiastic.'' According to the authors, ''humans can arrive at values by an intelligent process of choosing, prizing, and behaving.'' The book was written and the approach developed in response to the issues and problems the authors see confronting today's society: ''the pace and complexity of modern life have so exacerbated the problem of deciding what is good and what is right and what is worthy and what is desirable that large numbers of children are finding it increasingly bewildering, even overwhelming, to decide what is worth valuing, what is worth one's time and energy.''

The book focuses on the process individuals use to determine their values, rather than on the particular value outcomes of personal experiences. The valuing process involves seven essential components: choosing freely, choosing from among alternatives, choosing after thoughtful consideration of the consequences of each alternative, prizing and cherishing, affirming, acting upon choices, and repeating such action.

Values and Teaching is divided into four sections, followed by appendices, notes, bibliography, and index. Part One is an overview of the book. Part Two presents a theory of values in which the authors describe the difficulty of developing values, define *values* and *valuing,* and provide suggestions about teaching for value clarity. The third part, ''The Value Clarifying Method,'' describes 30 clarifying questions (for example, ''How did you feel when that happened?'' ''Can you give me some examples of that idea?'' and ''What other possibilities are there?'') accompanied by illustrative dialogues; presents examples of 13 values sheets and outlines the strategy for using them; and discusses classroom strategies (role play, thought sheets, action projects, and so on) for developing discussions on value-related issues. Part Four, ''Using the Value Theory,'' discusses problems, emotional needs, and research related to values education. Also included in this part are three observation instruments for determining the effect of values clarification on student behavior.

In general, the research findings described in the book indicate that students become more vital and purposeful when given opportunities to clarify their values. Various research studies of the value clarification approach at the college, high school, and elementary levels are summarized. Suggestions for teacher evaluation are outlined in an appendix, which presents a scheme for evaluating lesson plans and ways of coding specific questions.

Title: VALUES CLARIFICATION: A HANDBOOK OF PRACTICAL STRATEGIES FOR TEACHERS AND STUDENTS

Authors: Sidney B. Simon, Leland W. Howe, and Howard Kirschenbaum

Publisher: Hart Publishing Company, Inc., 15 West 4th St., New York, N.Y. 10012

Date: 1972

Grade Levels: K-12

Materials and Cost: Teacher's guide ($3.95)

This handbook contains 79 strategies that teachers and students can use to clarify their personal values. Each strategy is presented with a statement of purpose, an outline of the procedures, a note to the teacher, and additional suggested applications of the strategy. In order to help youngsters deal with widespread confusion and conflict over values, the authors provide opportunities for students to clarify their own values. Students are encouraged to choose freely from alternatives after thoughtful consideration of the consequences, prize their choices, publicly affirm their choices, and act upon them consistently. According to the authors, by following these processes, students will "behave in ways that are less apathetic, confused, and irrational and in ways that are more positive, purposeful, and enthusiastic." Specific objectives are identified for each strategy. For instance, the objective of the "Rank Order" strategy is to give "students practice in choosing from among alternatives and in publicly affirming and explaining or defending their choices."

The handbook begins with a brief explanation of the rationale and purpose of values clarification, followed by suggestions for using the book and descriptions of the 79 values strategies. The strategies emphasize the process of valuing as well as personal value issues and problems. Completing self-analysis worksheets and discussing value positions in small groups are the primary activities embodied in the strategies. The "Strength of Values" strategy, for example, encourages students to complete unfinished sentences such as, "I would be willing to fight physically for . . .," "I would be willing to die for . . .," and "I will share only with my friends my belief that . . ." Other lessons involve circle graphs in which students work with the "Pie of Life" to evaluate a typical day in their lives and how they might want to make that day better.

There are no provisions for student evaluation, although another book, *Values and Teaching* (analyzed earlier in this section), provides two observation instruments to help measure changes in student behavior related to values clarification. *A Handbook of Practical Strategies* has not been systematically fieldtested, but some of the strategies have been subject to some empirical studies (See Raths *et al.* 1966 and Superka 1973, p. 112). Most of these studies, although methodologically weak and somewhat inconclusive, do provide some basis for the authors' claim that students who use values clarification "become less apathetic, less flighty, less conforming as well as less overdissenting." Kirschenbaum (1974) discusses eleven recent studies which involve more sophisticated methodology and more emphasis on the clarification strategies found in the *Handbook*. Several other recent studies are summarized in the bibliography (Chapter VIII) of this Sourcebook.

Title: VALUES IN SEXUALITY: A NEW APPROACH TO SEX EDUCATION

Authors: Eleanor S. Morrison and Mila Underhill Price

Publisher: Hart Publishing Company, Inc., 719 Broadway, New York, NY 10003

Date: 1974

Grade Levels: 9-12

Materials and Cost: Teacher's guide ($4.95)

Values in Sexuality is intended to provide a structure within which high school and college students can openly explore and discuss their feelings about sexuality. The authors strongly believe that sexuality involves the cognitive as well as the affective domain. The biological facts of life, the personal value system, life style, self-image, communication skills, and understanding of human behavior are considered in relation to human sexuality. Teaching students the skills with which to clarify their own values and to make intelligent choices is the primary goal of this work.

Specific objectives for individual lessons include increasing self-awareness, promoting critical self-assessment, clarifying values, and improving thinking and communication skills. For example, in the chapter on sex roles, one objective is "to increase awareness of the different ways one could view male and female roles; to shed light on the options for individuals." The authors anticipate qualitative gains on the part of the student in terms of freedom to examine and discuss sexual issues; clarification of values; sensitivity to the importance of candidtalk about sex; consciousness of cultural and interpersonal expressions of sexuality; and appreciation for oneself, one's body, and one's sexuality.

All of the activities involve interaction in the form of discussion or role play and are intended for small groups composed of members of both sexes. The materials, developed for a six- to nine-week course, are divided into eleven chapters. The first focuses on group-building activities. Others deal with physiology, psychosexual development, sex roles, nonmarital sex, values clarification, and dimensions in relationships. For each exercise, there is information about materials needed, time required, objectives, rationale, and detailed procedural instructions. Most of the activities can be covered in an hour or less. The scope of the materials allows the teacher to supplement and adapt lessons to include such issues as abortion, pornography, venereal disease, and sex laws.

Self-evaluation is encouraged for each student. In the final chapter students are asked to identify their most valuable learning experiences and to relate what they have learned from such experiences. The purpose of this activity is to summarize and evaluate the course and what has been accomplished by it. The activities originated and have been used successfully for a number of years with students in a human sexuality course at Michigan State University.

Title: VALUING EXERCISES FOR THE MIDDLE SCHOOL (Resource Monograph #11)

Authors: J. Doyle Casteel, Linda H. Corbett, Wellesley T. Corbett, Jr., and Robert J. Stahl

Publisher: P. K. Yonge Laboratory School, College of Education, University of Florida, Gainesville, FL 32611 (Attn: Dr. J. B. Hodges)

Date: 1974

Grade Levels: 5-8

Materials and Cost: Teacher's guide (free on limited basis)

Valuing Exercises for the Middle School presents teachers with a usable format for teaching values clarification objectives. The authors believe that the main goal of middle schools is to help students acquire skills in the process of values clarification. The strategy they suggest for accomplishing this goal is the value sheet, a carefully planned written exercise. These sheets form the link between course content and the goal of values clarification. This monograph provides examples of six types of value sheets which teachers are encouraged to copy or modify and to try out in their own classes.

There are two major sections to this monograph. The first introduces and defines the value sheet, its purposes, and its objectives. The authors stress that value sheets are to be used in conjunction with ongoing courses of instruction, such as social studies, language arts, and science, so that a value sheet directly relates to a current topic of study. Each sheet must have a social or scientific context in which a situation for valuing is presented. Six formats for writing value sheets have been identified. These are standard, forced-choice, affirmative, rank-order, classification, and criterion (see the analysis of *Value Clarification in the Classroom: A Primer* earlier in this section for an explanation of the formats). In addition to the value sheets, four catagories of discussion questions are included: empirical, relational, valuing, and feeling.

In the second section of the monograph, examples of each format are given. These examples are specifically written for a unit on the Bill of Rights and deal with the concepts of justice and due process. Activities include reading, writing, role play, class discussion, and group work.

VI

action learning

Action learning is the least developed of the five values education approaches included in the typology. Derived from social-psychological concepts that stress moving beyond thinking and feeling to acting, this approach is related to the efforts of some social studies educators to emphasize community-based rather than classroom-based learning activities. This chapter explains the basic rationale, purpose, teaching methods, and instructional model of action learning. An activity illustrating the application of this approach is also provided. At present, this approach is not prevalent in many educational curricula. Those few materials that do relate to or reflect action learning are discussed here and analyzed.

Explanation of the Approach

Rationale and Purpose. The distinguishing characteristic of the action learning approach is that it provides specific opportunities for learners to act on their values. That is, it does not confine values education to the classroom or group setting but extends it to experiential learning in the community, where the interplay between choices and actions is continous and must be dealt with. As do those who favor clarification, proponents of action learning see valuing primarily as a process of self-actualization in which individuals consider alternatives; choose freely from among those alternatives; and prize, affirm, and act upon their choices. Action learning advocates, however, extend this concept in two ways. First, they place more emphasis on action-taking inside and outside the classroom than is reflected in the clarification approach. Second, the process of self-actualization is viewed as being tempered by social factors and group pressures. Values are seen to have their source neither in society nor in the individual but in the interaction between the person and the society.

The view of human nature that underlies this approach differs from the views upon which the other approaches are based. The other approaches consider the person either reactive (inculcation), active (analysis and clarification), or a combination of both (moral development). In contrast, the action learning approach perceives the individual as interactive.* The person is not totally

*This conception of human nature seems related to schools of thought in various academic disciplines: the positive relativists in philosophy (Dewey 1939; Bigge 1971), the field theorists in psychology and social psychology (Lewin 1935), the social-psychological personality theorists and therapists (A. Adler 1924; Horney 1950; Sullivan 1953), and the symbolic interactionists in sociology (Blumer 1969).

fashioned by the environment or vice versa. Neither does the person partly make the environment and the environment partly make the person. The person and environment, according to this theory, are mutual co-creators. The person, in fact, cannot be defined out of his or her context. In reinterpreting the ideas of the cognitive and social field psychologists, Bigge (1971, P. 40) clarifies this position:

> The basic principle of interaction is that nothing is perceivable or conceivable as a thing-in-itself; no object has meaning apart from its context. Hence, everything is construed in relation to other objects. More specifically, a thing is perceived as a figure against a background, experienced from a given angle or direction of envisionment. Persons in a given culture have a common social matrix, and a person devoid of a society is a rather meaningless concept. Still, each person is unique in both purposes and experiential background, and the reality upon which he bases intelligent action consists of himself and what he makes of the objects and events that surround him. Thus, in perception, a man and his perceived environment are coordinate; both are responsible for what is real.

Teaching Methods. Many of the teaching methods used in the analysis and clarification approaches are also applied in action learning. Two techniques unique to the action approach, however, are skill practice in group organization and interpersonal relations and action projects that provide opportunities to engage in individual and group action in the school and community.

Instructional Model. An instructional valuing model that illustrates the action approach is in the early stages of development by Anna Ochoa and Patricia L. Johnson at Florida State University. Their view is that the model is circular rather than linear—that is, one may enter at any of several points and work backward and forward in the steps presented in the model. The six steps are as follows:

1) *Becoming aware of a problem or issue:* Help students become conscious of a problem troubling others or themselves.

2) *Understanding the problem or issue and taking a position:* Help students to gather and analyze information and to take a personal value position on the issue.

3) *Deciding whether to act:* Help students to clarify values about taking action and to make a decision about personal involvement.

4) *Planning strategies and action steps:* Help students to brainstorm and organize possible actions; provide skill practice and anticipatory rehearsal.

5) *Implementing strategies and taking action:* Provide specific opportunities for carrying out plans either as individuals working alone or as members of a group.

6) *Reflecting on actions taken and considering next steps:* Guide students into considering the consequences of the actions for others, for themselves, and in relation to the problem. Also, guide students into thinking about possible next steps.

It would seem that this is really a linear model—that one would start at the beginning and progress through each step. But in real life this is rarely the case. Often people act impulsively after becoming aware of a problem and reflect later. It is for this reason that Ochoa and Johnson prefer to conceive of the model as circular rather than linear. As an instructional model it *progresses with the action;* it is not for use simply as preparation before the action.

Illustrative Learning Activity. The following activity has been developed by transforming a communtity action project from Jones (1971, pp. 26-29) into a valuing activity that illustrates the application of the instructional model for the action learning approach.

In a discussion of community problems, assume that students have expressed a concern about living costs for the poor. The teacher guides students in converting their expressed concern into a workable action problem by encouraging actual diagnosis of the real-life situation of the poor in their own community. For example, students might be asked to gather data through field research on the similarities and differences in merchandise and credit costs between low-income and middle-income neighborhoods. Two of Jones' survey charts, presented below, could be used to gather that data.

After comparing and contrasting differences on specific items such as radios and vacuum cleaners, the students discuss their results and formulate value questions. (Consider that, at this phase in the valuing process, learners are employing the methods of value analysis.) Once value questions have been generated, students employ value clarification techniques to discover their own positions on those questions.

Next the teacher assists students in devising feasible action projects consistent with the value positions they have taken. For example, if students decide after investigation that price and credit differences in different neighborhoods are wrong, they might be encouraged to consider possible action alternatives to alter the situation. They might come up with alternatives such as these: (1) write and distribute a community "Buyer's Guide" describing product values and the cost of credit; (2) inform the neighborhood of legal assistance office and inquire about the procedure for filing a class action suit against the store or finance agent; (3) write letters of complaint to local news media and government officials; or (4) use guerilla theater to dramatize fraudulent commercial practices. They would then judge these action alternatives according to their feasibility and appropriateness—a process requiring further value judgments. Once an action alternative is selected, students could proceed with planning and implementation.

In summary, this activity begins after students become aware of a possible problem involving unfair merchandise and credit costs for low-income neighborhoods. The activity then follows in sequence Steps 2 through 5 of the instructional model. The effectiveness of activities such as this one depends upon the feasibility of involving students in the alternative actions. Such

Retail Price Survey*

To compare retail mark-ups on merchandise in low-income and middle-income neighborhoods, choose an appliance store in each neighborhood and price each of the following items. (You may wish to choose several stores in each area and calculate an average price for each neighborhood.) If possible, price the same brand of each item in order to get an accurate comparison. If you can learn the wholesale prices of each item your survey will be more complete.

			Retail Price	
Item	Brand	Wholesale Price	Store in Low Income Neighborhood	Store in Middle Income Neighborhood
Radio				
Portable Color TV				
Stove				
Sewing machine				
Refrigerator				
Vacuum cleaner				
Washing machine				

*From Jones 1971, p. 26. Reprinted by permission.

Credit Practices*

To compare credit practices in the two neighborhoods, decide on a specific item (such as a color TV) and "shop" for it at a store in each neighborhood. Request to take home an unsigned contract or information about the store's credit program or finance company contract.

Evaluate the contract or information to determine what happens if you fail to make a payment. Place a check mark in the appropriate column if the answer is yes.

	Store in Low Income Area	Store in Middle Income Area
Will the item be taken from you?		
Must you pay the return charge?		
Will you forfeit all payments made up to that time?		
Will you be responsible for the unpaid balance?		
If the item is resold for more than the unpaid balance, can the store refuse to give your money back?		
Will you be responsible for any defect or damage to the item?		
Could the seller collect part of your wages?		
If the contract requires a co-signer, will he be liable for the debt?		
Could your property, or that of your co-signer, be taken and sold to pay toward the obligation?		
If a second item were added to the first contract, could the first item be taken if you miss payment on the second?		
If you complete payment before the due date can the store refuse to refund part of the finance charge?		
Does the contract contain a confession clause?		

*From Jones 1971, p. 27. Reprinted by permission.

practices are usually difficult to operationalize in traditional schools because of scheduling and, administrative and parental opposition.

Materials and Programs. Few materials or progams truly reflect the action learning approach to values education. Fred Newmann at the University of Wisconsin, Madison, has experimented with social action and community involvement projects in secondary schools. Based on that work, he has formulated and presented a rationale and general structure for including action learning as a fundamental part of the secondary curriculum (Newmann 1975). Considering values education one component of a citizen action curriculum, his new book, *Education for Citizen Action,* also includes the explication of a model for curriculum development, a discussion of various choices facing teachers involved in citizen action education, and a list of organizations and projects that support community involvement. The teacher text was received too late to be analyzed in this book.

Another recent effort related to the action learning approach to values education is the development of a junior high school curriculum package, *Skills for Ethical Action,* by the Humanizing Learning Program of the Research for Better Schools in Philadelphia. They are currently creating "a set of instructional materials designed to teach junior high school students a behavioral strategy, a step-by-step guide, which enables them to act ethically in their daily lives" (Chapman 1975, p. 1). Pilot testing of these materials is planned for January 1976.

Three other resources related to the action approach are analyzed in this chapter. They are: *Social Action,* one of the unit booklets in the *Public Issues Series* (Xerox), *Finding Community* (Jones 1971), and the teaching guide for the *Values Education Series* (McDougal, Littell). *Social Action* focuses on individual and group community action. Because the teacher's guide includes some suggestions for action projects, this material has been considered an action learning resource. It should be noted, however, that, like the other materials in the *Public Issues Series,* most of the questions and activities in the student booklet use the analysis approach.

Finding Community, one of the two teacher resources analyzed in this chapter, is really a guidebook for community action projects related to a variety of issues, including welfare, the police, buying and selling, and schools. Clearly embodying an activist value orientation and concentrating solely on actions against social abuses, this text is not really a values education work. It can, however, be used to implement some of the steps outlined in the action learning model.

Finally, the last resource analyzed is the teaching guide (Allen 1973) for the *Values Education Series.* Although the questions and activities in the student texts emphasize the clarification approach, the teacher's guide presents a rationale for values education based on "social self-realization" and community involvement—a purpose closely related to the rationale of action learning.

action learning: student materials

Title: SOCIAL ACTION: DILEMMAS AND STRATEGIES (*Public Issues Series)*

Directors: Fred M. Newmann and Donald W. Oliver

Publisher: Xerox Education Publications, Education Center, Columbus, OH 43216

Date: 1972

Grade Levels: 9-12

Materials and Cost: Student text ($0.50); teacher's guide (free with purchase of 10 or more student books)

Social Action: Dilemmas and Strategies is a booklet of case studies concerning actual student involvement in social action. Newmann and Oliver believe that an individual *can* influence public policy. The purpose of the book is not to get students involved in any particular social issue, but rather to have them discover where their own interests lie and to ask questions about social action projects concerning legitimacy of involvement, skills needed for effectiveness, strategies used, dilemmas faced, and personal commitments necessary. After dealing with such questions and analyzing their feelings about issues that arise, it is hoped that students will become involved in a social action project of their choice.

Social action, not to be confused with radicalism, is defined in these materials as "any deliberate attempt to influence an institution or public policy." As preparation for taking some action of their own, students read case studies of social action projects. These include a project in which young people organize to save a forest from housing developers and another case in which black students rally support for desegregating restaurants. Through the case studies, students gain insights into "choosing, participating in, and evaluating their involvement in social action projects." Students consider such factors as group solidarity and risks involved. They discuss alternative courses of action, methods, and, in the event of success or failure, the values of the action taken. After reading and discussing the case studies, and possibly role playing, students may enter the research and exploration stage to discover community issues that may be important to them. Activities such as field trips to community agencies, interviews of public officials and action group members, and surveys of community attitudes and needs are suggested in the teacher's guide. If the students discover a cause with which they can identify, they are encouraged to draw up a plan of action and to carry it through.

Actually carrying through with an action project will require school and parental support. The problem of a school's becoming involved in partisan politics is dealt with in the book, and one case includes student discussion of possible solutions to such a problem. Two student tests are included to evaluate the students' factual knowledge as well as their analytical skills in relation to social action.

DESCRIPTIVE CHARACTERISTICS

Grade Level

___ K-3
___ 4-6
___ 7-8
_X_ 9-10
_X_ 11-12

Materials

_X_ Student materials
_X_ Teacher guide
___ A-V kit
___ Tests
___ Other: ________________

Time

___ Curriculum (2 or more years)
___ Course (one year)
___ Semester (half year)
___ Minicourse (6-9 weeks)
_X_ Units (1-3 weeks)
_X_ Supplementary
___ Other: ________________

Medium Used

_X_ Readings
___ Worksheets
___ Films
___ Filmstrips
___ Records or tapes
___ Charts or posters
___ Transparencies
___ Other: ________________

PRECONDITIONS

Amount of Reading

_X_ Much
___ Moderate
___ Very little

Teacher Training

___ Provided in materials
___ Suggested by developers
_X_ Not mentioned
___ Other: ________________

Prejudice/Stereotyping

Much evidence = M
Some evidence = S

___ Racial or Ethnic
___ Sexrole
___ Other: ________________

EVALUATION INFORMATION

Provision for Student Evaluation

_X_ Instruments specified
___ Procedures specified
___ Guidelines suggested
___ Nothing provided
___ Other: ________________

Materials Evaluation

Materials tested = T
Results available = A

___ Fieldtested before publication
___ Fieldtested after publication
___ User feedback solicited
___ Other: ________________
_X_ Not evaluated

SUBSTANTIVE CHARACTERISTICS

Values Education Approach

___ Inculcation
___ Moral development
_X_ Analysis
___ Clarification
_X_ Action learning
___ Other: ________________

Values Education Emphasis

___ Major focus
_X_ One of several concerns
___ A minor concern

Process/Content Emphasis

_X_ Process of valuing
___ Content of valuing

Objectives

___ Stated specifically
_X_ Stated generally
___ Not stated

Student Activities

Used or stressed frequently = F
Used or stressed occasionally = O

_F_ Reading
_O_ Writing
_F_ Class discussion
_F_ Small-group discussion
___ Games
___ Simulations
_O_ Role playing
_F_ Action projects
___ Other: ________________

action learning: teacher materials

Title: FINDING COMMUNITY: A GUIDE TO COMMUNITY RESEARCH AND ACTION

Preparer: W. Ron Jones

Publisher: James E. Freel and Associates, 577 College Ave., Palo Alto, CA 94306

Date: 1971

Grade Levels: 9-12

Materials and Cost: Teacher's guide ($3.45)

The basic purpose of *Finding Community* is to help students explore how well existing institutions are serving the needs of the people. Its use, however, is not limited to form at all levels and can be used with community groups, individual citizens, or anyone interested in and concerned about contemporary social problems. As an instrument of learning, "it is based on the belief that a good way to learn about community is to get involved with it, and that taking action on problems is as important as finding out about them." The guide describes a variety of issues and then offers procedures for local research and action concerning these issues.

The book focuses on social topics, including food costs, selling practices, the welfare system, poverty, police, and the school system. Each of the 11 chapters is divided into four parts. The first part, entitled "Indictment," briefly describes the content of the chapter. The second part presents various readings that give evidence about an issue drawn from various sources, such as the writings of Michael Harrington, Neil Postman, and the Medical Committee for Human Rights. A third part, "Community Research and Action," provides surveys and procedures to help students determine if conditions described in the indictments can also be found in their community. The fourth section contains descriptions of what others are doing to respond creatively to the problems cited in the chapter. For example, reports on a buyers' boycott and on an alternative schools project are options listed in one chapter.

The activities included in the book involve research and action related to a specific problem. One of the activities included in the chapter on food costs and quality, for example, is a "Food Market Survey." A chart is provided for students to compare prices of selected items in low- and middle-income markets and food cooperatives. Students also investigate selling practices and credit abuse in their community.

Title: TEACHING GUIDE TO THE VALUES EDUCATION SERIES

Author: Rodney F. Allen

Publisher: McDougal, Littell and Company, Box 1667-B, Evanston, IL 60204

Date: 1974

Grade Levels: 7-12

Materials and Cost: Teacher's guide ($1.50)

Teaching Guide to the Values Education Series was originally developed as a guide to the Plover Books *Encounters with Life Series,* which is now published by McDougal, Littell under the title *The Values Education Series*. Although designed explicitly to accompany the three texts in the secondary series, the teacher's guide is a useful resource for anyone interested in values education.

The work is a 92-page narrative that discusses philosophical issues related to values education and explains certain procedures and processes that could be used to teach for value development. The ideas incorporated in the book integrate the analysis, moral development, and clarification approaches, and also emphasize action learning objectives. ''Social-self-realization'' is identified as the overall goal of the *Values Education Series*. Stressing that the highest conception of morality must incorporate the concept of community, the series is designed ''to get students out into the community . . . to get adults into schools to share concerns, wonder together, to work together on community problems and policies.''

Chapter 1 of the guide outlines various approaches to values education and explains the goal and purpose of the series. The next three chapters discuss the inadequacies of exclusively using a rational decision-making model; describe Clyde Kluckholn's (1951) model of goals, values, and ultimate concerns; explicate nine different orientations to justifying decisions; and discuss the nature of the ''moral person'' in relation to Maslow's (1962) hierarchy of needs, Wilson's (1967) six characteristics of the truly moral person, and Kohlberg's (1966) six stages of moral development.

The remaining four chapters focus more practically on the educational implication of value issues. The fifth chapter explicates the four dimensions of values education embodied in the *Values Education Series:* (1) critical-appreciative study of others' values, (2) personal awareness of one's own values and feelings, (3) ethical reasoning skills and, (4) life-style considerations. The sixth chapter outlines four processes, or strategies, for teaching values education through ethical cases. The last process is a nine-phase strategy developed by the author to encompass the other three processes. In Chapter 7 the author discusses various guidelines or rules for evaluating student growth in values education on both long-term bases (analysis of videotape discussion, self-analysis of student's work, determination of Kohlberg's stages) and short-term bases (teacher observation, written exercises). The last chapter briefly explains that the teacher should assume the role of an inquirer, evaluator, and facilitator of an open, probing classroom. Supplemental lists of readings and films related to the topics of the series are also provided.

VII
evocation and union

The five approaches to values education described in the previous chapters represent the range of alternatives reflected in existing curriculum materials and teaching resources. There are, however, two other approaches which, for lack of instructional resources, have not been included in the typology of approaches but are nevertheless valid alternatives in values education. Firmly grounded in philosophy and psychological theory, the "union" and "evocation" approaches are briefly explained below.

Evocation

Some theorists conceive of valuing as a process of emoting or feeling. Values are seen as personal emotions reflecting moral approval or disapproval. No set of values is thought to be better or worse than another. Except for measuring the strength of one's values, objective, empirical validation is impossible. People are valuing when they are actually evincing or expressing moral feelings, not when they are making statements or assertions about them. Valuing, according to this viewpoint, is the experience and expression of one's own intensely personal feelings about good and evil.

The values education approach based on such a conception of valuing is termed *evocation*. Its purpose is to help students evince and express their values genuinely and spontaneously without thought, hesitation, or discussion.

Probably the only pure example of a person valuing in the way the evocation approach suggests is the infant, who without thinking or hesitating knows what his or her organism wants and does not want, likes and dislikes, and approves and disapproves, and who spontaneously behaves by crying, cooing, or laughing. Carl Rogers (1964, pp. 160-67), in fact, sees this as the first stage in the development of a person's valuing process. He calls it "organismic valuing"—one's organism instinctively knows what is good for itself and what is not. Despite the possibility that only an infant can truly "evoke values" spontaneously, this approach is considered here for two reasons. First, the rationale upon which it is based has been supported by several philosophers and psychologists.* Second, some educators, Rogers included, believe that one

*The rationale for the evocation approach seems closely related to the ideas of philosophers such as Ayer (1946) and Westermarck (1932) and psychologists such as Combs and Snygg (1949) and Whitaker and Malone (1953). Each of these theorists stresses either the subjective or the emotional side of a person, or both. Psychotherapists Whitaker and Malone, in fact, directly attempt in their therap to help persons engage in spontaneous, autonomous choosing.

of the key goals of values education should be to help persons once again "get in touch" with their spontaneous, emotional, and organismically based valuing process and integrate it into their value system.

No one has developed an explicit teaching methodology or an instructional model to help teachers in applying the evocation approach to values education. Extreme proponents of this approach would consider a rigid set of procedures contrary to the essential purpose of evocation—to foster spontaneous, nonrational choicemaking.

Some methods that have been used by teachers do, however, seem to reflect this objective. The open school or classroom that emphasizes free exploration and reaction to the environment especially in terms of feelings would be one example. Another method that seems related to this approach is to present a series of provocative stimuli—for example, pictures, slides, filmstrips, movies, and/or readings—in order to elicit spontaneous, gut-level reactions from the students. The goal would not be to discuss or analyze these reactions, but to get students to react personally and genuinely to the situations in terms of their own values.

The basic technique of Transcendental Meditation (TM) also seems related to the evocation approach. The fundamental purpose of TM, as explained by the Research Coordinator of the International Center for Scientific Research at Maharishi International University, is to "develop the full potential of the individual effortlessly and spontaneously." He further writes that the technique involves "no contemplation or concentration . . . No analysis of thought takes place, nor does the meditator in any way attempt to manipulate or control mental or physical phenomena."*

While TM has become an accepted part of the curriculum in some states (Driscoll 1972), there are no curriculum materials or programs that directly manifest an evocation approach to values education. Several educational programs, such as "confluent education" (Brown 1971), "curriculum of effect" (Weinstein and Fantini 1970) and the Human Development Program (Palomares and Bessell 1970), stress awareness and expression of feelings, but they do not consider feelings as values. Moreover, contrary to the spirit of evocation, each of these programs emphasizes cognitive growth as well as affective development.

While not denying the importance of rationality, another curriculum project, Essentia, clearly focuses on the emotional and intuitive side of human learning. Although concentrating on the development of student and teacher resource materials for environmental education, the directors seem to propound a position on values education closely related to the evocation approach. Samples (1974, p. 49), for example, affirms that personal experiences and some research indicate that a person's most significant decisions are "based on emotion and intuition, not logic and rationality." He urges that teachers help students become "increasingly sensitive to the emotional drives that engage their value structures."

A few of the activities embodied in the environmental studies materials developed by Essentia, *Essence I* (1971) and *Essence II* (1975), seem to reflect evocation goals and methods. The *Essence* materials consist primarily of photo cards with several activities printed on one side. One card, for example, is a photograph of a student kneeling on the lawn in front of a building that looks like a traditional school. The activity is to "go outside and do something that you really want to do." The follow-up questions include: "How did you feel about doing your thing? While doing your thing?" A suggestion is made to "create something that expresses your feelings about doing your thing." While this activity, like all the activities in this program, does involve cognitive processes, it does encourage students to be spontaneous in their actions and feelings. Also the follow-up questions and activity minimize sequential, analytical thinking and focus on intuitive, metaphoric thinking. Thus, the "your thing" activity does represent the basic purpose and procedure of the evocation approach to values education.

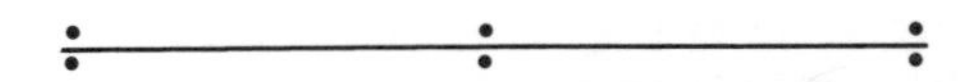

*These statements are from a letter written to Christine Ahrens by Nicholas Bedworth, Research Coordinator, ICSR, Maharishi International University, February 13, 1975.

Union

One group of theorists contends that values are eternal ideas that have their source in God. The popular interpretation of that viewpoint is that God is an absolute monarch who dictates the "right" spiritual values to His followers. Traditional Western Christianity reflects this view, and traditional approaches to Catholic education are examples of values education based on this idea. This conception of value indoctrination, however, does not necessarily fall outside the typology. From his viewpoint, valuing is considered a mystical socialization process in which values from an outside source, in this case God rather than the culture, are being instilled into persons. Thus, this interpretation is really a form of inculcation.

There is, however, another interpretation of the union approach which derives from a conception of God vastly different from the transcendent ruler concept. According to this view of union, God is seen as the "ultimate ground of being," the fundamental essence of things. The individual is not considered apart from God, but as one with God. This interpretation offers a distinctive view of human nature which is shared by many theorists.* Valuing, even if it involves ultimate, absolute values, cannot be an inculcation process according to this approach because there is no external force imposing values from without.* Rather, valuing is seen as a process of making contact with the core of being inside and outside oneself. This contact focuses on a feeling of "at-oneness" with the cosmos, variously termed *cosmic consciousness, individuation of the self, power of being, peak experience,* and the *You are It* feeling.

A variety of techniques exists to assist persons in achieving this experience. Some of these are Jungian dream analysis and psychotherapy, meditation, encountering transforming symbols, self-hypnosis, active and symbolic imagination, and Zen Buddhism. There are, however, no instructional models or materials to integrate this approach to values and valuing into the school curriculum. Translating the "union" or "cosmic consciousness" objectives into specific class activities is a difficult and delicate task. One might easily and unwittingly begin to use inculcation to try to instill a feeling of at-oneness in students. Or, if one tried to explain this unity of the cosmos by examining its chemical/physical aspects, one would be using analysis. Only if an activity led to an intuitive, transrational awareness of ultimate unity would the approach truly be union.

This is not to say that partial manifestations of this approach do not exist in educational theory and practice. Recent trends in Catholic education, such as "search retreats," strive to provide students with experiences emphasizing the unity of all peoples and things. Many environmental education programs stress similar viewpoints. "Confluent education" (Brown 1971) is one example of a nonreligious educational program exhibiting some concern for transcendent experiences and spiritual development (Assagioli 1971; Yeomans 1972).

Confluent education, which has already been mentioned as related to the evocation approach, derives part of its theoretical basis from Assagioli's "psychosynthesis." It therefore contains a "transpersonal" as well as personal component. The following fantasy trip is designed to help persons experience this "transpersonal self" by means of transforming symbols and active imagination. It is presented as recalled from a workshop with George Brown.

1) Close your eyes and relax. (pause)
2) Choose the first symbol that comes into your mind to represent your feelings. (pause) Picture it vividly. (pause) What does it tell you about your feelings? (pause)
3) Now choose a symbol for your mind.

---

*The following theorists reflect this view of human nature and existence: existentialists Tillich (1952) and Bugenthal (1965), Eastern philosophers Watts (1967) and Suzuki (1959), depth psychologists Jung (1939) and Progoff (1956), and the sociologist Pitrim Sorokin (1959).

**This points to an essential distinction between union and evocation. While evocation emphasizes intrinsic over extrinsic feelings and internal over external reality, the union approach stresses that dichotomies such as those are mostly illusions. Intrinsic and extrinsic or internal and external are two sides of the same fundamental reality.

The first one you think of. (pause) Picture it vividly. (pause) What does it tell you about your mind?

4) Now carry on a conversation between the two symbols. (pause) Now you can enter the conversation and talk to either or both. (pause)

5) OK. Now take one symbol in one hand and the other symbol in the other hand and imagine that you are walking along a road that gradually leads up a mountain. (pause) It's a bright clear day. Picture vividly what you see as you walk up the mountain. (pause)

6) The sun is bright and warm, but pleasantly warm. (pause) Now you are on top of the mountain. (pause) Picture the view vividly. (pause) Feel the warmth and brightness of the sun. (pause)

7) Now you look up at the sun and see a wise old man in it. You may walk up to him and ask him anything you want or you may stay on top of the mountain and feel the warmth and light. (pause) OK. If you were talking to the man, come down from the sun to the mountain top and feel the warmth and light once again. (pause)

8) Climb down the mountain. (pause) OK, you're down.

Questions:

1) What were your symbols? What did they tell about you? Did anything happen to them during the trip?

2) Did you feel the warmth and light of the sun? Whose was it really?

3) Did you talk to the wise old man? About what? Did he answer?

4) Were you able to get into this fantasy? Why or why not?

5) What was the most meaningful part of the fantasy for you? What does that say about your values?

Outside the educational system there have also been manifestions of this approach. Workshops and seminars conducted by the late Alan Watts and other similarly oriented theorists used a variety of methods to convey the message of oneness. Another effort to convey this fundamental unity of the cosmos is the Creative Initiative Foundation (2555 Park Blvd., Palo Alto, CA 94306). This community consists of families (largely in the San Francisco Bay area) who have committed much of their energies to group seminars, workshops, creative artistic productions, and personal activities designed to deepen and broaden the feeling of oneness with the universe.

Many spiritual groups in North America who have based their ideas on one or more of the Eastern religions seem to have purposes similar to the union approach to values education. The Yasodhara Ashram Society of British Columbia, Canada, for example, offers educational programs designed to help persons discover and actualize their true Self. One activity, "life seals" (Radha 1973), seems to reflect union purposes and methods. This exercise involves choosing and drawing symbols to represent some of your characteristics—your five senses, six positive and six negative qualities, and so on. The symbols are then arranged around a small dot that symbolizes your essential being. You can then merely let that picture make an imprint on your mind or think about the relationships among and the meanings of the symbols. This activity then uses symbolic imagination and creative art in an attempt to stimulate unconscious as well as conscious processes and to lead to a new awareness of Self.

Except in the religiously oriented periodicals and books, the union approach seems to receive scant attention in the educational literature. One exception is an article by Harman in *Approaches to Education for Character* (1969, pp. 301-14), which identifies the process of cosmic consciousness and confrontation with transforming symbols as two significant approaches to self-image transformation. Another is an article by Foster in *Values in an Age of Confrontation* (1970, pp. 119-23) which stresses the need to view valuing essentially as a religious experience.

Drews and Lipson (1971) also acknowledge the possibility that values have their source in an ultimate ground of being. They contend that one might become attuned to "goodness" by experiencing cosmic consciousness (Drews and Lipson 1971, p. 68). They envision education as creative growth affirming "the unity of all and the cosmic consciousness which apprehends it . . . Each person is regarded as both a unique entity and a part of the universal order"

(Drews and Lipson 1971, p. 153).

Finally, a recent anthology of readings entitled *Four Psychologies Applied to Education* (Roberts 1975) contains one section of articles focusing on transpersonal psychology and its educational implications. Three articles particularly relate to the union approach because of their emphasis on educating for ultimate values and for the realization of the ''essential unity with all being.'' These articles are: ''Education for Transcendence'' (Murphy 1975), ''An Outline of Transpersonal Psychology: Its Meaning and Relevance for Education'' (McWaters 1975), and ''Some Applications of Psychosynthesis in the Educational Field'' (Crampton 1975).

Generally, however, it appears that the union approach to values education is being manifested primarily outside the educational system. Some of these manifestations, such as the efforts of the Creative Initiative Foundation, could be used as bases for developing and refining such a values education approach as an integral part of the existing educational structure.

VIII

a bibliography of values education materials

This bibliography is divided into two parts. The first section is organized according to approach and contains annotated references for four categories of values education materials: student materials, teacher materials, theoretical background materials, and research studies and articles. An asterisk (*) precedes those materials that have been analyzed in this book. To locate the analysis, note the title of the asterisked material and check the Index of Materials.

The second part is a selective bibliography of works related to values and values education that the authors of this paper have not classified by approach. Included in this section are lists of other bibliographies on values, student and teacher materials related to values education, catalogs containing films dealing with values, and other background materials on values and values education.

Both sections of the bibliography contain works that are indexed in the ERIC system. These are identified in the citation by their acquisition number (e.g., ED 684 352). If a nearby library or resource center has a complete ERIC microfiche collection, you may use the ED number for locating the document and reading it on the library's microfiche reader. If you would like to order a microfiche or "hardcopy" (xerography) of the document, write to the ERIC Document Reproduction Service (EDRS), P.O. Box 190, Arlington, VA 22210. EDRS will advise of the price for microfiche and hardcopy. You should refer to the ED number when requesting price information or ordering. The price is also indicated in the resume of the document found in the monthly ERIC index, *Resources in Education*. Articles from educational journals are also included in this bibliography. They have been selected from the *Current Index to Journals in Education,* ERIC's monthly index of educational journals. You should refer directly to the journals cited for these articles.

annotated bibliography of values education materials classified by approach

A. Inculcation

1. Student Materials: Inculcation

*a. Blanchette, Zelda Beth, *et al. The Human Values Series.* Austin, TX: Steck-Vaughn, 1970, 1973.

K-6: A set of supplementary textbooks, this series is designed to help students think about and develop eight basic human values, including affection, respect, well-being, and enlightenment.

*b. *Character Education Curriculum: Living with Me and Others.* San Antonio, TX: American Institute for Character Education, 1974

K-5: This character education program consists of a teacher's handbook, a teacher's guide, student worksheets, illustrations, evaluation instruments, and posters for each grade level. The materials are designed to encourage students to adopt the standards of behavior embodied in Russell C. Hill's *Freedom Code* (be honest, be kind, do your fair share to help those in need, make creditable use of your time and talents, etc.).

*c. *Freedom and Responsibility: A Question of Values.* White Plains, NY: The Center for Humanities, 1973.

9-12: This audiovisual kit contains 160 slides in two carousel cartridges, two cassettes or two records, and a teacher's guide. Part I focuses on freedom and shows various ways in which human potentialities are limited. Part II centers on responsibility and the consequences of accepting responsibility for decisions made.

*d. Leonard, Blanche A. *Building Better Bridges with Ben.* Santa Monica, CA: Sunny Enterprises, 1974.

4-8: This teacher's guide and student book attempt to encourage students to act in accordance with 11 of Ben Franklin's virtues, including humility, justice, sincerity, frugality, and industry.

e. Mitsakos, Charles, general ed. *The Family of Man: A Social Studies Program.* Newton, MA: Selective Educational Equipment, 1971-74.

K-5: Prepared by the University of Minnesota Project Social Studies, these multimedia, hands-on kits are designed to teach skills, generalizations, and concepts, as well as values and attitudes. Values such as curiosity, respect for evidence, appreciation and respect for cultural diversity, and human dignity are emphasized.

f. Senesh, Lawrence. *Our Working World.* Chicago, IL: Science Research Associates, 1973.

1-6: Titles in this program include *Families, Neighborhoods, Cities, Regions of the United States, The American Way of Life, Regions of the World,* and the rationale book, *New Paths in Social Science Curriculum Design.* The purpose of the program "is to develop children's imagination and willingness to work to build a world where people live harmoniously together and harmoniously with their environment." Values emphasized in addition to harmony include interdependence, the recognition and acceptance of individual and cultural differences, and the need for laws.

2. Teacher Materials: Inculcation

*a. Bensley, Marvin L. *Coronado Plan: Teacher's Guides.* San Diego, CA: Pennant, 1974.

K-12: These grade-level teacher's guides integrate the Rucker values education approach with a drug abuse curriculum and outline activities for various subject areas, including social studies and English. The guides were developed as part of a drug abuse project in the Coronado, California, school district.

*b. Brayer, Herbert O., and Zella W. Cleary. *Valuing in the Family: A Workshop Guide for Parents.* San Diego, CA: Pennant, 1972.

This handbook outlines actions parents can take to develop family relationships around sharing the eight values first postulated by Rucker *et al.* (1969) and embodied in *The Human Values Series* textbooks.

*c. Hargraves, Richard B. *Values: Language Arts.* Miami, FL: Dade County Public Schools, 1971. ED 064 738.

7-12: Designed for a values program based on a study of literature, including "The Man Without a Country" and "I Am a Rock," this curriculum guide attempts to help students become aware of and develop a value system that incorporates a positive self-image and the values of peace, justice, and freedom.

*d. Hawley, Robert C. *Human Values in the Classroom: Teaching for Personal and Social Growth.* Amherst, MA: Education Research Associates, 1973.

K-12: Stressing the need to shift from a competitive to a cooperative value system, this guidebook contains discussions and suggested activities to help teachers focus on basic values such as love, trust, interdependence, and joy. Topics covered in the book include human values and needs, achievement motivation, communication skills, values clarification, and decision making.

e. *Lakota Woskate: Curriculum Materials Resource Unit 6.* Spearfish, SD: Black Hills State College, 1972. ED 066 240.

9: Utilizing games and sports, this unit is designed to teach ninth-grade children of the Oglala Sioux people the values of endurance, risk, desire to excel, and respect for others

f. Los Angeles City Schools. *The Teaching of Values: An Instructional Guide for Kindergarten, Grades 1-14.* Los Angeles, CA: Division of Instructional Services, Los Angeles City Schools, 1966.

K-14: This curriculum guide is designed to help teachers encourage students to develop certain values, such as love, respect for law and order, reverence, justice, and integrity.

g. Pasadena City Schools. *Moral and Spiritual Values.* Pasadena, CA: Division of

Instructional Services, Pasadena City Schools, 1957.

K-12: This curriculum guide is based on the conviction that the school should instill certain moral and spiritual values into students.

*h. Rucker, W. Ray, *et al. Human Values in Education.* Dubuque, IA: Kendall/Hunt, 1969.

K-12: This is the teacher text upon which programs embodying the eight value categories of Lasswell and Rucker (well-being, rectitude, affection, . . .) are based. It identifies classroom practices that tend to promote those eight values. In addition, discussions of order and discipline, the enhancement of self-image, and the measurement of value growth are included. A report of a school project using this approach to values education is also provided.

*i. Simpson, Bert K. *Becoming Aware of Values.* San Diego, CA: Pennant, 1973.

K-12: A teacher handbook for applying the Rucker approach to the classroom, the book contains a discussion of the principles and processes involved in this approach, as well as summaries of activities, materials (especially games), and evaluation instruments based on this approach.

j. *United States History: From Community to Society. Teacher's Guide, Grade Six, Project Social Studies.* Minneapolis, MN: University of Minnesota, 1968. ED 068 383.

6: This teacher's guide to the sixth-grade component of a sequential K-12 social studies curriculum contains seven units designed to help students learn scholarly values, democratic values, and the value of human dignity.

3. Theoretical Background Materials: Inculcation

a. Sears, Robert R., *et al. Patterns of Child Rearing.* Evanston, IL: Row, Peterson, 1957.

The book presents a Freudian interpretation of the process of valuing whereby the child forms an ego-ideal within his or her own personality which corresponds to the values of the parents.

b. Whiting, John William. "Socialization Process and Personality." In *Psychological Anthropology,* Francis L. K. Hsu, ed. Homewood, IL: Dorsey, 1961, pp. 355-99.

In reviewing various cross-cultural studies of child rearing practices from infancy to later childhood, the author finds evidence to support the hypothesis that personality is determined by the maintenance systems and child training practices of the culture.

4. Selected Research Studies and Articles: Inculcation

a. Abrams, Macy L., and James A. Saxon. "VIDAC: A Computer Program for Value Identification and Classification." Unpublished doctoral dissertation. San Diego, CA: United States International University, 1969. (Abstracted in *Dissertation Abstracts International* 31: 2224-25A, November 1970)

In this study a content analysis dictionary and computer program were developed to interpret written responses according to the Lasswell/Rucker value framework.

b. Bandura, Albert, and Fredrick J. McDonald. "The Influence of Social Reinforcement and the Behavior of Models in Shaping Children's Moral Judgments.'' *Journal of Abnormal and Social Psychology,* 67 (1963) pp. 274-284.

This is the classic and controversial study by two social learning theorists which demonstrated that children's bases for judging moral acts (by consequences or intentions) according to Piaget's stages could be altered by modeling and reinforcement.

c. Carney, Richard C. ''An Evaluation of the Effect of a Value-Oriented Drug Abuse Education Program Using the Risk Taking Attitude Questionnaire.'' Coronado, CA: Coronado Unified School District, 1971.

This study attempted to determine whether the use of the *Coronado Plan Teacher's Guides* would change students' risk-taking and drug abuse attitudes.

d. Crane, Valerie, and Bennie L. Ballif. ''Effects of Adult Modeling and Rule Structure on Responses to Moral Situations of Children in Fifth Grade Classrooms.'' *The Journal of Experimental Education,* 41 (1973) pp. 49-52.

In this study, inner-city fifth graders imitated models who provided reasons for their responses to open-ended value conflict situations more often than models who did not provide reasons.

e. Murphy, Maribeth L. ''Measurement of Values through Responses to Selected Visual Stimulus Materials.'' Unpublished doctoral dissertation. San Diego, CA: United States International University, 1970. (Abstracted in *Dissertation Abstracts International* 30: 529A, June 1970)

This study developed and piloted the *Murphy Inventory of Values,* which has since been used to measure student growth in values development according to the Lasswell/Rucker framework.

B. Moral Development

1. Student Materials: Moral Development

*a. Bender, David, and Gary McCuen. *Photo Study Cards: Meaning and Values*. Anoka, MN: Greenhaven, 1974.

8-12: The five photo cards are entitled ''Who Are You?'', ''Who Would You Like to Be?'', ''What Do You Value?'', ''You and Authority'', and ''You and Social Responsibility.'' Each card has pictures and activities on both sides. One side is based on moral development, the other on clarification activities.

*b. Fenton, Edwin, ed. *Holt Social Studies Curriculum*. New York, NY: Holt, Rinehart and Winston, 1969-75. Includes the following titles: *Comparative Political Systems, Comparative Economic Systems, The Shaping of Western Society, Tradition and Change in Four Societies, A New History of the United States, The Humanities in Three Cities,* and *Introduction to the Behavioral Sciences*.

9-12: The seven courses in this curriculum contain several Kohlbergian moral dilemmas with topics relevant to their particular subject matter emphases. The teacher's guides contain brief explanations of Kohlberg's theory.

*c. Kohlberg, Lawrence, and Robert Selman. *First Things: Values*. New York, NY: Guidance Associates, 1972. Includes the following titles: *The Trouble*

With Truth, That's No Fair!, You Promised!, But It Isn't Yours . . ., and *What Do You Do About Rules?*

1-5: Five sets of sound-filmstrips that present children in moral dilemma situations are included. Teacher's guides provide guidelines for leading discussions so that students develop more complex moral reasoning patterns. A teacher training component, *A Strategy for Teaching Values,* is also included.

*d. Lockwood, Alan. *Moral Reasoning: The Value of Life.* Columbus, OH: Xerox, 1972.

9-12: This booklet is one of the *Public Issues Series* (see entry C-1-n). It contains short readings describing various moral dilemmas related to the value of human life. Also included is a short explanation of Kohlberg's theory of moral development.

e. *Rules.* Boulder, CO: Biological Sciences Curriculum Study, 1974.

4-7: *Rules* is one of the modules in the *Human Sciences Program.* In it, observations of natural phenomena that exhibit regularity as well as rules governing human social behavior are examined. The 44 activities in this module are grouped into three problem areas: "Is There a Rule?", "What Should I Do?", and "How Do Rules Change?" A large-scale simulation game is included as an integrative activity. Many of these activities are specifically designed to stimulate moral reasoning.

*f. Selman, Robert L., *et al. First Things: Social Reasoning.* New York, NY: Guidance Associates, 1974. Series includes the following titles: *How Do You Know What Others Will Do?, How Would You Feel?, How Do You Know What's Fair?,* and *How Can You Work Things Out?*

1-5: Four sets of sound-filmstrips present children in social problem situations. Teacher's guides provide suggestions for leading discussions so that students will advance in their levels of social reasoning (egocentric, informational, self-reflective, and mutual perspective taking). A teacher training component, *A Strategy for Teaching Social Reasoning,* is also included.

2. Teacher Materials: Moral Development

a. *Catalogue of Teaching and Research Materials in Moral Education.* Vancouver, British Columbia, Canada: Association for Values Education and Research (A.V.E.R.), University of British Columbia, 1975.

This catalogue contains curriculum materials, including moral dilemmas and role-playing activities, research articles and notes, and other resources gathered by A.V.E.R., formerly known as the Moral Education Center. Order copies from Professor W. A. Bruneau, A.V.E.R., Faculty of Education.

b. Galbraith, Ronald E., and Thomas M. Jones. *Moral Reasoning: Teaching Strategies for Adapting Kohlberg to the Classroom.* Anoka, MN: Greenhaven, (in press).

Developed by the Values Education Project, a joint effort of the Social Studies Curriculum Center of Carnegie-Mellon University and the Laboratory of Human Development of Harvard University, this manual presents a classroom teaching process for stimulating group discussion of Kohlberg-type moral dilemmas. The book also contains sample dilemmas for elementary and secondary students, instructions for teachers to create their own dilemmas, and a selected bibliography of additional resources.

c. Galbraith, Ronald E., and Thomas M. Jones. "Teaching Strategies for Moral Dilemmas: An Application of Kohlberg's Theory of Moral Development to the Social Studies Classroom." *Social Education,* 39 (January 1975) pp. 16-22.

This article explains Kohlberg's theory of moral development and describes a detailed teaching process for using moral dilemmas in the classroom.

d. Hickey, J. "Designing and Implementing a Correctional Program Based on Moral Development Theory." In *Moralization: The Cognitive Developmental Approach,* Lawrence Kohlberg and Elliott Turiel, eds. New York, NY: Holt, Rinehart and Winston, in press.

This article presents an account of an attempt to establish Kohlberg-type discussion groups inside a prison. Instead of using hypothetical moral dilemmas, however, the prisoners use their own real dilemmas and problems.

*e. Lickonia, Thomas. *A Strategy for Teaching Values.* New York, NY: Guidance Associates, 1972.

1-5: This is the teacher training component for the *First Things: Values* series. It contains three sound-filmstrips and a teacher's guide designed to help teachers apply Kohlberg's theory of moral development to the elementary classroom. Part 1 discusses the rationale of the moral development approach; Part 2 shows the teacher's role in implementing this approach; and Part 3 depicts a classroom discussion and debate based on this approach.

*f. Mattox, Beverly A. *Getting It Together: Dilemmas for the Classroom.* San Diego, CA: Pennant, 1975.

1-12: An explanation of Lawrence Kohlberg's theory of moral development as well as suggestions for classroom application are included in this guidebook. Moral dilemmas for students in primary, elementary, junior high, and senior high grades are given, along with suggestions for writing original dilemmas.

g. Pagliuso, Susan. *A Workbook: Understanding Stages of Development.* Toronto, Ontario, Canada: Ontario Institute for Studies in Education, 1975.

This workbook has been developed to help teachers understand and apply Kohlberg's theory of moral development.

h. Piburn, Michael D. "Moral Dilemmas and the Environment." 1973. ED 091 261. Paper presented at the annual meeting of the National Council for the Social Studies, San Francisco, November 19-24, 1974.

9-12: Introductory remarks outline the six stages of moral development, as researched by Jean Piaget and Lawrence Kohlberg. Following are four environmental dilemmas. A series of questions leading to investigation of the moral issue is raised for each dilemma.

*i. Porter, Nancy, and Nancy Taylor. *How to Assess the Moral Reasoning of Students.* Toronto, Ontario, Canada: The Ontario Institute for Studies in Education, 1972.

4-12: This manual explains how to interpret a student's responses to several of Kohlberg's moral dilemmas in order to determine his or her stage of moral development.

*j. Selman, Robert L., *et al. A Strategy for Teaching Social Reasoning.* New York, NY: Guidance Associates, 1974.

1-5: This is the teacher training component for the *First Things: Social Rea-*

soning series. It includes three sound-filmstrips explaining the theory of social reasoning and depicting a teacher leading elementary students in the discussion of interpersonal dilemmas.

3. Theoretical Background Materials: Moral Development

a. Bull, Norman J. *Moral Education.* Beverly Hills, CA: Sage, 1969.

This book explains McDougall's theory of moral development and its implications for education. This theory postulates four levels of development: premorality, external morality, external-internal morality, and internal morality.

b. Kohlberg, Lawrence. "Moral Education in the Schools: A Developmental View." *School Review,* 74 (1966) pp. 1-30.

Kohlberg's theory of moral development and its implications for education are described in detail in this article.

c. Kohlberg, Lawrence. "The Child as a Moral Philosopher." *Psychology Today,* 7 (1968) pp. 25-30.

This short article introduces Kohlberg's theory of moral development.

d. Kohlberg, Lawrence. "Moral Development and the New Social Studies." *Social Education,* 37 (May 1973) pp. 369-375.

The article relates Kohlberg's theory of moral development to the new social studies and discusses stages of moral reasoning as they relate to high school students.

e. Kohlberg, Lawrence, and Elliot Turiel. "Moral Development and Moral Education." In *Psychology and Educational Practice,* G. Lesser, ed. Chicago, IL: Scott, Foresman, 1971, pp. 410-465.

A discussion of the relationship of moral development to other forms of moral education, a presentation of the research findings related to Kohlberg's theory, and a rationale for using the moral development approach in the schools are included in this article.

f. Perry, William G., Jr. *Forms of Intellectual and Ethical Development in the College Years.* New York, NY: Holt, Rinehart and Winston, 1970.

This book presents findings from research on adolescents and post-adolescents and describes a nine-stage scheme of ethical development.

g. Piaget, Jean. *Moral Judgment of the Child.* New York, NY: Collier, 1962.

This book was the first to postulate the theory that structural change bases for moral judgment existed within the person and were rooted both in the experience of the person and in a developmental sequence determined largely by genetics. From clinical studies of children's conceptions of rules in various common games and of their ideas about cheating and justice in hypothetical dilemmas, Piaget first formulated a developmental theory of morality that included four stages: premoral, obedience to adult authority, autonomous-reciprocity, and autonomous-ideal reciprocity.

h. Rest, James. "Developmental Psychology as a Guide to Value Education: A Review of Kohlbergian Programs." *Review of Educational Research,* 44 (1974) pp. 241-259.

This article includes a critical discussion of the fundamental ideas of cognitive developmental psychology, of Kohlberg's own educational programs, of several other programs related to moral development (e.g., the Sprinthall-Mosher psychological education program), and of future prospects for using developmental psychology as a guide to values education.

4. Selected Research Studies and Articles: Moral Development

a. Blatt, Moshe. "The Effects of Classroom Discussion Programs upon Children's Level of Moral Development." Unpublished doctoral dissertation. Chicago, IL: University of Chicago, 1969.

One of the early studies that indicated that students who participated in group discussions based on Kohlberg-type dilemmas progressed more than those who did not. The progression was also found to be sequential—that is, from Stage 2 to Stage 3 or from Stage 4 to Stage 5.

b. Leming, James S. "An Exploratory Inquiry into the Multifactor Theory of Moral Behavior Applied to Values Education." Paper presented at the annual meeting of the American Educational Research Association, Washington, D.C., March 31, 1975. ED 110 354.

The purpose of this study was to determine if and to what degree several factors defined by John Wilson as being related to moral behavior were related to stages of moral reasoning as defined by Kohlberg and to choice of right action. One of the findings suggests "that stage of moral reasoning when dealing with classical moral dilemmas [e.g., Helga in Nazi Germany] is more likely to be determined by developmental considerations than is stage of moral reasoning on practical dilemmas" (those relevant to students' life space).

c. Lieberman, Marcus. "Evaluation of a Social Studies Curriculum Based on an Inquiry Method and a Cognitive-Developmental Approach to Moral Education." Paper presented at the annual meeting of the American Educational Research Association, Washington, D.C., April 1975. ED 106 175.

This study evaluated the effect of a social studies curriculum based on an integration of Fenton's materials (see entry B-1-b) and Kohlberg's moral dilemmas. One finding indicated a significant difference in moral maturity scores between classes that had moral discussions and those that did not. No difference was found between teachers who attended a five-day workshop and those who read a manual.

d. Simpson, Elizabeth Léonie. "Moral Development Research: A Case Study of Scientific Cultural Bias." *Human Development,* 17 (1974) pp. 81-106.

In this article the author critically examines the research upon which Kohlberg's hierarchy of moral development is based. The findings indicated "that the definitions of stages and the assumptions underlying them, including the view that the scheme is universally applicable, are ethnocentric and culturally-biased."

e. Turiel, Elliott. "An Experimental Test of the Sequentiality of Developmental Stages in the Child's Moral Judgment." *Journal of Personality and Social Psychology,* 3 (1966) pp. 611-618.

This is one of the first studies of Kohlberg's theory to indicate that students can be stimulated to develop to the next stage of moral reasoning by hearing arguments from that higher stage. The study also demonstrated that contact with reasoning below or more than one stage above the stage of an individual will not lead to moral development.

f. Turiel, Elliott. "Stage Transition in Moral Development." In *Second Handbook of Research on Teaching,* R.M.W. Travers, ed. Chicago, IL: Rand-McNally, 1973, pp. 732-758.

In this article the author discusses some of the research upon which Kohlberg's theory of moral development is based. In addition, the Bandura and MacDonald (1963) study of social learning versus Piaget's stages is criticized and replication studies are discussed.

C. Analysis

1. Student Materials: Analysis

*a. Allender, Donna S., and Jerome S. Allender. *I Am the Mayor.* Philadelphia, PA: Center for the Study of Federalism, Temple University, 1971.

4-7: These inquiry materials, in which each student plays the role of the mayor, are intended for the study of city government. Students are presented with problems, questions, decisions, and information to introduce them to a mayor's duties and expose them to the issues related to city government. A teacher's guide is included.

*b. Bender, David L., and Gary E. McCuen, eds. *Opposing Viewpoints Series.* Anoka, MN: Greenhaven, 1971-74.

8-12: These seven sets of materials provide a basis for student exploration into values, conflict, and change. Eight topics are explored: race, welfare, ecology, philosophy, foreign policy, the penal system, the sexual revolution, and problems of death.

*c. Berlak, Harold, and Timothy R. Tomlinson. *People/Choices/Decisions.* New York, NY: Random House, 1973. Includes the following titles: *A Village Family* and *One City Neighborhood.*

4-6: These multimedia materials focus on change in various societies and the types of social and ethical problems arising as a result of such change. Ten additional six- to eight-week units are being prepared.

*d. Brandwein, Paul F. *The Social Sciences: Concepts and Values.* New York, NY: Harcourt Brace Jovanovich, 1970-75.

K-8: The conceptually structured content of this curriculum focuses on five social science disciplines at each grade level, becoming increasingly more sophisticated in the higher grades. Values in their own as well as in other cultures are explored by the students. All materials emphasize inquiry and analysis and are activity oriented.

e. Brown, Richard, and Van R. Halsey, eds. *Amherst Project Units in American History.* Menlo Park, CA: Addison-Wesley, 1970-74. Values-related units are: *Freedom and Authority in Puritan New England; Thomas Jefferson, The Embargo, and the Decision for Peace; Lincoln and Slavery: Ideals and the Politics of Change; Hiroshima: A Study in Science, Politics and the Ethnics of War; Korea and the Limits of Limited War; Imperialism and the Dilemma of Power; The Western Hero: A Study in Myth and American Values; God and Government: The Uneasy Separation of Church and State; Conscience and the Law: The Uses and Limits of Civil Disobedience;* and *Communism in America: Liberty and Security in Conflict.*

9-12: The development of these units was initially sponsored by Amherst College and later by Hampshire College, Amherst, Massachusetts, and the Newberry Library, Chicago, Illinois, with grants from the U.S. Office of Education. Authentic historical evidence drawn from American experience is used to pursue inquiries concerning human issues, problems, questions, and values.

*f. Durkin, Mary C., and Anthony H. McNaughton. *The Taba Program in Social Science*. Menlo Park, CA: Addison-Wesley, 1972-74.

K-7: Using social science concepts, this multimedia program places heavy emphasis on thinking skills, which are divided according to three student tasks: forming concepts, inductively developing generalizations, and applying principles. While encouraging students to understand their own values, the materials include activities enabling them to infer the values of others from their reasoning and behavior in specific situations.

g. Fraenkel, Jack R., series ed. *Perspectives in World Order*. New York, NY: Random House, 1973, 1975. Includes the following titles: *Peacekeeping* and *The Struggle for Human Rights: A Question of Values.*

8-12: These are the first two of a series of six booklets being developed (in cooperation with the Institute for World Order) to deal with a global system of world order. The other four booklets will focus on arms policies and arms control, methods of settling disputes, economic development, and the long-range political and social impact of science and technology. All six are interrelated and overlap in their methodology, their futuristic outlook, and their emphasis on world order values.

*h. *Human Values in an Age of Technology*. White Plains, NY: The Center for Humanities, 1972.

9-12: This audiovisual kit contains 160 slides in two carousel cartridges, two cassettes or two records, and a teacher's guide. The program outlines the technological progress of humankind from prehistoric times to the present. Both positive and negative implications of technology are brought out.

*i. *Law and Justice for Intermediate Grades: Making Value Decisions*. New Rochelle, NY: Pathescope Educational Films, 1973.

4-8: Three color sound-filmstrips compose this program. Social issues which are important in the area of law but which require personal decisions based on facts and values are presented.

*j. Lippitt, Ronald, Robert Fox, and Lucille Schaible. *Social Science Laboratory Units*. Chicago, IL: Science Research Associates, 1969.

4-6: This seven-unit package of materials confronts students with social realities and encourages them to gather, organize, and use data on human behavior.

k. Mehlinger, Howard, and John J. Patrick. *American Political Behavior*. Lexington, MA: Ginn, 1974.

9-12: *American Political Behavior* intends to provide an alternative to traditional civics and government courses, incorporating insights from the disciplines of political science, sociology, and anthropology. Critical thinking and inquiry skills are emphasized. Students learn to gather, classify, and interpret information; to consider value claims rationally; and to make reasoned value judgments.

*l. *Moral Dilemmas of American Presidents: The Agony of Decision.* New Rochelle, NY: Pathescope Educational Films, 1974.

10-12: Each of the five color sound-filmstrips in this program presents a critical social or political issue and a crucial decision faced by a president of the United States. Alternatives are presented, and students must decide which course of action they would take in the same situation. A teacher's guide is included.

*m. Nelson, Jack L., series ed. *American Values Series: Challenges and Choices.* Rochelle Park, NJ: Hayden, 1974-75. Includes the following titles: *City Life, Dissent and Protest, The Environment: A Human Crisis, The Poor, The Rights of Women, Urban Growth, War and War Prevention,* and *Values and Society.*

9-12: Each of the eight books in this series presents a framework for examining a social issue in contemporary society. Each presents case studies, factual information, divergent views and opposing value judgments, futuristic scenarios, and recommendations for further study. A teacher's guide, *An Introduction to Value Inquiry: A Student Process Book* (see entry C-2-h) has also been developed.

*n. Oliver, Donald, and Fred M. Newmann. *The Public Issues Series.* Columbus, OH: Xerox, 1967-74.

9-12: This series was developed by the Harvard Social Studies Project. Through 30 unit books students learn to examine and analyze the origins of social conflict and to discuss the value dilemmas of public controversy. Students explore such concepts as due process, separation of powers, and human dignity.

*o. *Origins of American Values: The Puritan Ethic to the Jesus Freaks.* White Plains, NY: The Center for the Humanities, 1973.

9-12: This two-part sound-slide program examines value systems to help students understand the ethical structure of America. The 160 slides focus on the values of such groups as the Puritans and the Utopians and present many aspects of American culture, including spirituality, war, and materialism.

p. Quigley, Charles N., and Richard P. Longaker. *Voices for Justice: Role Playing in Democratic Procedures.* Lexington, MA: Ginn, 1970.

9-12: This book and accompanying teacher's guide are intended to provide students with the opportunity to act out the decision-making processes inherent in a democratic society. In each of the eight cases, students must identify the interests and values involved.

q. Rice, Marion J., and Wilfrid C. Bailey, project directors. *Political Anthropology: Values, Socialization, Social Control, and Law.* Athens, GA: Anthropology Curriculum Project, University of Georgia, 1968.

8-9: This supplementary text focuses on how social controls, in the form of laws and values, help people to live together effectively.

*r. Rogers, Vincent R. *The Values and Decisions Series.* Columbus, OH: Xerox, 1972-74.

7-12: These ten student booklets examine the value conflicts behind crucial decisions in America's history, including the Cuban missile crisis, the Boston Tea Party, the Vietnam buildup, and the Mexican War of 1846-48. Teacher's guides are included.

*s. Ruggiero, Vincent Ryan. *The Moral Imperative*. Port Washington, NY: Alfred Publishing, 1973.

12: The 12 chapters of this book each explore avenues by which ethical and moral issues can be anlyzed. The content focuses on moral questions students often raise.

*t. Sayre, Joan. *Teaching Moral Values Through Behavior Modification: Intermediate Level*. Danville, IL: Interstate, 1972.

3-5: This is a 54-page book containing 21 situation stories. It includes suggestions for guiding discussion of those stories. A set of 84 picture cards accompanies it. The units focus on prejudice, personal ethics, responsibility, and respect for authority.

u. Sayre, Joan M., and James E. Mack. *Teaching Moral Values Through Behavior Modification: Primary Level*. Danville, IL: Interstate, 1973.

K-2: This program, patterned after the Intermediate Level program, includes a teacher's guide with situation stories, plus a set of four picture cards to accompany each story. Since the major teaching strategy is group discussion, suggestions to facilitate such discussions are included with each group of stories. Vocabulary, problems, and concepts are geared specifically for students in the primary grades.

*v. Shaver, James P., and A. Guy Larkins. *Analysis of Public Issues Program*. Boston, MA: Houghton Mifflin, 1973.

9-12: The problem booklets and multimedia materials present concepts and case studies to help students make rational decisions about public issues.

*w. Tooni, Linda. *Law and Order: Values in Crisis*. Pleasantville, NY: Warren Schloat, 1971.

9-12: These six color filmstrips deal with the nature of law, values, justice, and order in our changing society.

*x. Turner, Sheila, ed., and Cornell Capa, series coordinator. *Images of Man I and II*. Englewood Cliffs, NJ: Scholastic, 1972, 1973.

7-12: Each of these two "concerned photography programs" contains four sound-filmstrips, a packet of 11" x 14" photo reproductions, and a teacher's guide. The focus is on social issues, social values, and the human experience.

y. *Values in Mass Communication*. Boston, MA: Allyn and Bacon, 1974.

10-12: This is one of the *Episodes in Social Inquiry Series* developed by Sociological Resources for the Social Studies. In this particular episode students have the "opportunity to explore the manner in which social values are embodied in communications from the mass media." Although the focus is on the Western, suggestions are provided in the teacher's guide for applying the same process to other art forms, such as the TV family situation comedy.

2. Teacher Materials: Analysis

*a. Barr, Robert D. *Values and Youth (Teaching Social Studies in an Age of Crisis –No. 2).* Washington, D.C.: National Council for the Social Studies, 1971.

7-12: By focusing on the value dilemmas present in today's society, the book aims to help teachers seriously consider the dilemmas of today's youth and focus their social studies courses on significant issues. Included are articles by students and by leading values educators such as Oliver, Shaver, Newmann, and Simon.

b. Conner, Shirley, *et al. Social Studies in the School Program: A Rationale and Related Points of View.* Towson, MD: Baltimore County Board of Education, 1970. ED 066 393.

K-12: One of the papers included in this rationale focuses on values and valuing, stating that "providing students with techniques for value examination, clarification, and evaluation is more important than inculcating a particular set of values."

*c. Evans, W. Keith, *et al. Rational Value Decisions and Value Conflict Resolution: A Handbook for Teachers.* Salt Lake City, UT: Granite School District and the Value Analysis Capability Development Programs, University of Utah, 1974.

7-12: Using the conceptual framework found in *Values Education: Rationale, Strategies, and Procedures* (see entry C-2-e), this handbook provides teachers with ways for developing student capability in making and/or justifying value decisions and resolving value conflict.

d. *The Good Man, Good Life, and Good Society. Social Studies and Language Arts: 6448.17.* Miami, FL: Dade County Public Schools, 1972. ED 073 962.

10-12: This nine-week unit introduces students to differing views and cultures. By focusing on three value issues—What is a good man? a good life? a good society?—students examine the geographic, political, economic, and social settings of Athens, Florence, and New York.

*e. Metcalf, Lawrence E., ed. *Values Education: Rationale, Strategies, and Procedures.* 41st Yearbook. Washington, D.C.: National Council for the Social Studies, 1971.

K-12: Containing four essays on teaching values, the book stresses the goals, teaching procedures, and strategies for analyzing values and suggests methods for resolving value conflicts.

f. Meux, Milton, *et al. Value Analysis Capability Development Programs: Final Report.* Salt Lake City, UT: Granite School District and the Value Analysis Capability Development Programs, University of Utah, 1974.

7-12: This report, based on the theories described in *Values Education: Rationale, Strategies, and Procedures,* presents instructional materials to help students develop competence in rational value analysis.

*g. Miller, Harry G., and Samuel M. Vinocur. "A Method for Clarifying Value Statements in the Social Studies Classroom: A Self-Instructional Program." 1972. ED 070 687.

9-12: Designed to aid social studies teachers with values clarification, this self-instructional program includes teaching strategies and examples for stimulating and clarifying student value statements.

*h. Nelson, Jack L. *An Introduction to Value Inquiry: A Student Process Book*. Rochelle Park, NJ: Hayden, 1974.

9-12: This is the teacher's guide for the *American Values Series* (see entry C-1-m). Focusing on the inquiry process, this book proposes a way for developing a questioning attitude toward social problems and a framework for seeking solutions. The exercises, case studies, and illustrations describe connections between facts and values and discuss values in ways that assist in clarifying value problems.

*i. Payne, Judy R. *Introduction to Eastern Philosophy, Social Studies: 6414.23*. Miami, FL: Dade County Public Schools, 1971. ED 071 937.

10-12: By comparing and contrasting five major Eastern religions—Hinduism, Buddhism, Confucianism, Taoism, and Shintoism—this course aims to guide students in their universal search for values and beliefs about the meaning of life.

j. Swenson, William G. *The Search for Values Through Literature: A Practical Teaching Guide*. New York, NY: Bantam, 1973.

10-12: The course outlined in this book is based on works of literature that deal with "Values and the System," "Values and Others," "Values and the Meaning of Life and Death," and "Values and Understanding One's Self." Through such works as *A Doll's House* by Henrik Ibsen, students examine values, value sources, and value conflicts. Objectives and discussions of seven works of literature are included. Other materials are also suggested. The book concludes with strategies for integrating the course.

k. *Values: Teacher's Edition*. Oakland, CA: Oakland Unified School District, 1972.

8-12: This curriculum guide explains the value analysis model presented in the 41st NCSS Yearbook (Metcalf 1971—see entry C-2-e) and describes 28 learning activities that apply the model. The activities deal with multi-ethnic topics such as stereotypes, Black capitalism, the grape strike, and Chinatown. A separate *Student's Edition* contains the readings and discussion questions for each activity.

l. Social Studies Methods Texts with Some Emphasis on Value Analysis:

1) Banks, James A. *Teaching Strategies for the Social Studies: Inquiry, Valuing, Decision Making*. Reading, MA: Addison-Wesley, 1973.

2) Brubaker, Dale. *Secondary Social Studies for the '70s*. New York, NY: Crowell, 1973.

3) Fraenkel, Jack. *Helping Students Think and Value*. Englewood Cliffs, NJ: Prentice-Hall, 1973.

4) Hunt, Maurice P., and Lawrence E. Metcalf. *Teaching High School Social Studies*. New York, NY: Harper, 1968.

5) Joyce, Bruce P. *New Strategies for Social Education*. Chicago, IL: Science Research Associates, 1972.

6) Massialas, Byron G., and C. Benjamin Cox. *Inquiry in Social Studies*. New York, NY: McGraw-Hill, 1966.

7) Michaelis, John U. *Social Studies for Children in a Democracy*. Englewood Cliffs, NJ: Prentice-Hall, 1972.

8) Oliver, Donald, and James Shaver. *Teaching Public Issues in the High School*. Boston, MA: Houghton Mifflin, 1966.

9) Smith, Frederick, and C. Benjamin Cox. *New Strategies and Curriculum in Social Studies*. Chicago, IL: Rand-McNally, 1969.

10) Taba, Hilda, *et al. A Teacher's Handbook to Elementary Social Studies: An Inductive Approach*. Menlo Park, CA: Addison-Wesley, 1971.

3. Theoretical Background Materials: Analysis

a. Gray, Charles E. ''Curricular and Heuristic Models for Value Inquiry.'' 1972. ED 070 737.

A rationale is presented for a social studies program that emphasizes the analysis of value systems and value judgments and explains and illustrates two models for value inquiry: (1) a curricular model designed to assist teachers in developing a values-oriented social studies curriculum and (2) a heuristic model consisting of a set of instructional strategies for dealing with value judgments.

b. Handy, Rollo. *Value Theory and the Behavioral Sciences*. Springfield, IL: Charles C. Thomas, 1969.

This discussion focuses on several theories of value, including those of Pepper, R.B. Perry, Dewey, and the author himself, each of which reflects the rational and empirical orientation of the analysis approach to values education.

c. Scott, William A. *Values and Cognitive Systems*. Bethesda, MD: National Institute of Mental Health, 1972. ED 073 407.

This document explains and discusses an approach to the study and measurement of values based on a research model and strategy designed to examine ''natural cognitions'' or ideas entertained by people before an experimenter has disturbed their thought.

d. Scriven, Michael. *Student Values as Educational Objectives*. Boulder, CO: Social Science Education Consortium, 1966.

This paper focuses on the problem of dealing with values in the schools. It deals specifically with the role of values in the curriculum.

e. Scriven, Michael. ''Values, Morality, and Rationality.'' In *Concepts and Structures in the New Social Studies,* Irving Morrissett, ed. New York, NY: Holt, Rinehart and Winston, 1966, pp. 133-146. (See also ''Values in the Curriculum,'' pp. 127-132.)

In a roundtable discussion with several other scholars, Scriven presents the argument for a rational basis of morality. In the previous chapter, he discusses the relation of values to education and the curriculum and suggests ''it is still an open question whether any values are needed that go beyond that which is supportable by rational appeal to logical analysis.''

f. Shaver, James P. *Values and Schooling: Perspectives for School People and Parents*. Logan, UT: Utah State University, 1972. ED 067 320.

The role of the school in relation to students' values is discussed and the suggestion is made that teachers can help students build their values on a firm rational basis within the framework of a democratic society.

g. Related works:

1) Blackham, H.J. *Humanism*. Baltimore, MD: Penguin, 1968.

2) Ellis, Albert. *Reason and Emotion in Psychotherapy*. New York, NY: Lyle Stuart, 1962.

3) Kelly, George A. *The Psychology of Personal Constructs*. New York, NY: W.W. Norton, 1955.

4) Pepper, Stephen G. *The Sources of Value*. Berkeley, CA: University of California Press, 1958.

5) Scriven, Michael. *Primary Philosophy*. New York, NY: McGraw-Hill, 1966.

6) Toulmin, Stephen E. *An Examination of the Place of Reason in Ethics*. Cambridge, England: Cambridge University Press, 1950.

4. Selected Research Studies and Articles: Analysis

a. Bond, David J. ''A Doctoral Theses: An Analysis of Valuation Strategies in Social Science Education Materials.'' Unpublished doctoral dissertation. Berkeley, CA: School of Education, University of California, 1970.

This study determined that few social studies materials published before 1970 embodied a strictly rational-analytical model of valuing. Various definitions of *value* used by social studies educators are also discussed.

b. Kelly, Joseph T. ''Values and Valuing in Recent Social Studies Textbooks.'' Unpublished doctoral dissertation. Berkeley, CA: School of Education, University of California, 1970.

This study involved a content analysis of social studies textbooks to determine the degree to which a valuing model is incorporated into the content and methodology of the texts.

c. Meux, Milton, *et al. Value Analysis Capability Development Programs: Final Report*. Salt Lake City, UT: Granite School District and the Value Analysis Capability Development Programs, University of Utah, 1974.

This study evaluated the effect of a program based on the handbook *Rationale Value Decisions and Value Conflict Resolution* (see entry C-2-c) upon students' ego strength, degree of dogmatism, and capabilities in and attitudes toward value analysis. The only significant differences between the experimental and the control students involved capability and disposition for certain values analysis tasks.

d. Oliver, Donald W., and James P. Shaver. ''An Experimental Curriculum Project Carried Out Within the Jurisprudential Framework.'' In *Teaching Public Issues in the High School*. Boston, MA: Houghton Mifflin, 1966.

This chapter describes an exploratory and inconclusive effort to determine the effect of a social studies curriculum based largely on the *Public Issues Series* booklets (see entry C-1-n) on junior high students' analytic competence, knowledge of subject matter, and interest in public problems. The differential impact of recitation and Socratic teaching styles and the relationship between various personality traits and an ability to analyze public issues were also studied.

e. Shaver, James P., and A. Guy Larkins. *The Analysis of Public Issues: Concepts, Materials, Research. Final Report*. Logan, UT: Utah State University, 1969. ED 037 475.

This study was designed as a systematic replication of the Oliver and Shaver (1966) study of the Harvard Social Studies Project *(Public Issues Series)* materials (see entry C-1-n). Using the same measurement instruments for teaching style, cognitive learning, and personality traits and using the *Analysis of Public Issues Program* with high school students, the investigators found no significant treatment effects.

D. Clarification

1. Student Materials: Clarification

*a. Allen, Rodney F., *et al. Deciding How to Live on Spaceship Earth: The Ethics of Environmental Concern*. Evanston, IL: McDougal, Littell, 1973.
Series (see also entries D-1-f and D-1-ff), consists primarily of short case studies and value-clarifying activities related to various environmental issues, such as noise pollution, the energy crisis, the use of natural resources, and the politics of environmental development. A teacher's guide for the entire series is available.

*b. Anderson, Judity L., *et al. Focus on Self-Development. Stage One: Awareness; Stage Two: Responding; and State Three: Involvement*. Chicago, IL: Science Research Associates, 1970, 1971, 1972.

K-6: This is a three-part multimedia series. The filmstrips, story records, and photoboards in the *Stage One* (grades one-two) program are designed to help children understand themselves, others, and their environments. Children are made aware that some of their experiences are common to others and are encouraged to express themselves freely. *Stage Two* (grades three-four) is designed to stimulate active response to a variety of situations ranging from a child's doing something because it is expected to pursuing something on his or her own and getting satisfaction from it. The 18 units in *Stage Three* (grades five-six) aim to help students become aware of their own involvement and the involvement of others, to relate behavior to values, to accept and understand others, and to make decisions concerning future involvement.

*c. Argus Filmstrips. Niles, IL: Argus Communications, 1974.

7-12: These 16 color sound-filmstrips and accompanying teacher's guides all deal with personal and social values. The content is varied, but for each, discussion questions and activities that get to the point of the filmstrip are suggested.

*d. Brandwein, Paul. *Self Expression and Conduct: The Humanities*. New York, NY: Harcourt Brace Jovanovich, 1974-75.

1-3: This multimedia, activity-centered, sequentially structured humanities program is designed to help children learn to use various modes of expression—including art, dance, drama, music, and language—to convey their feelings about themselves and their world. Each of the lessons and activities explores one or more of the fundamental values of humanity: truth, beauty, justice, love, and faith. Instead of inculcating these values, however, the activities help students to clarify their own concepts of these values and to make decisions according to those beliefs.

e. Caprio, Betsy. *Poster Ideas for Personalized Learning*. Niles, IL: Argus Communications, 1974.

4-12: This book suggests ways to use posters as a teaching tool and resource to stimulate student interest and creativity. Teaching strategies and activities, coordinated with 200 posters also available from Argus, are designed to increase awareness, value clarification, and communications skills.

*f. Carey, Mauren, *et al. Deciding on the Human Use of Power: The Exercise and Control of Power in an Age of Crisis.* Evanston, IL: McDougal, Littell, 1974.

9-12: Consisting primarily of short case studies and value clarifying activities, this text from the *Values Education Series* (see also entries D-1-a and D-1-ff) focuses on the use and control of various kinds of power, including individual, group, political, and economic power.

*g. Church, John G. *A Probe into Values.* New York, NY: Harcourt Brace Jovanovich, 1973.

4-6: The series of 40 pamphlets accompanying *The Social Sciences: Concepts and Values* (see entry C-1-d) describes a variety of dilemmas drawn from everyday experiences of young children and includes questions to stimulate group discussion of alternative solutions to the problems.

*h. *Clarifying your Values: Guidelines for Living.* White Plains, NY: The Center for Humanities, 1974.

9-12: This audiovisual kit contains 160 slides in two carousel cartridges, two cassettes or two records, and a teacher's guide. It describes specific situations involving the risks and advantages of acting in accordance with one's own values.

*i. Curwin, Gerri, *et al. Dimensions of Personality: Search for Values.* Dayton, OH: Pflaum, 1972.

9-12: This kit, containing 44 lessons and 77 spirit masters, is designed to help students examine their behavior and clarify their values in relation to time, competition, authority, personal space, commitment, relationships, and images.

*j. *Deciding Right from Wrong: The Dilemma of Morality Today.* White Plains, NY: The Center for Humanities, 1974.

9-12: This audiovisual kit contains 160 slides in two carousel cartridges, two cassettes or two records, and a teacher's guide. The program examines circumstances under which some crucial historical and literary decisions have been made, the persons making the decisions, and the social implications that followed.

*k. *Decision-Making: Dealing with Crises.* White Plains, NY: The Center for Humanities, 1974.

9-12: Two carousel cartridges containing 160 slides, two cassettes or two records, and a teacher's guide are included in this program. The content deals with personal problems young people often encounter while growing up—drinking, pregnancy, problems at school and at home.

*l. Dinkmeyer, Don. *Developing Understanding of Self and Others (DUSO), D-1, D-2.* Circle Pines, MN: American Guidance Service, 1970, 1973.

K-4: The units in these two sets of materials provide personal development tasks designed to help students with their self-images. The students examine their own feelings, the feelings of others, and their relationships with others.

*m. Dupont, Henry, *et al. Toward Affective Development* (*TAD*). Circle Pines, MN: American Guidance Service, 1974.

3-6: *TAD,* a multimedia kit, may be used with average students integrated into the regular curriculum or with students in guidance or remedial programs. The five sections include "Reaching In and Reaching Out," "Your Feelings and Mine," "Working Together," "Me: Today and Tomorrow," and "Feeling, Thinking, and Doing."

*n. *Dynamic Consumer Decision Making.* New York, NY: Educational and Consumer Relations Department, J.C. Penney Company, 1972.

9-12: This material focuses on consumer decision making. The program includes introductory information for the teacher and a variety of student activities. Three general types of decision-making activities are presented: probing, processing information, and clarifying values.

*o. Elder, Carl A. *Making Value Judgments: Decisions for Today.* Columbus, OH: Charles E. Merrill, 1972.

7-12: The 14 chapters in this book focus on important problems, including drugs, crime, prejudice, and personal relationships, to help youth clarify their values and give them a better understanding of decision making so they can learn how to make their own personal value judgments.

*p. *Environmental Values Action Cards.* St. Paul, MN: Minnesota State Department of Education, 1974.

1-6: Intended as a source of ideas for teachers, these cards attempt to make children aware of themselves and of others and to encourage children to explore intrinsic and extrinsic values and means of expression that are significantly different from those normally used in the classroom.

*q. Fischer,Carl, and Walter Limbacher. *Dimensions of Personality.* Dayton, OH: Pflaum, 1969-70, 1972. Includes the following titles: *Let's Begin, Now I'm Ready, I Can Do It, What About Me?, Here I Am, I'm Not Alone, and Becoming Myself.*

K-6: These materials are designed to help primary and intermediate students with their physical, social, and emotional development. The seven units for each primary grade level present activities for developing self-concepts, such as "Making Friends," "Solving Problems," and "Thinking about My Feelings." Through various readings, cartoons, and pictures, the intermediate program helps children know and understand themselves by engaging in activities and discussions on such things as self-awareness, emotion, heredity, environment, growth, behavior, prejudice, learning, and self-image. A teacher's guide and spirit masters accompany the student books for each title.

*r. Gelatt, H. B., *et al. Deciding.* New York, NY: College Entrance Examination Board, 1972.

7-9: This course of study contains three sections that include activities designed to present students with a decision-making process that can be applied directly to their life choices. The materials include a student book and a leader's guide.

*s. Gelatt, H.B., *et al*. *Decisions and Outcomes*. New York, NY: College Entrance Examination Board, 1973.

10-12: The four sections in this program provide role plays, simulations, and discussion activities of various real-life situations, helping stŭdents to learn more about themselves and their peers by developing and applying decision-making skills.

*t. Goodykoontz, William F. *Contact*. New York, NY: Scholastic, 1968-74.

7-12: This multi-unit reading series presents various anthologies to which students react by expressing their thoughts and feelings in a logbook, in class discussion, or in simulation activities. A teacher's guide, posters, and a record are also included with each unit. The program is designed for students with less than average reading abilities.

u. Hall, Brian. *Valuing: Exploration and Discovery*. San Diego, CA: Pennant, 1971.

12: This audiovisual kit, containing background text, graphic materials, and taped situations, emphasizes listening and communication skills and interpersonal experiences. Unit titles are as follows: Unit 1—"Values and Change"; Unit 2—"Values in Listening"; Unit 3—"Examining Personal Values"; and Unit 4—"Applying Values."

*v. Hanley, Jim, and Don Thompson. *Searching for Values: A Film Anthology*. New York, NY: Learning Corporation of America, 1972.

9-12: Fifteen major motion pictures, adapted and edited for classroom use, are included in this series. Each film is approximately 16 minutes and deals with a particular value problem—loneliness (from *Five Easy Pieces*), killing (from *Bless the Beasts and Children*), truth (from *On the Waterfront*), and so on. Teacher's guides with specific values clarification activities are provided for each film.

*w. *Hard Choices: Strategies for Decision-Making*. White Plains, NY: The Center for Humanities, 1975.

9-12: Two carousel cartridges containing 160 slides, two cassettes or two records, and a teacher's guide are included in this program. The program emphasizes the importance of defining a decision, establishing values, recognizing alternatives, gathering information, and applying decision-making strategies based on risks and probabilities.

*x. Harmin, Merrill. *Making Sense of Our Lives*. Niles, IL: Argus Communications, 1974.

7-12: Consisting of cassettes, posters, and 74 value sheets, this multimedia program provides experiences to help students clarify their values, to make thoughtful choices in real-life situations, to listen to others, and to express personal convictions with confidence.

*y. Harmin, Merrill. *People Projects*. Menlo Park, CA: Addison-Wesley, 1973.

4-8: The three sets of project cards composing this program are designed to help students think about personal events, find satisfaction in such thinking, clarify their confusions and inconsistencies, appreciate others' experiences, develop small-group skills, develop abilities for responsible self-direction, and develop mature value thinking. A teacher's guide is included with each card set.

z. Howard, Robert. *Roles and Relationships: Exploring Attitudes and Values.* New York, NY: Westinghouse Learning, 1973.

11-12: An individualized course, including a student text and an instructor's kit, this program focuses on interaction between a person and his or her environment, particularly the human environment. The goal is to increase awareness of self, of relationships with others, of roles, and of attitudes and values through questioning and discussion activities.

*aa. Klein, Ronald, *et al. Dimensions of Personality: Search for Meaning.* Dayton, OH: Pflaum, 1974.

7-8: The 36 lessons in this junior high program are designed to provide students with opportunities to reflect on their lives and to clarify their personal values in relation to external forces, internal drives, and relationships with others. A teacher's guide and spirit masters are included.

*bb. *Man and His Values.* White Plains, NY: Center for the Humanities, 1973.

9-12: This sound-slide program traces the historical concepts of good and evil, presents students with situations for making value decisions, and includes activities in which students list and rank their own values.

*cc. McPhail, Peter, *et al. Lifeline.* Niles, IL: Argus Communications, 1975.

7-12: This program of moral education contains three phases, "In Other People's Shoes," "Proving the Rule," and "What Would You Have Done?" Through discussion of open-ended, everyday situations, students are encouraged to examine alternatives, weigh consequences, and make decisions consistent with what they value. Students are urged to take the needs, interests, and feelings of others into account as well as their own.

dd. Miguel, Richard J. *Decision: A Values Approach to Decision Making.* Columbus, OH: Charles E. Merrill, 1974.

7-12: This audiovisual kit, designed to help students analyze decision-making processes and clarify their values, includes activity cards, spirit masters, a sound-filmstrip, and cassettes. Also included are a handbook that explains in detail how to use the kit and resource materials, including *Making Value Judgements* by Carl A. Elder and *Values and Teaching* by Raths, Harmin, and Simon.

ee. *The New Model Me.* Lakewood, OH: Meeting Modern Problems Project, Lakewood City Public School System, 1973

9-12: A student book and teacher's guide are included in this high school curriculum. It is composed of a series of activities divided into six units: "Human Behavior," "Controls," "Real Self," "Values," "Response," and "Change." The intent of the course is to provide basic skills and understanding for dealing with difficult situations in life.

*ff. O'Fahey, Sheila, *et al. Deciding How to Live as Society's Children: Individual Needs and Institutional Expectations.* Evanston, IL: McDougal, Littell, 1974.

9-12: This text from the *Values Education Series* (see also entries D-1-a and D-1-f) consists largely of short case studies and clarification activities related to femininity/masculinity, education, work, and family. The last chapter encourages students "to consider ways in which individuals and groups can bring about significant change in the structure of society."

*gg. Paulson, Wayne. *Deciding for Myself: A Values-Clarification Series*. Minneapolis, MN: Winston, 1974

6-12: These materials, which include three sets of student booklets and a teacher's guide, organize strategies around key elements of the valuing process as defined by Raths *et al* (see entry D-2-s): "prizing, alternatives, consequences, acting on beliefs, speaking out, choosing freely, and acting with a pattern." The focus is on clarifying personal values and making everyday choices and on how students feel about important social issues. A formula for creating new valuing experiences is also suggested.

*hh. Raths, Louis E. *Exploring Moral Values*. Pleasantville, NY: Warren Schloat, 1969.

2-6: Containing 15 filmstrips, this program provides opportunities for students to discuss human realities in a variety of relevant life situations requiring moral or ethical judgments and to explore and clarify their responses.

*ii. Shaftel, Fannie, and George Shaftel. *Values in Action*. Minneapolis, MN: Winston, 1970.

4-6: This audiovisual package, consisting of ten filmstrips and three records, presents problem situations and encourages students to think about, discuss, and role play possible solutions to those problems.

*jj. Simon, Sidney B. *Meeting Yourself Halfway: 31 Value Clarification Strategies for Daily Living*. Niles, IL: Argus Communications, 1974.

7-12: Materials include a book for either the students or the teacher and a set of 31 spirit masters. The group-oriented strategies focus on the processes involved in choosing, prizing, and acting. These, according to Simon, are the three integral parts of the values clarification process.

*kk. Smith, M.F. *The Valuing Approach to Career Education*. Waco, TX: Education Achievement Corporation, 1973-74.

K-8: This is a multimedia instructional system divided into three series, K-2, 3-5, and 6-8. It is designed to teach several value-clarifying skills, various thinking skills, and certain career concepts to elementary children. The materials include color filmstrips, tape cassettes, storybooks, games, posters, puppets, and tests. The teacher's guides contain detailed lesson plans for each series.

ll. *Values Series*. Santa Monica, CA: BFA Educational Media, 1972.

1-6: This series consists of sixty-four 12" x 18" color picture cards with teaching suggestions on the reverse side. Everyday values problems are pictured. It is recommended that the children be allowed to work through them in a nonjudgmental atmosphere; however, in some cases leading questions emphasize value concepts such as responsibility, safety, honesty, and sharing.

mm. Wrenn, C. Gilbert, and Shirley Schwarzrock. *Coping With Series*. Circle Pines,

MN: American Guidance Service, 1973.

7-12: This set of 23 books presents many relationships and problems often confronted by young people. The teacher's manual contains information about the entire series as well as the rationale, objectives, role of the teacher, suggested procedures, and a supplementary bibliography for each book. The series may be used for individual reading, as a background for class discussion, or for group counseling and guidance sessions. The books are concerned with getting along with others, understanding of self, and problems with drugs, alcohol, smoking, food, and other crutches.

2. Teacher Materials: Clarification

*a. Casteel, J. Doyle, and Robert J. Stahl. *Value Clarification in the Classroom: A Primer*. Pacific Palisades, CA: Goodyear, 1975.

9-12: Designed for use in undergraduate, graduate, and inservice teacher education courses, the major part of this book is devoted to a strategy called "the value sheet." Six formats are suggested with examples, and directions for developing new or modified value sheets are given.

*b. Casteel, J. Doyle, *et al*. *Valuing Exercises for the Middle School*. Gainesville, FL: P.K. Yonge Laboratory School, College of Education, University of Florida, 1974.

5-8: The first part of this monograph introduces and defines the value sheet. In the second section the six formats identified in Casteel and Stahl's *Value Clarification in the Classroom: A Primer* are applied to the middle school. Examples of each format are given, designed specifically for a unit on the Bill of Rights.

*c. Cole, Richard. *A New Role for Geographic Education: Values and Environmental Concerns*. Oak Park, IL: National Council for Geographic Education, 1974.

3-12: This monograph suggests guidelines and a variety of strategies for teachers interested in applying values clarification techniques to the study of geography.

d. Curwin, Richard L., and Gerri Curwin. *Developing Individual Values in the Classroom*. Palo Alto, CA: Learning Handbooks, Education Today, 1974.

K-6: This handbook is one of a series of teacher resource books published by *Learning Magazine*. Focusing on values education, this book explains the theory and practice of the clarification approach and provides various activities to assist teachers in building trusting atmospheres, helping students "discover their true self," "integrating values and curriculum areas," creating their own clarifying activities, and evaluating students' progress. An annotated bibliography of values and humanistic education resources is also included.

*e. Dunfee, Maxine, and Claudia Crump. *Teaching for Social Values in the Social Studies*. Washington, D.C.: Association for Childhood Education International, 1974.

K-6: A resource for elementary teachers, this book illustrates the application of various value-clarifying techniques and strategies in relation to student self-concept, prejudice, friendship, the environment, and democracy.

f. *Experiences in Decision Making: Elementary Social Studies Handbook*. Edmonton, Alberta, Canada: Alberta Department of Education, 1971.

K-6: The five parts of this handbook include objectives and references for a new social studies program, elaboration of components of the program, suggestions for planning instructional units, learning activities, and sample units. The rationale incorporates the belief that human values and the valuing process should be the major focus of the new social studies.

g. Glashagel, Char, and Jerry Glashagel. *Valuing Families*. Akron, OH: Youth Values Project, Akron Y.M.C.A., 1974.

K-12: A resource for family life education, these materials consist of 24 different strategies and exercises for family groups. They are intended to help develop self-esteem, to provide practice for effective communication, and to sharpen decision-making skills.

h. Glashagel, Char, and Jerry Glashagel. *Valuing Youth*. Akron, OH: Youth Values Project, Akron Y.M.C.A., 1974.

K-6: Intended for persons working with elementary-age children, these materials suggest four basic valuing strategies, as well as strategies for specific value issues. An underlying assumption is that alcohol and drug use and abuse are related to a person's value system. Included in the materials package is a training program for leaders.

i. Hall, Brian. *Values Clarification as Learning Process*. Paramus, NJ: Paulist Press, 1973.

12: This series of three books is designed to help teachers implement the clarification approach. *Book 1–Sourcebook* examines values and how people apply them in their own lives; *Book 2–Guidebook* contains descriptions of projects and exercises to help people examine and clarify their values; and *Book 3–Handbook for Christian Educators* presents guidelines for using values clarification in religious education.

*j. Harmin, Merrill, *et al*. *Clarifying Values Through Subject Matter: Applications for the Classroom*. Minneapolis, MN: Winston, 1973.

6-12: The use of various clarification techniques in 20 subject-matter areas, including social studies, biology, earth science, mathematics, health, art, and music, are illustrated in this book.

*k. Hawley, Robert C. *Value Exploration Through Role Playing: Practical Strategies for Use in the Classroom*. New York, NY: Hart, 1975.

7-12: The six chapters of this book attempt to give teachers specific information and strategies for implementing role play in the classroom.

*l. Hawley, Robert C., *et al*. *Composition for Personal Growth: Values Clarification Through Writing*. New York, NY: Hart, 1973.

7-12: The application of various clarification strategies in secondary English composition programs is explained and illustrated. Activities focus on the topics of identity, interpersonal relations, and personal growth.

m. Howe, Leland W., and Mary Martha Howe. *Personalizing Education: Values Clarification and Beyond*. New York, NY: Hart, 1975.

The authors feel that in order to personalize education, values clarification should form an integral part of every dimension of the classroom. With this purpose in mind, this teacher resource provides over 100 strategies in addition to worksheets.

n. Knapp, Clifford E. ''Teaching Environmental Education with a Focus on Values.'' 1972. ED 070 614.

4-12: This short paper illustrates the application of several clarification techniques to environmental issues. Strategies used include value sheets, role playing, contrived incidents, values continuum, values voting, and rank orders. This paper also appears in *Readings in Values Clarification* (Simon and Kirschenbaum, 1973, pp. 161-74).

*o. Kuhn, David J. "Value Education in the Sciences: The Step Beyond Concepts and Processes." 1973. ED 080 317.

7-12: This short paper discusses how students' values can be clarified in science classes and illustrates the application of various techniques to science topics. The techniques used include simulations, role playing, sensitivity modules, and attitudinal surveys.

p. McPhail, Peter, *et al. Moral Education in the Secondary School.* London, England: Longmans, 1972.

7-12: Part I of this work discusses the nature of adolescence and the rationale for stressing moral education. Part II deals with the practical aspects of implementing a program of moral education. It outlines and describes the *Lifeline* program and discusses the teacher's role, curriculum planning, and school organization in relation to the program. The appendices provide suggestions for extending the *Lifeline* approach in areas such as sex education, racial relations, and community services and present some research findings based on the work of the authors.

*q. Morrison, Eleanor S., and Mila Underhill Price. *Values in Sexuality: A New Approach to Sex Education.* New York, NY: Hart, 1974.

9-12: This book offers a course structure within which high school and college students can openly explore and discuss their feelings about sexuality. Units focus on group building activities, physiology, psycho-sexual development, sex roles, nonmarital sex, values clarification, and dimensions in relationships.

r. Paine, Doris M., and Diana Martinez. *Guide to Religious Thought: An Examination of Spiritual Value Systems.* New York, NY: Bantam, 1974.

10-12: This guide suggests a program for helping students to examine their own system of values and beliefs and to compare them with those of others. In this sense the course reflects the analysis approach. However, the valuing process emphasized encourages the development of communications skills in the area of feelings and emotions. A major objective of the course is values clarification. This is to be achieved through small-group processes and discussion.

*s. Raths, Louis E., *et al. Values and Teaching: Working with Values in the Classroom.* Columbus, OH: Charles E. Merrill, 1966.

K-12: This is the first teacher resource published on the clarification approach to values education. The authors explain their theory of values, illustrate the use of several strategies to help students clarify their values, discuss guidelines and problems in applying this approach, and review the early research on values clarification.

*t. Shaftel, Fannie R., and George Shaftel. *Role-Playing for Social Values: Decision-Making in the Social Studies.* Englewood Cliffs, NJ: Prentice-Hall, 1967.

K-8: Part I of this text explains the theory, rationale, and methodology of role playing. Included are a discussion of the social studies objectives that can be attained through role playing, suggestions for guiding the role-playing process, and descriptions of various uses of this dramatic technique. Part II consists of problem stories that can serve as the stimuli to the role-playing activity. The stories deal with individual integrity, group responsibility, and self-acceptance.

*u. Simon, Sidney B., and Jay Clark. *More Values Clarification: A Guidebook for the Use of Values Clarification in the Classroom*. San Diego, CA: Pennant, 1975.

7-12: This extension of *Values Clarification* (see w. below), presents new strategies geared for helping teenagers and young adults clarify their values. (To be retitled *Beginning Values Clarification).*

v. Simon, Sidney B., and Howard Kirschenbaum, eds. *Readings in Values Clarification*. Minneapolis, MN: Winston, 1973.

K-12: Readings related to values in general and the clarification approach in particular are included in this anthology. The first section, "Values Clarification and Other Perspectives," includes articles by Rogers, Rokeach, and Kohlberg, as well as several by Simon and his associates. The second section of the book consists of articles discussing the application of values clarification to various subject areas, including history, environmental education, foreign languages, and English. Other parts contain articles relating values clarification to religious education, the family, administration, and group dynamics. The book concludes with an annotated bibliography on values clarification.

*w. Simon, Sidney B., *et al. Values Clarification: A Handbook of Practical Strategies for Teachers and Students*. New York, NY: Hart, 1972.

K-12: This manual consists of 79 values clarification activities and strategies for elementary and secondary students and adults. Each strategy is explained in terms of its purpose and procedure. Additional suggestions and applications are also provided.

x. Walz, Garry R., ed. *Communique: Resources for Practicing Counselors*. 2 (May 1973). Ann Arbor, MI: ERIC/CAPS, School of Education, University of Michigan. ED 075 766.

K-12: Part of this issue of *Communique* contains a description of the values clarification process and of specific techniques for use by teachers and counselors.

y. Williams, Elmer. *Values and the Valuing Process: Social Studies for the Elementary School, Proficiency Module #5*. Athens, GA: Department of Elementary Education, University of Georgia, 1972. ED 073 990.

K-6: This teacher training module is designed to help prospective teachers become aware of the affective domain and develop competence in using clarification strategies with their students. The first part deals with Bloom's taxonomy of affective objectives. The second part focuses on the valuing process. The last section is a teaching strategy built around an unfinished story that will help children identify alternatives in a problem situation and examine the possible consequences of each alternative. Appendices include additional activities and a bibliography of materials.

z. *Y Circulator*. 4 (Spring 1973). New York, NY: National Council of YMCAs. ED 080 403.

7-12: This issue of the *Y Circulator* details the process used to plan and implement a program of values clarification at a Hi-Y Conference in Blue Ridge, North Carolina.

3. Theoretical Background Materials: Clarification

a. Maslow, Abraham H., ed. *New Knowledge in Human Values*. New York, NY: Harper and Row, 1959.

This collection of 15 articles is based on addresses delivered to the First Scientific Conference on New Knowledge in Human Values organized by the Research Society for Creative Altruism. Contributors include Bronowski, Hartman, and Margenaw, who reflect a naturalistic or scientific orientation to values; Allport, Maslow, Fromm, and Goldstein, who reflect a humanistic viewpoint; and Tillich, Suzuki, and Weisskopf, who propound an ontological (spiritual) orientation. The first group of scholars relate to the analysis approach to values education, the second group to clarification, and the final group to the union approach.

b. Moustakas, Clark. *The Authentic Teacher: Sensitivity and Awareness in the Classroom*. Cambridge, MA: Howard A. Doyle, 1966.

A theoretical basis for teachers helping students to develop as healthy, whole persons, as well as classroom illustrations, are presented in this publication. Emphasis is placed upon understanding children in terms of their own values and meanings rather than in terms of external diagnosis and evaluation.

*c. Raths, Louis E., *et al*. *Values and Teaching: Working with Values in the Classroom*. Columbus, OH: Charles E. Merrill, 1969.

Part Two, "A Theory of Values," presents the theoretical basis for values clarification. (See also entry D-2-s.)

d. Rogers, Carl. *Freedom to Learn*. Columbus, OH: Charles E. Merrill, 1969.

This book offers an explanation of how and why classrooms should be organized to allow students to be free to learn. It contains Rogers' article originally published in the *Journal of Abnormal and Social Psychology* (1964, pp. 160-167) elaborating a theory of the evolution of the valuing process which relates directly to the clarification approach to values education.

e. Related Works:

1) Allport, Gordon. *Becoming: Basic Considerations for a Psychology of Personality*. New Haven, CT: Yale University Press, 1955.

2) Allport, Gordon. "Values and Youth." In *Studies in Adolescence*, Robert E. Grunder, ed. New York, NY: Macmillan, 1963, pp. 17-27.

3) Fromm, Erich. *Man for Himself: An Inquiry into the Psychology of Ethics*. New York, NY: Holt, Rinehart and Winston, 1947.

4) Murphy, Gardner. *Human Potentialities*. New York, NY: Basic Books, 1958.

4. Selected Research Studies and Articles: Clarification

a. Clegg, Ambrose, Jr., and James L. Hills. "A Strategy for Exploring Values and Valuing in the Social Studies." In *Readings on Elementary Social Studies:*

Emerging Changes, Jonathon C. McLendon, ed. Boston, MA: Allyn and Bacon, 1970, pp. 375-84.

This exploratory study found that several cognitively oriented teaching strategies developed by Taba could be used to teach three of Rath's valuing processes (choosing, reflection, and affirmation) to fifth-grade students.

b. Covault, Thomas J. "The Application of Value Clarification Teaching Strategies with Fifth Grade Students to Investigate their Influence on Students' Self-concept and Related Classroom Coping and Interactive Behaviors." Unpublished doctoral dissertation. Columbus, OH: Ohio State University, 1973. [Reported in the *Values Education Newsletter,* 1 (February 1974) pp. 1-2.]

This study found that fifth-grade students who participated in 11 one-hour values clarification sessions made the following significant changes as compared with a control group who had physical education taught by the same investigator: improved self-concept, positive attitude toward learning, and less acute and infrequent apathetic, uncertain, and inconsistent behavior.

c. Gray, Russell Dent, III. "The Influence of Values Clarification Strategies on Student Self Concept and Sociometric Structures in Selected Elementary School Classrooms." Unpublished doctoral dissertation. Los Angeles, CA: School of Education, University of Southern California, 1975.

This study found that using an outside specialist for teaching one hour of values clarification lessons per week for 15 weeks is not an effective method for changing self-concept and most sociometric structures in sixth-grade students.

d. Kingman, Barry. "The Development of Value Clarification Skills: Initial Efforts in an Eighth Grade Social Studies Class, Part II." Occasional Paper 75-1. Stony Brook, NY: American Historical Association History Education Project, State University of New York, 1975.

In discussing his efforts to teach values clarification to a group of eighth-grade students, the author reports his limited quantitative findings and his various problems and failures. He concludes "that value clarification is an enormously complex process riddled with technical and theoretical problems."

e. Raths, James. "Clarifying Children's Values." *The National Elementary Principal,* 42 (November 1962) pp. 35-39.

Of the 100 students in grades five through eight who acted as their own controls, this early study of values clarification found that 88 made significant changes in "raising questions and alternatives," "active participating," "initiation and self-direction of classroom activity," and "attitudes toward learning."

E. Action Learning

1. Student Materials: Action Learning

*a. Newmann, Fred M., and Donald W. Oliver. *Social Action: Dilemmas and Strategies (Public Issues Series).* Columbus, OH: Xerox, 1972.

9-12: This booklet investigates the ways young people can influence public policy and suggests value dilemmas regarding what types of social and political actions are appropriate for youth.

2. Teacher Materials: Action Learning

*a. Allen, Rodney F. *Teaching Guide to the Values Education Series*. Evanston, IL: McDougal, Littell, 1974.

9-12: This teacher's guide presents some theoretical background on values and an instructional model for values education to be used with the *Values Education Series* (see entries D-1-a, D-1-f, and D-1-ff). The emphasis on "social self-realization" and community, which is reflected in this teacher work but not in the student materials, is the reason why it is classified under the action learning approach.

b. Citizenship Education Clearing House (CECH). P.O. Box 24220, St. Louis, MO 63130.

CECH is a nonprofit organization that will furnish information on establishing action programs for young people.

*c. Jones, W. Ron. *Finding Community: A Guide to Community Research and Action*. Palo Alto, CA: James E. Freel, 1971.

9-12: Admittedly biased toward an activist philosophy, this book is valuable mainly as a source of possible community action projects related to welfare, food costs, consumer prices, the police, and schools.

d. National Commission on Resources for Youth. *New Roles for Youth in the School and Community*. New York, NY: Citation Press, 1974.

This publication describes 70 community action and service projects carried out by students.

e. Newmann, Fred M. *Education for Citizen Action: Challenge for Secondary Curriculum*. Berkeley, CA: McCutchan, 1975.

9-12: This teacher resource presents a rationale, curriculum model, and suggested guidelines for developing a secondary-level educational program around the central objective of enhancing "student ability to exert influence in public affairs." The author argues that this ability is a crucial aspect of the broader goal of developing environmental competence and that the school is uniquely suited to achieving this objective. The curriculum development model identifies those areas of competence related to this objective: formulating policy goals (which includes "moral deliberation"), working for support of goals, and resolving psycho-philosophic concerns. The appendix includes a list of organizations and projects throughout the country that support citizen action and community involvement programs.

3. Theoretical Background Materials: Action Learning

a. Aoki, T. "Controlled Change: A Crucial Curriculum Component in Social Education." Paper presented at the annual meeting of the National Council of the Social Studies, Denver, November 1971. ED 065 404.

This paper advocates a "transactional" approach to social education which focuses on the interaction between students and their significant world and calls for students' participatory commitment to the process of change.

b. Bigge, Morris L. *Positive Relativism: An Emergent Educational Philosophy*. New York, NY: Harper and Row, 1971.

This book postulates the educational philosophy of positive relativism, which stresses that "a person is a psycho-social being" and that "personal development is largely a matter of individual-social development." The discussion of the nature of values reflects this viewpoint.

c. Blumer, Herbert. *Symbolic Interactionism: Perspective and Method*. Englewood Cliffs, NJ: Prentice-Hall, 1969.

The ideas of George Herbert Mead are interpreted from a sociological perspective in this book. Blumer contends that a person is not fully determined by the society or culture. The possession of a "self," according to Blumer, makes the person "a special kind of actor," who can help guide his or her own behavior within the social context.

d. Cherryholmes, Cleo H. *Toward a Theory of Social Education.* Washington, D.C.: Office of Education, U.S. Department of Health, Education and Welfare, 1971. ED 065 373.

This paper explains a theory of social education based on the axiom that "students are social actors engaged in purposive decision making who process information in acquiring and acting upon normative and empirical beliefs about social phenomena." Normative assumptions of this theory are that social education should increase the ability of students to (1) make socially effective choices, (2) systematically assess alternative social futures, and (3) be continuous social learners.

e. Dewey, John. *Theory of Valuation (International Encyclopedia of Unified Science,* Vol. II, Pt. 4). Chicago, IL: University of Chicago, 1939.

This work postulates a theory of valuing to which educators and theorists from other values education approaches claim to be related. Dewey was classified as an "action learning" theorist because of his emphasis on the social and personal aspects of valuing, as reflected in the following: Valuing "is as much a matter of interaction of a person with his social environment as walking is an interaction of legs with a physical environment"; "We must realize both the degree to which moral beliefs are a product of social environment and the degree to which thinking can alter that environment."

f. Raup, R. Bruce, *et al. The Improvement of Practical Intelligence.* New York, NY: Harper, 1950.

A model for making group value judgments which emphasizes both the nature of the situation (environment) and the "moods" of the characters (person) is presented in this book.

g. Ubbelohde, Robert. *Social Studies and Reality: A Commitment to Intelligent Social Action.* Greensboro, NC: Humanistic Education Project, University of North Carolina, 1973. ED 081 711.

This essay argues that practices allowing teachers to help students deal with society in an effort to bring about needed social change and action would include values clarification techniques, the methods of the social and physical sciences, and the dialectical method.

F. Other Approaches

1. Evocation

a. Ayer, Alfred J. *Language, Truth, and Logic.* London, England: Victor Gollancy, 1946.

An "emotive theory of values" is propounded, contending that values "are simply expressions of emotion which can be neither true nor false" and, thus, are unverifiable.

b. Combs, Arthur W., and Donald Snygg. *Individual Behavior: A Perceptual Approach*. New York, NY: Harper and Row, 1949.

This classic work on phenomenological psychology emphasizes that there is no objective reality, merely reality as perceived through subjective frames of reference.

c. Driscoll, Francis. "TM as a Secondary School Subject." *Phi Delta Kappan*. 54 (December 1972) pp. 236-37.

A New York superintendent discusses how and why transcendental meditation (TM) has been made available to students and teachers in his school district.

d. *Essence Cards*. Menlo Park, CA: Addison-Wesley, 1971, 1975. Includes the following: *Essence I* and *Essence II*.

K-12: Developed by the Environmental Studies Project, now known as Essentia, these materials are designed to develop more effective, humane environments. Creativity and inventiveness are encouraged. The teacher's guides suggest ways for creating an accepting, open, trusting atmosphere in the classroom. *Essence I* consists of 78 assignment cards intended to develop awareness of self, others, and the total environment. *Essence II* consists of approximately 200 awareness cards divided into eleven mini-units: Communicate, Creature, Coping with Complexity, Movement, Astronomy/Astrology, Community, Peephole, Evolution, People, Patterns, and Enviros. Also included is a game that requires invention.

e. Rogers, Carl. "Toward a Modern Approach to Values." *Journal of Abnormal and Social Psychology*. 68 (1964) pp. 160-67.

Rogers presents a theory of valuing that claims that the valuing process within a person has an "organismic" base and evolves through three stages—infant, adult, and self-actualizing adult. The first stage, which conceives of valuing as a flexible, changing, unconscious, and fully organismic process, closely relates to the evocation approach to values education.

f. Samples, Robert E. "Value Prejudice: Toward a Personal Awareness." *Media & Methods,* 11 (September 1974) pp. 14-18, 49-52.

Samples contends that since most important decisions are "based on emotion and intuition, not logic and rationality," teachers should focus on the emotional drives that underlie a person's value structure rather than on the rational expression of those values. He is co-director of an educational group called Essentia, located at Evergreen State College in Olympia, Washington. This group is developing student and teacher curriculum materials designed to focus on the intuitive as well as analytical processes.

g. Westermarck, Edward. *Ethical Relativity*. New York, NY: Harcourt, Brace, 1932.

A theory of values is presented that conceives of values as moral emotions indicating approval or disapproval. Since values or moral principles are grounded in emotion, Westermarck contends that morality is relative and that moral principles have no objective validity.

h. Whitaker, Carl A., and Thomas P. Malone. *The Roots of Psychotherapy*. New York, NY: Blakiston, 1953.

This book elaborates the authors' "experiential or non-rational" psychotherapy, which stresses the feeling experience of the patient rather than the intellect and which strives to have the patient develop the ability to make spontaneous, unconscious, autonomous choices without rational thinking.

i. Whitaker, Carl A., and Thomas P. Malone. ''Experiential or Non-Rational Psychotherapy.'' In *Psychotherapy and Counseling,* Joseph Sahakian, ed. Chicago, IL: Rand-McNally, 1969, pp. 414-436.

A concise summary of the ''experiential'' approach to psychotherapy is presented in this article.

2. Union

a. Crampton, Martha. ''Some Applications of Psychosynthesis in the Educational Field.'' In *Four Psychologies Applied to Education: Freudian, Behavioral, Humanistic, and Transpersonal,* Thomas B. Roberts, ed. New York, NY: Wiley, 1975, pp. 453-462.

This article describes a curriculum project, Integrative Qualities, designed to develop educational materials that stress transpersonal elements such as ''higher intuition'' and ''ultimate values.'' Some of these materials are available from the Canadian Institute of Psychosynthesis, Inc., 3496 Avenue Marlow, Montreal 260, Quebec, Canada.

b. Foster, Arthur L. ''Valuing as Religious Experience.'' In *Values in an Age of Confrontation,* Jeremiah W. Canning, ed. Columbus, OH: Charles E. Merrill, 1970, pp. 119-123

This essay discusses various other definitions of valuing then contends that valuing is essentially a religious experience of making contact with the Godhead.

c. Harman, Willis W. ''Experience with a Graduate Seminar on Personal Growth.'' In *Approaches to Education for Character,* Clarence H. Faust and Jessica Feingold, eds. New York, NY: Columbia University Press, 1969, pp. 301-314.

In this essay three processes of transforming the self are discussed, two of which relate directly to the union approach to values education—the use of imagination and transforming symbols and the experience of cosmic consciousness.

d. Hartoonian, H. Michael. ''A Disclosure Approach to Value Analysis in Social Studies Education: Rationale and Components.'' Paper presented at the Third Annual Conference on Social Education and Social Science. Lansing, MI: Kellogg Center, Michigan State University, 1973. ED 083 059.

This paper presents a rationale for a disclosure approach to value analysis, which involves the student construction of value profiles of his or her own mythic thought.

e. Jung, Charles C. ''The Next Revolution: Education and the Evolution of Self.'' Paper presented at the annual meeting of the American Educational Research Association, Chicago, 1973. ED 063 546.

This paper postulates a theory of the ''evolution of the social-psychological self'' which closely resembles other developmental theories. However, the last stage—the creative self—seems to reflect a view of the person similar to that of the union approach to values education.

f. McWaters, Barry. ''An Outline of Transpersonal Psychology: Its Meaning and Relevance for Education.'' In *Four Psychologies Applied to Education: Freudian, Behavioral, Humanistic, and Transpersonal,* Thomas B. Roberts, ed. New York, NY: Wiley, 1975, pp. 448-452.

The author outlines a new classification scheme of educational domains that includes a transpersonal dimension composed of four modes of experience: intuitional, psychic, mystical, and personal/transpersonal integrative. Examples of the content of each mode and the methods of developing each mode of experience are also provided.

g. Murphy, Michael H. ''Education for Transcendence.'' In *Four Psychologies Applied to Education: Freudian, Behavioral, Humanistic, and Transpersonal,* Thomas B. Roberts, ed. New York, NY: Wiley, 1975, pp. 438-447.

The author discuses some recent psychological research (including that of Laing at the Tavistock Clinic in London and Kamiya at the Langley Porter Neuropsychiatric Institute in San Francisco and some psychotherapy methods used in Gestalt therapy and encounter groups) which he believes could be applied to the educational goal of transcending the ego and experiencing cosmic oneness.

h. Radha, Swami Sivananda. ''Life Seals.'' *ASCENT: The Journal of Yasodhara Ashram Society,* 5 (Spring 1973) pp. 10-15.

Swami Radha describes a procedure she uses with groups to help individuals gain ''new understanding about the Self.'' It employs art, symbolism, and intuition. (This procedure is discussed in Chapter VII of this book.)

i. Suzuki, D. T. ''Human Values in Zen.'' In *New Knowledge in Human Values,* Abraham H. Maslow, ed. New York, NY: Harper and Row, 1959, pp. 94-106.

The article presents a Zen Buddhist conception of the nature of values, which sees the ultimate source of values and valuing in the ''isness'' of things. In typical Zen master fashion, Suzuki claims that ''the value is a value when it is a no-value.''

j. Tillich, Paul. ''Is a Science of Human Values Possible?'' In *New Knowledge in Human Values,* Abraham H. Maslow, ed. New York, NY: Harper and Row, 1959, pp. 189-196.

Discussion focuses on the ontological foundation of values, which, according to Tillich, are derived from ''man's own essential being.''

k. Watts, Alan W. *The Book: On the Taboo Against Knowing Who You Are.* New York, NY: Collier, 1967.

With frequent use of parables and stories from Eastern philosophy and religion, Watts discusses in Western terms the task, meaning, and value of attaining cosmic consciousness—the feeling that you are IT (at one with God).

l. Yeomans, Thomas. *Search for a Working Model: Gestalt, Psychosynthesis, and Confluent Education.* Occasional Paper No. 22, Santa Barbara CA: Development and Research in Confluent Education (DRICE), University of California, 1972.

Attempting to establish a theoretical basis for the program of ''confluent education,'' this paper summarizes the key ideas of Perls' Gestalt therapy and Assagioli's psychosynthesis. In using the ideas of the latter psychologist, the advocates of confluent education seem to be affirming that ''transpersonal experience and development are . . . legitimate and natural directions of growth'' and, thus, legitimate and natural concerns for education.

m. Related Works:

1) Assagioli, Robert. *Psychosynthesis.* New York, NY: Viking, 1971.

2) Bugenthal, J.F.T. *The Search for Authenticity.* New York, NY: Holt,

Rinehart and Winston, 1965.

3) Jung, Carl G. *The Integration of the Personality*. New York, NY: Farrar and Rinehart, 1939.
4) Maslow, Abraham H. *Religions, Values, and Peak Experiences*. New York, NY: Viking, 1970.
5) Progoff, Ira. *The Death and Rebirth of Psychology*. New York, NY: Julian, 1956.
6) Sorokin, Pitirim A. ''Reply to Professor Wiesskopf.'' In *New Knowledge in Human Values,* Abraham H. Maslow, ed. New York, NY: Harper and Row, 1959, pp. 224-232.
7) Tillich, Paul. *The Courage to Be*. New Haven, CT: Yale University Press, 1952.
8) Weisskopf, Walter A. ''Comment.'' In *New Knowledge in Human Values,* Abraham H. Maslow, ed. New York, NY: Harper and Row, 1959, pp. 199-223.

selected bibliography of related works on values and values education

A. General Bibliographies on Values

1. Albert, Ethel M., and Clyde Kluckhohn. *A Selected Bibliography on Values, Ethics, and Esthetics, in the Behavioral Sciences and Philosophy, 1920-1958*. Glencoe, IL: Free Press, 1959.

2. *A Guide to Selected Curriculum Materials on Interdependence, Conflict, and Change: Teacher Comments on Classroom Use and Implementation*. Denver, CO: Center for Teaching International Relations, Denver University; and New York: Center for War/Peace Studies, New York Friends Group, Inc., 1973. ED 096 236

3. Hearn, D. Dwain, ed., and Sandy Nicholson. *Values, Feelings and Morals. Part 1: Research and Perspectives. Part 2: An Annotated Bibliography of Programs and Instructional Materials*. Washington, D.C.: American Association of Elementary, Kindergarten, and Nursery Educators, 1974. ED 095 472.

4. *Moral and Values Education. Bibliographies in Education, No. 44*. Ottawa, Ontario, Canada: Canadian Teacher's Federation, 1974. ED 097 269.

5. *Reading List for the Theme Center "The Individual's Quest for Universal Values." Curriculum Research Report*. Brooklyn, NY: Bureau of Curriculum Research, New York City Board of Education, 1960. ED 089 251.

6. Thomas, Walter L. *A Comprehensive Bibliography on the Value Concept*. Grand Rapids, MI: Project on Student Values, Northview Public Schools, 1967. ED 024 064.

B. Bibliographies Related to Specific Approaches

1. Glaser-Kirschenbaum, Howard, and Barbara Glaser-Kirschenbaum. "An Annotated Bibliography on Values Clarification." In *Readings in Values Clarification,* Sidney B. Simon and Howard Kirschenbaum, eds. Minneapolis, MN: Winston, 1973, pp. 366-385. (Clarification)

2. *Report No. 2: Moral Education: A Bibliography* and *Annotations*. Vancouver, British Columbia, Canada, 1974. (Moral Development)

3. *Selective Bibliography on Valuing as an Educational Approach to Drug Abuse and Other High Risk Behavior*. Coronado, CA: Coronado Unified School District, 1973. (Inculcation)

C. Student Materials Related to Values Education

1. Abbey, David S. *Valuing: A Discussion Guide for Personal Decision Making.* Chicago, IL: Human Development Institute, Instructional Dynamics Incorporated, 1974.

   11-12: *Valuing* is a self-contained program that teaches the fundamentals of the process involved in making choices and decisions to groups of nine to 12 participants. It permits people to share information about themselves only when they wish to do so without the assistance of a trained leader. The complete program includes an audio cassette, a manual, six figures books, and an exercise book.

2. *The Adventures of the Lollipop Dragon.* Chicago, IL: Singer Education and Training Products, Society for Visual Education, 1970. Includes the following titles: *How the Lollipop Dragon Got His Name (Sharing), Working Together, Avoiding Litter, Care of Property, Taking Turns,* and *Kindness to Animals.*

   1-3: This set of color sound-filmstrips is illustrated in cartoon style. The characters, including the Lollipop Dragon and the children of Tum Tum, demonstrate the values and conduct implied in the titles. Script guides and the *Lollipop Dragon Coloring Book* are also available.

3. Campbell, Alexander, and Ralph H. Ojemann. *Learning to Decide Program.* Cleveland, OH: Educational Research Council of America, 1970.

   4-6: This multimedia program consists of a teacher's book for each of the three grade levels, students' stories, a question booklet, a decision-making booklet, filmstrips, and tapes. Also included is a packet entitled *Readings in Human Behavior.*

4. Campbell, Alexander, and Ralph H. Ojemann. *Values and Decision Making Program.* Cleveland, OH: Educational Research Council of America, 1972, 1975.

   7-12: This program includes a junior high component and a senior high component. A student booklet, a teacher's guide, and a packet, *Readings in Human Behavior,* are included in each component.

5. *Developing Basic Values.* Chicago, IL: Singer Education and Training Products, Society for Visual Education, 1964. Includes the following titles: *Respect for Property, Consideration for Others, Acceptance of Differences,* and *Recognition of Responsibilities.*

   3-6: These color sound-filmstrips present stories and sample class discussions illustrating the basic values reflected in the titles.

6. Jackson, Dorothy J. *Career Decision Making: A Mini Course.* Ithaca, NY: Cornell Institute for Occupational Education, New York State College of Agriculture, Cornell University, forthcoming January 1976.

   9-12: The course includes three packets, each with a student booklet and a leader's guide. Areas covered include "Values," "Occupational Information," and "Decision Points." The aim of the course, which includes both individual and group activities, is to help students build career decision-making skills. It is presently being piloted.

7. *Open-Ended Stories.* Lakeland, FL: Imperial Film, 1970. Includes the following titles: *The Painting, The Open Gate, The New Building, The Purse,* and *The Warning Blinker.*

1-6: Each of the sound-filmstrips presents an unresolved conflict situation. Some alternative solutions are presented. The values involved are integrity, self-responsibility, responsibility for others, friendship, and courage. A summary of filmstrip content and suggested questions are given in the study guide.

8. *Posters Without Words*. Niles, IL: Argus Communications, 1973.

   7-12: Materials include six color and six black-and-white posters, 14" x 21", two spirit masters, and a teacher's direction sheet. The posters are designed to encourage personal reflection, creative expression, and group discussion.

9. Price, Roy. *Concepts for Social Studies*. New York, NY: Macmillan, 1974.

   9-12: Included in this set of 21 paperback books for social studies are four on values concepts: *The Arena of Values, A Walk in My Neighbor's Shoes, The Crux of the Matter,* and *The Cement of Societies*. Cartoons, photographs, and illustrations supplement the readings, and a teacher's guide is available for each title.

10. *They Need Me*. Lakeland, FL: Imperial Film, 1968. Includes the following titles: *My Friends Need Me, My Mother and Father Need Me, My Dog Needs Me,* and *My Baby Sister Needs Me*.

    1-6: These four captioned filmstrips present children's interdependence upon those around them. Situations in which a child could be of help are explored, and children must decide on a course of action. The solution is then pictured.

11. *Two Sides to Every Story*. Lakeland, FL: Imperial Film, 1970. Includes the following titles: *Is Anyone to Blame?, Have You Felt Hurt?, A Place in the Family,* and *Have You Wanted to Be Alone?*

    1-6: These color, captioned filmstrips attempt to deal, through open-ended situations, with conflicts involving hurt feelings, misunderstandings, and relations with brothers and sisters.

12. *Understanding Values*. Jamaica, NY: Eye Gate, 1973. Includes the following titles: *Stealing, Cheating and Chiseling, Lies, Half-Truths and Untold Truths, Other's Values/Your Values, Who Cares/Staying Involved,* and *Right, Wrong, or Maybe*.

    6-12: These six sound-filmstrips present open-ended situations dealing with the subjects mentioned in the titles.

D. Teacher Materials Related to Values Education

1. Bessell, Harold, and Uvaldo Palomares. *Human Development Program*. San Diego, CA: Human Development Training Institute, 1973, 1974.
2. Brown, George. *Human Teaching for Human Learning: An Introduction to Confluent Education*. New York, NY: Viking, 1971.
3. Epstein, Charlotte. *Affective Subjects in the Classroom: Exploring Race, Sex, and Drugs*. Scranton, PA: Intext, 1972.
4. Kuhns, William. *Themes Two: One Hundred Short Films for Discussion*. Dayton, OH: Pflaum, 1974.
5. Schrank, Jeffrey. *Media in Value Education: A Critical Guide*. Niles, IL: Argus Communications, 1970.

6. Weinstein, Gerald, and Mario D. Fantini. *Toward Humanistic Education: A Curriculum of Affect*. New York, NY: Praeger, 1970.

E. Theoretical Background Materials Related to Values and Values Education

1. *The Acquisition and Development of Values: Perspectives on Research*. Bethesda, MD: National Institute of Child Health and Human Development, 1968.

2. Baier, Kurt, and Nicholas Rescher, eds. *Values and the Future*. New York, NY: Free Press, 1969.

3. Barrett, Donald N., ed. *Values in America*. South Bend, IN: University of Notre Dame Press, 1961.

4. Bauer, Nancy W. "Development of Effective Moral Decision-Making Through Social Studies." Paper presented to the College and University Faculty Assembly of the National Council for the Social Studies, Chicago, November 1974.

5. Beck, Clive M. *Moral Education in the Schools: Some Practical Suggestions*. Toronto, Ontario, Canada: Ontario Institute for Studies in Education, 1971.

6. Beck, Clive M., *et al. (eds). Moral Education: Interdisciplinary Approaches*. Toronto, Ontario, Canada: University of Toronto Press, 1971.

7. Belok, Michael, *et al. Approaches to Values in Education*. Dubuque, IA: William C. Brown, 1966.

8. Berkowitz, Leonard. *Development of Motives and Values in the Child*. New York, NY: Basic Books, 1964.

9. Brameld, Theodore, and Stanley Elam, eds. *Values in American Education*. Bloomington, IN: Phi Delta Kappa, 1964.

10. Broudy, Harry S. *Enlightened Cherishing: An Essay on Aesthetic Education*. Urbana, IL: University of Illinois Press, 1972.

11. Buttimer, Sister Annette. *Values in Geography*. Washington, D.C.: Commission on College Geography, Association of American Geographers, 1974. ED 098 137.

12. Combs, Arthur, ed. *Perceiving, Behaving and Becoming*. Washington, D.C.: Association for Supervision and Curriculum Development, 1962.

13. Dahlke, H. O. *Values in Culture and Classroom*. New York, NY: Harper and Row, 1958.

14. Drews, Elizabeth M., and Leslie Lipson. *Values and Humanity*. New York, NY: St. Martins, 1971.

15. Faust, Clarence H., and Jessica Feingold, eds. *Approaches to Education for Character: Strategies for Change in Higher Education*. New York, NY: Columbia University Press, 1969.

16. Hall, Everett W. *What Is a Value?* New York, NY: Humanities Press, 1952.

17. Hunt, Mate G. *Values: Resource Guide*. Oneonta, NY: American Association of

Colleges for Teacher Education, 1958.

18. Katz, Martin. *Decisions and Values*. Princeton, NJ: College Entrance Examination Board, 1963.

19. Krathwohl, David, *et al*. *Taxonomy of Educational Objectives: The Classification of Educational Goals. Handbook II: Affective Domain*. New York, NY: David McKay, 1964.

20. Lyon, Harold C., Jr. *Learning to Feel–Feeling to Learn*. Columbus, OH: Charles E. Merrill, 1971.

21. Meddin, Jay. "Attitudes, Values, and Related Concepts: A System of Classification." *Social Science Quarterly,* 55 (March 1975) pp. 889-900.

22. Niblett, W. R., ed. *Moral Education in a Changing Society*. London, England: Faber and Faber, 1963.

23. Peterson, James A. *Counseling and Values: A Philosophical Examination*. San Diego, CA: Pennant, 1972.

24. Rokeach, Milton. *Beliefs, Attitudes, and Values*. San Francisco, CA: Jossey-Bass, 1970.

25. Rokeach, Milton. *The Nature of Human Values*. New York, NY: Free Press, 1973.

26. Sahakian, William S. *Systems of Ethics and Value Theory*. New York, NY: Philosophical Library, 1963.

27. Simpson, Elizabeth L. *Democracy's Stepchildren*. San Francisco, CA: Jossey-Bass, 1971.

28. Smith, Philip G. *Theories of Value and Problems of Education*. Urbana, IL: University of Illinois Press, 1970.

29. Wilson, John. *The Assessment of Morality*. London, England: NFER Publishing, 1973.

30. Wilson, John, *et al*. *Introduction to Moral Education*. Baltimore, MD: Penguin, 1967.

F. Film Catalogs with Values - Related Materials

For the catalogs listed below ordering addresses have been provided. Values-related films are generally listed in these catalogs under such categories as guidance, values education, human relations, ethics, social values, and contemporary issues.

1. *BFA Educational Media: Catalog of 16mm Films*. Available from BFA Educational Media, A Division of Columbia Broadcasting System, Inc., 2211 Michigan Ave., Santa Monica, CA 90404.
2. Bosustow Productions Film Catalog. Available from Bosustow Productions, 1649 Eleventh St., Santa Monica, CA 90404.
3. *Britannica Films*. Catalog No. 39, 1974-75. Available from Encyclopaedia Britannica Education Corporation, 425 N. Michigan Ave., Chicago, IL 60611.
4. Carousel Film Catalog. Available from Carousel Films, Inc., 1501 Broadway,

Suite 1503, New York, NY 10036.

5. *Coronet Films*. Available from Coronet Instructional Media, 65 East South Water St., Chicago, IL 60601.

6. Eccentric Circle Film Catalog. Available from Eccentric Circle, P.O. Box 1481, Evanston, IL 60204.

7. *Educational Motion Pictures*. Available from Indiana University, Audio-Visual Center, Bloomington, IN 47401, Attention: NET Film Service.

8. *Film and Multi-Media Catalog: Mass Media*. Available from Mass Media, 1720 Chouteau Ave., St. Louis, MO 63103.

9. Film Images Catalog. Available from Film Images, A Division of Radim Films, Inc., 17 West 60th St., New York, NY 10023.

10. *Film List: Center for Teaching International Relations*. Available from Colorado Division, UNA-USA-UNESCO, 1600 Logan St., Denver, CO 80203.

11. *Films for Junior and Senior High School Social Studies*. Available from Indiana University, Audio-Visual Center, Bloomington, IN 47401.

12. *Films on the Future: A Selective Listing*. Available from World Future Society, P.O. Box 30369, Bethesda Branch, Washington, D.C. 20014.

13. Gilbert Films Catolog. Available from Gilbert Films, Erector Square, New Haven, CT 06506.

14. *Guidance Associates Instructional Media Catalog: Social Studies 1975* (section on "Motion Media"). Available from Guidance Associates/Motion Media, 757 Third Ave., New York, NY 10017.

15. *Learning Corporation of America: Searching for Values: A Film Anthology*. Available from Learning Corporation of America, 711 Fifth Ave., New York, NY 10022.

16. *Lifelong Learning Films,* 44 (March 31, 1975). Available from Lifelong Learning, University Extension, University of California, Berkeley, CA 94720.

17. *Mountain Plains Educational Media Council, Film Catalog*. Available from University of Colorado, Bureau of Audiovisual Instruction, Boulder, CO 80302, Attention: Booking Clerk.

18. *NBC Educational Enterprises: 16mm Film Catalog. 1974-1975*. Available from NBC Educational Enterprises, 30 Rockefeller Plaza, New York, NY 10020.

19. New Day Films Catalog. Available from New Day Films, P.O. Box 315, Franklin Lakes, NJ 07417.

20. Perennial Education Film Catalog. Available from Perennial Education, Inc., 1825 Willow Rd., P.O. Box 236, Northfield, IL 60093.

21. *Perspective Films: Unique Visual Statements on the World Around Us*. Available from Perspective Films, 369 West Erie St., Chicago, IL 60610.

22. *Pictura 16mm Educational Film Catalog*. Available from Pictura Film Distribution Corporation, 43 West 16th St., New York, NY 10011.

23. *Pyramid Films*. Available from Pyramid Films, Box 1048, Santa Monica, CA 90406.

24. *Sterling Educational Films Catalog*. Available from Sterling Educational Films, A Division of the Walter Reade Organization, Inc., 241 East 34th St., New York, NY 10016.

25. *Time Life Films Catalog*. Available from Time Life Films, 43 West 16th St., New York, NY 10011.

26. *United Nations Films and Filmstrips Catalog*. Available from Colorado Division, UNA-USA-UNESCO, 1600 Logan St., Denver, CO 80203.

27. *Wombat Productions Film Catalogs: Films that Reach*. Available from Wombat Productions, Inc., 77 Tarrytown Rd., White Plains, NY 10607.

28. *Wombat Productions: Your 1974-'75 Catalog Update*. Available from Wombat Productions, Inc., 77 Tarrytown Rd., White Plains, NY 10607.

G. Selected Documents on Values Education in the ERIC System

1. Allen, Rodney F. "But the Earth Abideth Forever: Values in Environmental Education." No date. ED 099 300.

2. Bradley, R. C. "Values and Reading." Paper presented at the Annual Convention of the International Reading Association, New Orleans, 1974. ED 088 007.

3. Burgess, Evangeline. *Values in Early Childhood Education*. Washington, D.C.: National Education Association, 1965. ED 088 565.

4. Casteel, J. Doyle, *et al. The Science Observation Record: A Theoretical Model Relevant to Value Clarification in Mathematics, Science, and Social Studies*. Gainesville, FL: Institute for Development of Human Resources, University of Flordia, 1974. ED 093 959.

5. Christopher, Lochie B., and Orvis A. Harrelson, eds. *Inside Out: A Guide for Teachers*. Bloomington, IN: National Instructional Television Center, 1973. ED 081 199.

6. Del Prete, Richard P., and Peter P. Twining. "Value Development Employment Module." 1973. ED 091 645.

7. DeMarte, Patrick J., and Margo I. Sorgman. "A Pilot Study to Investigate the Effects of Courses in Humanistic Education on the Self-Perceptions of Preservice Teachers." Paper presented at the annual meeting of the National Council for the Social Studies, San Francisco, November 1973. ED 090 109.

8. Denys, Larry. "Beyond Progress and Development." 1972. ED 068 434.

9. Dubois, Sheilagh, ed. *Values in the Curriculum*. Windsor, Ontario, Canada: Ontario Association for Curriculum Development Annual Conference, 1971. ED 081 965.

10. *Education for Student Concerns. Affective Education Research Project*. Philadelphia, PA: Office of Curriculum and Instruction, Phildelphia School District, 1968. ED 093 725.

11. *Focus on Man: A Prospectus. Social Studies for Utah Schools.* Salt Lake City, UT: Utah State Board of Education, 1971. ED 065 383.

12. Fraenkel, Jack R. "Teacher Approaches to the Resolution of Value Conflicts." Paper presented at the annual meeting of the National Council for Social Studies, Boston, November 1972. ED 092 445.

13. Fraenkel, Jack R. "Values: Do We or Don't We Teach Them?" 1971. ED 065 388.

14. Frank, Peter R. "An Effective Approach to Drug Education." Paper presented at the annual meeting of the American Educational Research Association, Chicago, 1974. ED 092 823.

15. Frost, Reuben B., and Edward J. Sims, eds. *Development of Human Values Through Sports.* Washington, D.C.: American Alliance for Health, Physical Education, and Recreation, 1974. ED 099 352.

16. Greenberg, Polly, and Bea Epstein. *Bridge-To-Reading. Section 3: Feelings, Thoughts, Understandings, Solving Problems, Values.* Morristown, NJ: General Learning Corporation, 1973. ED 093 489.

17. *A Guide to Selected Curriculum Materials on Interdependence, Conflict, and Change: Teacher Comments on Classroom Use and Implementation.* Denver, CO: Center for War/Peace Studies; and New York, NY: New York Friends Group, Inc., 1973. ED 096 236.

18. Holdrege, Craig, *et al. Sunshine Unfolding.* Boulder, CO: Social Science Education Consortium, 1972. ED 081 708.

19. *Humanities III: The Future of Man.* Wilmington, DE: Stanton School District, 1971. ED 065 431.

20. Jones, John A. "The Curriculum Accommodation Questionnaire, Form S." Paper presented at the annual meeting of the American Educational Research Association, Chicago, 1974. ED 091 437.

21. Jones, John A. "Validation of the Curriculum Accommodation Questionnaire." Paper presented at the annual meeting of the American Educational Research Association, Chicago, 1974. ED 091 436.

22. Kerlinger, Fred N. "The Study and Measurement of Values and Attitudes." Paper presented at the annual meeting of the American Educational Research Association, Chicago, 1972. ED 079 618.

23. Kingman, Barry. *The Development of Value Clarification Skills: Initial Efforts in an Eighth Grade Social Studies Class.* Occasional Paper 74-3. Stony Brook, NY: American Historical Association History Education Project, State University of New York, 1974. ED 090 128.

24. Kuhmerker, Lisa. "We Don't Call It Moral Education: American Children Learn About Values." 1973. ED 092 467.

25. Leming, James S. "An Empirical Examination of Key Assumptions Underlying the Kohlberg Rationale for Moral Education." Paper presented at the annual meeting of the American Educational Research Association, Chicago, 1974. ED 093 749.

26. Madison, John P. "An Analysis of Values and Social Action in Multi-Racial Children's Literature." Unpublished doctoral dissertation. Urbana, IL: University of Illinois, 1972. ED 083 611.

27. *Man and His Relationship to the Natural and Cultural Environment: The United States. A Resource Guide*. Honolulu, HI: Office of Instructional Services, Hawaii State Department of Education, 1972. ED 091 268.

28. *Man's Changing Values and a World Culture–New Directions and New Emphases for Educational Programs: A Report on the 1971 Phi Delta Kappa Conference on World Education*. Glassboro, NJ: Phi Delta Kappa, 1971. ED 079 190.

29. Meux, Milton, *et al*. *The Development of a Value Observation System for Group Discussion in Decision Making: Final Report*. Salt Lake City, UT: University of Utah, 1972. ED 066 389.

30. Molnar, Alex. "Modes of Values Thinking in Curriculum." Paper presented at the annual meeting of the Association for Supervision and Curriculum Development, Minneapolis, 1973. ED 077 131.

31. *Moral Education: Development of a Model. Final Report*. Princeton, NJ: Educational Testing Service, 1972. ED 085 285.

32. Mukerji, Rose, and Ruth S. Pollak. *Ripples* and *Guide for Ripples*. Bloomington, IN: National Instructional Television Center, 1971. ED 079 987.

33. Murphy, Patricia D., *et al*. *Consumer Education Curriculum Modules: A Spiral-Process Approach. 2. Valuing Process*. Fargo, ND: College of Home Economics, North Dakota State University, 1974. ED 095 269.

34. Olmo, Barbara G. "Values Education in the New Jersey Secondary Curriculum." 1974. ED 099 263.

35. Pracejus, Eleanor L. *The Effect of Value Clarification on Reading Comprehension*. Ann Arbor, MI: University Microfilms, 1974. ED 098 557.

36. *Project Social Studies: Twelve Grade Units*. Minneapolis, MN: Minnesota University, 1967-68. ED 083 103, 083 104, 083 105, 083 106, 083 108, 083 109, 083 110.

37. Ruud, Josephine B. *Teaching for Changed Attitudes and Values*. Washington, D.C.: Home Economics Education Association, 1971. ED 078 203.

38. Satterlie, Arthur L. *Human Dignity Through History*. Vallejo, CA: Vallejo Unified School District, 1971. ED 066 397.

39. Schmidt, Fran, and Grace Adams. *American Culture, Social Studies, Language Arts: 6426.01*. Miami, FL: Dade County Public Schools, 1971. ED 070 685.

40. Troyer, Maurice E., *et al*. "Purposes, Processes, and Consequences of Three Space 1-unit Seminars on the Nature and Meaning of Values." Paper presented at the annual meeting of the American Educational Research Association, New Orleans, 1973. ED 077 797.

41. Ubbelohde, Robert. "Value Problems and Curriculum Decisions." Paper presented at the annual meeting of the Association for Supervision and Curriculum Development, Minneapolis, 1973. ED 075 926.

42. Vuicich, George, and Joseph Stoltman. *Geography in Elementary and Secondary Education: Tradition to Opportunity*. Boulder, CO: ERIC Clearinghouse for Social Studies/Social Science Education; Social Science Education Consortium, Inc., 1974. ED 097 243.

43. Wells, Leora Wood. *The Acquisition and Development of Values: Perspectives on Research*. Bethesda, MD: National Institute of Child Health and Human Development, National Institutes of Health, 1968. ED 066 414.

44. Whitehurst, Keturah E. "Techniques and Processes of Socialization of the Black Child." Paper presented at the Institute in the Black Perspective, Washington, D.C., 1972. ED 097 963.

H. Selected Articles on Values Education from Educational Journals

(Annotations are from ERIC's Current Index to Journals in Education.)

1. Allen, Rodney F. "Student Concerns and Commitments." *Social Education,* 38 (April 1974) pp. 349-355.

   This article suggests activity in which students examine life-style implications of diverse commitments and values in order to help them deal with both social and personal concerns.

2. Alley, Louis E. "Athletics in Education: The Double-Edged Sword." *Phi Delta Kappan,* 56 (October 1974) pp. 102-105, 113.

   School athletics can be an exceedingly potent tool for developing desirable behavior patterns—but only if directed by coaches of resolute integrity. Illustrative anecdotes are offered.

3. Berdie, Ralph F., *et al.* "And Man Created God in His Own Image." *Counseling and Values,* 19 (October 1974) pp. 10-18.

   This study explores the hypothesis that there is "a positive relationship between an individual's self-concept and his concept of God." The article is followed by a contrary opinion by R. B. Nordberg and by the author's rejoinder.

4. Betof, Edward H., and Howard Kirschenbaum. "A Valuing Approach." *School Health Review,* 5 (January/February 1974) pp. 13-14.

   The article describes the use of facts, concepts, and values in teaching students the importance of feeling, thinking, choosing, and acting in their daily lives.

5. Boggs, David L. "An Interpretive Review of Social Science Research on Behaving-Valuing Patterns of Low Status People." *Adult Education,* 24 (Summer 1974) pp. 293-312.

   This study is an inductive analysis of the relationship between stated purposes for adult education programs and the behaving-valuing process of potential low-status clients as revealed in social science research.

6. Cogan, John, and John H. Litcher. "Social Studies after Curriculum Reform: Some Unfinished Business." *Elementary School Journal,* 75 (October 1974) pp. 55-61.

   The need for a coordinated approach to social studies curriculum development is discussed. Issues to be considered include goals, personalizing programs through active learner participation, human-centered programs, values and the valuing process, a broadening of the range of content resources available, and the teacher education program.

7. Crabtree, Walden. "Establishing Policy in the Values Education Controversy." *Contemporary Education,* 46 (February 1974) pp. 24-27.

   This article offers a brief description of some values education programs in order to clarify reactions to criticisms of these efforts to educate for character.

8. Dalis, Gus T., and Ben B. Strasser. "The Starting Point for Values Education." *School Health Review,* 5 (January/February 1974) pp. 2-5.

9. Della Pave, L. Richard. "Success Values: Are They Universal or Class-Differentiated?" *American Journal of Sociology,* 80 (July 1974) pp. 153-169.

   This study, using Hyman Rodman's concept *value stretch* in an attempt to resolve the long-standing controversy over the existence of universal versus class-differentiated success values in American society, surveys white boys from four Massachusetts high schools.

10. Dickens, Mary Ellen. "Values, Schools, and Human Development." *Clearing House,* 48 (April 1974) pp. 473-77.

    How are values imparted to children? Are they taught? Are they learned by example? What is the appropriate role for the school? And so these questions go on. The author offers some thoughts on this subject.

11. Dillman, Phillip L. "The Humanities at Pine Crest School." *Humanities Journal,* 8 (December 1974) pp. 5-9.

    This secondary humanities curriculum is based on four assumptions: the humanities are for all students; they must be interdisciplinary and presented through multimedia; they must deal with real issues affectively as well as cognitively; and they must involve value judgments and decision making.

12. Dreischmeier, William B. "Teaching for a Change in Attitude: Values Clarification." *Agricultural Education Magazine,* 47 (December 1974) pp. 129-130, 136.

    According to this article teachers need to do more to help students in the process of value development.

13. Edwards, Larry W. "Elementary School Students Should Make Value Judgments." *Music Educators Journal,* 61 (September 1974) pp. 40-44.

    The article discusses a guide to a curriculum through which school children can develop their sensitivity and independence.

14. Farrell, Edmund J. "Choosing Values and Valuing Choices." *ADE Bulletin,* 40 (March 1974) pp. 51-56.

    The role of teaching and of teachers in determining and asserting our values and in exploring alternatives and their consequences is discussed.

15. "Focusing on Everyday Problems: Consumer Education." *Social Education,* 38 (October 1974) pp. 500-505.

    Suggestions for incorporating consumer awareness into the usual civics or government courses are made with reference to values clarification and the needs and experiences of the student.

16. Forbes, Jack D. "The Americanization of Education in the United States." *Indian Historian,* 7 (September 1974) pp. 15-21.

The goals of education for Native Americans should be based upon the development of the individual and the maintenance or re-establishment of the native community in harmony with the universe (the Powhatan Goals of Education), according to this article.

17. Forcinelli, Joseph, and Thomas S. Engeman. "Value Education in the Public School." *Thrust for Education Leadership,* 4 (October 1974) pp. 13-16.

The authors attempt to give the reader a general understanding of the basis and goals of value-oriented programs in addition to considering their practical applicability in the classroom.

18. Galbraith, Ronald E., and Thomas M. Jones. "Teaching Strategies for Moral Dilemmas: An Application of Kohlberg's Theory of Moral Development to the Social Studies Classroom." *Social Education,* 39 (January 1975) pp. 16-22.

An outline of Lawrence Kohlberg's theory of cognitive moral development prefaces an application of the teaching plan developed by the Social Studies Curriculum Center at Carnegie-Mellon University for leading discussions of moral dilemmas.

19. Genge, Betty Anne, and John J. Santosuosso. "Values Clarification for Ecology." *Science Teacher,* 41 (February 1974) pp. 37-39.

A value clarification exercise developed for a unit on pollution is presented. In it students are given or prepare a number of items to rate from desirable to undesirable or from undesirable toward desirable.

20. Goodman, Arnold M. "Potential for Growth and Development: A Rabbinic View." *Counseling and Values,* 19 (October 1974) pp. 30-35.

According to the author the entire thrust of the Jewish Rabbinic Tradition is to accept the reality of development. Behavior reflects values, and values come from the study of the Torah.

21. Graves, Clare W. "Human Nature Prepares for a Momentous Leap." *Futurist,* 8 (April 1974) pp. 72-87.

A psychological theory that holds that human beings live at different levels of existence contains implications for education, management, and social services.

22. Gray, James U. "A Teaching Strategy for Clarifying Aesthetic Values." *Art Education,* 27 (October 1974) pp. 11-14.

The purpose of this article is to demonstrate that important aspects of aesthetic education are neither technical nor abstruse and that elementary school teachers particularly can develop in children an openness to aesthethic experience.

23. Greenberg, Herbert J. "The Objectives of Mathematics Education." *Mathematics Teacher,* 67 (November 1974) pp. 639-643.

Literacy, values, and—stemming from these—purposeful action are seen as the basic and inseparable educational objectives. The mathematics curriculum, behavioral objectives, and the affective domain are discussed in light of these. Statements from various national committees and advisory boards are included.

24. Hinkemeyer, Michael T. "Societal Values: A Challenge to the Curriculum

Specialist.'' *Social Studies,* 65 (March 1974) pp. 114-18.

The challenge to the curriculum specialist is to determine objectives for citizenship that consider the varied democratic principles and societal value demands and to create a cooperative professional relationship between college-level and school-level curriculum specialists.

25. Hobbs, Jack. ''The Problem of Language and Values in Aesthetic Education.'' *Studies in Art Education,* 15 (February 1973) pp. 5-9.

26. Hopp, Joyce W. ''VC for Sixth Graders.'' *School Health Review,* 5 (January/February 1974) pp. 34-35.

    This article describes the use of values clarification in teaching sixth graders health education.

27. Huggins, Kenneth B. ''Alternatives in Values Clarification.'' *National Elementary Principal,* 54 (November/December 1974) pp. 76-79.

    Within a carefully structured situation, students can be allowed greater choice than they now have. This can be accomplished without making them feel lost and confused. The balance between direction and freely offered alternatives is a delicate one, but the teacher need not be afraid of it.

28. Kneer, Marian E. ''How Human Are You? Exercises in Awareness.'' *Journal of Health, Physical Education and Recreation,* 45 (June 1974) pp. 32-34.

    The author sees teacher value awareness as a prerequisite for humanism in teaching. A values inventory from the book *Values Clarification* by Simon, Howe, and Kirschenbaum is included.

29. Kniker, Charles R. ''The Values of Athletics in Schools: A Continuing Debate.'' *Phi Delta Kappan,* 56 (October 1974) pp. 116-120.

    Neither the proponents nor the critics of athletics can offer substantial evidence to prove that athletics per se are either beneficial or harmful. A summary of the research to date is presented.

30. Koch, Susan. ''Technology, Television, and Values.'' *English Journal,* 63 (October 1974) pp. 24-25.

    Teachers must develop an ethical perspective on the uses of technology, according to this article.

31. Kuhn, David J. ''Value Education in the Sciences: The Step Beyond Concepts and Processes.'' *School Science and Mathematics,* 74 (November 1974) pp. 583-88.

32. Liles, Jesse. ''A Dilemma of Teaching Values to Young Children.'' *Contemporary Education,* 45 (Summer 1974) pp. 296-98.

33. Matson, Hollis N. ''Values: How and From Where?'' *School Health Review,* 5 (January/February 1974) pp. 36-38.

34. Matthews, Esther. ''Values and Counseling: One Perspective.'' *Counseling and Values,* 19 (October 1974) pp. 37-41.

    The author maintains that counselors must design their services around the development and clarification of values in an environment conducive to human growth.

35. McAulay, J. D. "Values and Elementary Social Studies." *Social Studies,* 65 (February 1974) pp. 61-64.

An elementary social studies program should help a child develop an awareness of significant personal social values. Values pertinent to the child from age four to 11 are pointed out. Four principal activities in which the child must engage to develop each of these values into behavioral patterns are discussed.

36. McGrath, Earl J. "Careers, Values and General Education." *Liberal Education,* 60 (October 1974) pp. 281-303.

The three functions of the undergraduate college relate to careers, values, and general education, and the willingness of most independent colleges to provide these services will determine their survival.

37. Mitchell, John J. "More Dilemmas of Early Adolescence." *School Counselor,* 22 (September 1974) pp. 16-22.

Some of the moral dilemmas facing adolescents and some problems counselors face when dealing with adolescents are discussed. In particular, the author mentions the difficulty of distinguishing normal developmental growing pains from personality disturbance.

38. Moon, Linda Lee. "Search for Self—The Counselor in the Classroom." *School Counselor,* 22 (November 1974) pp. 121-23.

In an effort to humanize education and counseling, the author relates experiences with a nine-week course entitled "Search for Self," which was team-taught by another teacher and herself. Both the literature and the group activities centered around trustbuilding, communication skills, strengthbuilding, values clarification, and selfstudy.

39. Osman, Jack D. "The Use of Selected Value-Clarifying Strategies in Health Education." *Journal of School Health,* 44 (January 1974) pp. 21-25.

The results of this investigation combined with feedback from students leads to the conclusion that the use of selected value-clarifying strategies in a health education course for future teachers is feasible. Strategies include value sheets and thought cards.

40. Osman, Jack D. "Value Growth Through Drug Education." *School Health Review,* 5 (January/February 1974) pp. 25-30.

41. Ozbek, Nicky and R. Forehand. "Factors Influencing the Moral Judgment of Retardates." *Journal of Mental Deficiency Research,* 17 (September/December 1973) pp. 255-261.

42. Perron, Jacques. "Les Valeurs en education: Vers un portrait psycho-social de l'étudiant Quebeçois." *Canadian Counsellor,* 8 (January 1974) pp. 23-35.

This article presents a psychological definition of values and defines ways of measuring them. It also reports results of a study dealing with the evolution of educational values of different groups of students at high school and college levels (N=400) and a comparison between the students' values and those of a group of teachers.

43. Pine, Gerald, and Angelo Boy. "Counseling and the Quest for Values." *Counsel-*

ing and Values, 19 (October 1974) pp. 42-47.

No field of endeavor that touches human lives can afford to leave its philosophical presuppositions unexamined. The psychologically whole counselor lives his values as well as reflects on them. This article discusses this ongoing process of forming values as it relates to counseling.

44. Raisner, Arnold. ''The Left Hand of Science.'' *Science and Children,* 11 (May 1974) pp. 7-9.

    The author suggests that science instruction should allow students to see science not only as a technical speciality of geniuses but also as a legitimate feature of every man's daily concerns and a tool for the development of moral and social values.

45. Raymond, Boris. ''A Sword with Two Edges: The Role of Children's Literature in the Writings of N.K. Krupskaia.'' *Library Quarterly,* 44 (July 1974) pp. 206-218.

    This article focuses on the use of children's books for instilling prevailing moral, political, and social values in children, particularly in Russia.

46. Rest, James. ''Developmental Psychology as a Guide to Value Education: A Review of 'Kohlbergian' Programs.'' *Review of Educational Research,* 44 (Spring 1974) pp. 241-259.

    Consideration is given to the way in which the foundational ideas of Kohlberg, Dewey, and Piaget have been extended in educational practice in relation to the way in which conclusions from research are used to guide program construction.

47. Ruiz, Eleazar M. ''Want to Combat Drugs? Try the PCT Approach.'' *Journal of Drug Education,* 4 (Spring 1974) pp. 111-17.

    The Parent-Child-Teacher Approach, through the Interactive Learning Process Model, provides a philosophical orientation which allows viable communication to occur among parents, students, and teachers in resolving serious people-related drug problems. It focuses on the dilemma faced by youth who must adjust to their peer-group value system and also cope with that of the home and the school.

48. Samples, Robert E. ''Value-Prejudice: Toward A Personal Awareness.'' *Law in American Society,* 3 (November 1974) pp. 32-37.

    A few techniques are suggested for the use of teachers and students to increase the level of personal awareness and to receive a picture of values and prejudices.

49. Schlaadt, Richard G. ''Implementing the Values Clarification Process.'' *School Health Review,* 5 (January/February 1974) pp. 10-12.

50. Schmidtlein, Frank A. ''Decision Process Paradigms in Education.'' *Educational Researcher,* 3 (May 1974) pp. 4-11.

    The article illustrates and describes the historical roots and major characteristics, including environmental conditions and value orientation dilemmas, of two competing models of organizational decision making used in educational operations and research and development: the comprehensive/prescriptive paradigm and the incremental/remedial paradigm.

51. ''Section II: Dealing with Conflict—The Element of Personal Choice: Personal Choice in the American Revolution.'' *Social Education,* 38 (February 1974) pp. 132-153.

An introductory and a negotiations exercise offer activities related to the choices open to the participants in the American Revolution. The choices are discussed from the viewpoint of Roger Fisher, a law professor.

52. "Section III: Examining American Values: Value Choices Since Revolutionary Times." *Social Education,* 38 (February 1974) pp. 154-173.

    The statements of Erik Erickson and Urie Bronfenbrenner on American values are followed by a values clarification exercise and an activity based on biographical sketches of five Americans who lived before and after the American Revolution.

53. Shannon, John R. "Help Basic Business Students Identify Their Values." *Business Education Forum,* 29 (November 1974) pp. 26-27.

54. Shuman, R. Baird. "Values and the Teaching of Literature." *Clearing House,* 47 (December 1973) pp. 232-38.

    The article discusses the study of literature as a means of understanding the techniques of literature as well as helping students to understand themselves.

55. Strong, William. "Unself." *Media and Methods,* 11 (November 1974) pp. 8-16, 56-57.

    The author maintains that personal happiness and social cohesion depend on individuals' committing themselves to something larger than themselves—a cause or the ideal of helping others.

56. Taichinov, M. B., and Kh. Kh. Ianbulatov. "The Role of Words in the Moral Education of School Pupils." *Soviet Education,* 17 (November 1974) pp. 66-81.

    The special role of words in the formation of moral consciousness and behavior is explored.

57. Thurner, Majda, *et al.* "Value Confluence and Behavioral Conflict in Intergenerational Relations." *Journal of Marriage and the Family,* 36 (May 1974) pp. 308-318.

    The author describes findings of an investigation of values and interpersonal perceptions of high school seniors and parents of high school seniors. The findings support the notion that there is relatively little value conflict and that the "generation gap" within middle- and lower-middle-class families is largely a myth.

58. Warren, Carrie L. "Value Strategies in Mental Health." *School Health Review,* 5 (January/February 1974) pp. 22-24.

59. Yawkey, T. D., and E. L. Aronin. "The Living Circle Approach in the Social Studies." *Social Studies,* 65 (February 1974) pp. 71-75.

    Social studies programs are increasing their focus upon social and interpersonal awareness. This article discusses the teacher's role in teaching about values in social studies classes at the primary and secondary levels. The technique known as the "living circle," or "group guidance," is explained.

60. Yogeshananda, Swami. "Moral Education: A Hindu View." *Journal of Moral Education,* 3 (February 1974) pp. 135-36.

    The article investigates the possibility of teaching a nonsectarian morality in the multicultural school while benefiting Muslim, Humanist, Hindu, and Jew.

61. Young, David P. "Science and Values Belong Together." *Journal of College Science Teaching,* 4 (November 1974) pp. 111-13.

Three courses designed to bring science and values together in the science classroom are described.

62. Zosimovskii, A. V. "Age-Related Characteristics in the Moral Development of Children." *Soviet Education,* 17 (November 1974) pp. 5-21.

A more precise picture of the characteristics of the moral development of children in the Soviet Union is offered in a scheme of classification of development according to age.

afterword

Two decades ago few educators were advocating or providing ways for dealing directly with values in the social studies classrooms. A decade later many social studies educators were putting forth eloquent, reasoned pleas for teachers to help students work with values and value issues in school. Usually these rationales included explanations of one or more of the following factors: the rapid rate of social change, the wide range of value alternatives available to young people in our modern society, the mind-boggling developments related to ecology and nuclear destruction, and the failure to other institutions to deal effectively with the value confusion and conflict among youth. At that time, however, few educators offered any specific methods, activities, or materials to achieve the aim. Since then a vast amount of curriculum and teacher background materials in values education has been developed and distributed. Thus, while there was a dearth of resources to help teachers work with values in the classroom ten years ago, a large number of materials now exists, making it extremely difficult for teachers to review and select values education resources thoughtfully and carefully. Educators must now begin to focus their energies on comprehending, evaluating, and using these materials more purposefully and effectively.

This publication is one effort to help with these tasks. The central aims of our work have been to collect, organize, and analyze the vast number of materials in values education and to communicate this information so that educators can evaluate and choose resources that are most appropriate for their needs. We have attempted to achieve these objectives by providing the following: a typology of major values education approaches, a framework for analyzing values education materials, analyses for 84 sets of materials, three preliminary exercises to help educators determine their priorities in relation to approaches and materials, and a bibliography, largely annotated, of more than 400 resources in values education.

We realize that these items will not solve all the problems involved in dealing with such a large quantity of materials. We also realize that there are other critical problems that must be confronted in values education upon which this book has not even touched. Two of these are briefly discussed below as recommendations for other efforts needed in values education.

One need with which this book has dealt only slightly is for more and better ways to evaluate student growth in values education. Because of the twin trends toward accountability and a return to traditional education, teachers must be able to obtain evidence that efforts at teaching values and valuing skills have been successful. From the evaluative data sections of the analyses in Chapters II-VI, one can see that the availability of quality instruments and techniques to evaluate values growth varies according to the approach. While few instruments exist to measure clarification and action learning objectives, several complicated systems have been devised for inculcation and moral development. Proponents of the former approaches should devote their energies to developing better evaluation procedures. Educators from the latter two approaches need to make their systems simpler and more usable.

A second vital need is for experienced, qualified, and committed persons to work with teachers and students on a long-term, in-depth basis in establishing, maintaining, and improving values education programs and values education within existing programs. One-, two-, or even five-day workshops are insufficient. These persons must be willing to work throughout the year for several years in order to help teachers on a concrete, realistic basis to develop the approaches and valuing activities most suited to their instructional styles and needs. Charles Kniker at Iowa State University (Ames, Iowa) is one educator who has been engaged in such an effort. The result of his work, including guidelines for building one's own approach to values education, will be published soon. More efforts like this are needed if the many curriculum materials designed to teach values and valuing are to be used effectively.

references

Adler, Alfred. *The Practice and Theory of Individual Psychology*. New York, NY: Harcourt Brace Jovanovich, 1924.

Adler, Franz. "The Value Concept in Sociology." *American Journal of Sociology,* 62 (November 1956) pp. 272-79.

Allport, Gordon. *Becoming: Basic Considerations for a Psychology of Personality*. New Haven, CT: Yale University Press, 1955.

Asch, Solomon E. *Social Psychology*. Englewood Cliffs, NJ: Prentice-Hall, 1952.

Assagioli, Robert. *Psychosynthesis*. New York, NY: Viking, 1971.

Ayer, Alfred Jules. *Language, Truth, and Logic*. London, England: Victor Gollancy, 1946.

Banks, James A. *Teaching Strategies for the Social Studies: Inquiry, Valuing, Decision Making*. Reading, MA: Addison-Wesley, 1973.

Bensley, Marvin L. *Coronado Plan: Teacher's Guides*. San Diego, CA: Pennant, 1974.

Berlak, Harold, and Timothy R. Tomlinson. *The Development of a Model for the Metropolitan St. Louis Social Studies Center*. Final Report, Project No. Z-004. St. Louis, MO: Washington University, 1967. ED 012 390.

Bigge, Morris L. *Positive Relativism: An Emergent Educational Philosophy*. New York, NY: Harper and Row, 1971.

Blackham, H. J. *Humanism*. Baltimore,MD: Penguin, 1968.

Blanchette, Zelda Beth, *et al. The Human Values Series*. Austin, TX: Steck-Vaughn, 1970, 1973.

Blatt, Moshe. "The Effects of Classroom Discussion Programs upon Children's Level of Moral Development." Unpublished doctoral dissertation. Chicago, IL: University of Chicago, 1969.

Blumer, Herbert. *Symbolic Interactionism: Perspective and Method*. Englewood Cliffs, NJ: Prentice-Hall, 1969.

Bond, David J. "A Doctoral Thesis: An Analysis of Valuation Strategies in Social Science Education Materials." Unpublished doctoral dissertation. Berkeley, CA: School of Education, University of California, 1970.

Brown, George. *Human Teaching for Human Learning: An Introduction to Confluent Education*. New York, NY: Viking, 1971.

Bugenthal, J. F. T. *The Search for Authenticity*. New York, NY: Holt, Rinehart and Winston, 1965.

Bull, Norman J. *Moral Education*. Beverly Hills, CA: Sage, 1969.

Canning, Jeremiah W., ed. *Values in an Age of Confrontation*. Columbus, OH: Charles E. Merrill, 1970.

Chapman, Marian L. "Skills for Ethical Action Instructional Materials: An Overview." Philadelphia, PA: Humanizing Learning Program, Research for Better Schools, 1975.

Charles, Cheryl, and Ronald Stadsklev, eds. *Learning with Games: An Analysis of Social Studies Educational Games and Simulations*. Boulder, CO: Social Science Education Consortium, 1972.

Church, John G. *The Social Sciences: Concepts and Values. A Probe into Values*. New York, NY: Harcourt Brace Jovanovich, 1973.

Combs, Arthur W., and Donald Snygg. *Individual Behavior: A Perceptual Approach.* New York, NY: Harper and Row, 1949.

Crampton, Martha. "Some Applications of Psychosynthesis in the Educational Field." In *Four Psychologies Applied to Education: Freudian, Behavioral, Humanistic, and Transpersonal,* Thomas B. Roberts, ed. New York, NY: Wiley, 1975, pp. 453-462.

Dewey, John. *Theory of Valuation (International Encyclopedia of Unified Science,* Vol. II). Chicago, IL: University of Chicago, 1939.

Drews, Elizabeth M., and Leslie Lipson. *Values and Humanity.* New York, NY: St. Martins, 1971.

Driscoll, Francis. "TM as a Secondary School Subject." *Phi Delta Kappan,* 54 (December 1972) pp. 236-37.

Dukes, William F. "Psychological Studies of Values." *Psychological Bulletin,* 3 (1955) pp. 24-50.

Dunfee, Maxine, and Claudia Crump. *Teaching for Social Values in Social Studies.* Washington, D.C.: Association for Childhood Education International, 1974.

Ellis, Albert. *Reason and Emotion in Psychotherapy.* New York, NY: Lyle Stuart, 1962.

Erikson, Erik H. *Childhood and Society.* New York, NY: W. W. Norton, 1950.

Essence I and *Essence II.* Menlo Park, CA: Addison-Wesley, 1971, 1975.

Evans, W. Keith, *et al. Rational Value Decisions and Value Conflict Resolution: A Handbook for Teachers.* Salt Lake City, UT: Granite School District, 1974.

Foster, Arthur L. "Valuing as Religious Experience." In *Values in an Age of Confrontation,* Jeremiah W. Canning, ed. Columbus, OH: Charles E. Merrill, 1970, pp. 119-123.

Fraenkel, Jack. *Helping Students Think and Value.* Englewood Cliffs, NJ: Prentice-Hall, 1973.

Fromm, Erich. *Man for Himself: An Inquiry into the Psychology of Ethics.* New York, NY: Holt, Rinehart and Winston, 1947.

Galbraith, Ronald E., and Thomas M. Jones. "Teaching Strategies for Moral Dilemmas: An Application of Kohlberg's Theory of Moral Development to the Social Studies Classroom." *Social Education,* 39 (January 1975) pp. 16-22.

Gelatt, H. B., *et al. Decisions and Outcomes.* New York, NY: College Entrance Examination Board, 1973.

Goodykoontz, William. *Contact.* New York, NY: Scholastic Book Services, 1968-74.

Handy, Rollo. *Value Theory and the Behavioral Sciences.* Springfield, IL: Charles C. Thomas, 1969.

Harman, Willis W. "Experience with a Graduate Seminar on Personal Growth." In *Approaches to Education for Character,* Clarence H. Faust and Jessica Feingold, eds. New York, NY: Columbia University Press, 1969, pp. 301-314.

Harmin, Merrill, *et. al. Clarifying Values Through Subject Matter: Applications for the Classroom.* Minneapolis, MN: Winston, 1973.

Harvey, O. J., D. E. Hunt, and H. M. Schroder. *Conceptual Systems and Personality Organization.* New York, NY: Wiley, 1961.

Hawley, Robert C. *Human Values in the Classroom: Teaching for Personal and Social Growth.* Amherst, MA: Education Research Associates, 1973.

Hawley, Robert C., *et al. Composition for Personal Growth: Values Clarification Through Writing.* New York, NY: Hart, 1973.

Horney, Karen. *Neurosis and Human Growth.* New York, NY: W. W. Norton, 1950.

Hunt, Maurice P., and Lawrence E. Metcalf. *Teaching High School Social Studies.* New York, NY: Harper, 1968.

Inhelder, Barbel, and Jean Piaget. *The Growth of Logical Thinking from Childhood to Adolescence.* New York, NY: Basic Books, 1958.

Jones, W. Ron. *Finding Community: A Guide to Community Research and Action.* Palo Alto, CA: James E. Freel, 1971.

Jung, Carl G. *The Integration of the Personality.* New York, NY: Farrar and Rinehart, 1939.

Kelly, George A. *The Psychology of Personal Constructs.* New York, NY: W. W. Norton, 1955.

Kirschenbaum, Howard. *Recent Research in Values Clarification.* Upper Jay, NY: National Humanistic Education Center, 1974.

Kluckhohn, Clyde. "Values and Value-Orientations in the Theory of Action: An Explanation in Definition and Classification." In *Toward a General Theory of Action,* Talcott Parsons and Edward A. Shils, eds. Cambridge, MA: Harvard University Press, 1951, pp. 388-433.

Kohlberg, Lawrence. "Moral Education in the Schools: A Developmental View." *School Review,* 74 (1966) pp. 1-20.

Kohlberg, Lawrence, with Phillip Whitten. "Understanding the Hidden Curriculum." *Learning, the Magazine for Creative Teaching,* 1 (December 1972) pp. 10-14.

Kohlberg, Lawrence, and Robert Selman. *First Things: Values.* New York, NY: Guidance Associates, 1970.

Kohlberg, Lawrence, *et al.* *"The Justice Structure of the Prison: A Theory and an Intervention." In Collected Papers on Moral Development and Moral Education,* Lawrence Kohlberg, ed. Cambridge, MA: Moral Education and Research Foundation, Harvard University, 1973, pp. 3-14.

Krathwohl, David, *et al. Taxonomy of Educational Objectives. The Classification of Educational Goals. Handbook II: Affective Domain.* New York, NY: David McKay, 1964.

Lepley, Ray, ed. *Value: A Cooperative Inquiry.* New York, NY: Columbia University Press, 1949.

Lewin, Kurt. *A Dynamic Theory of Personality.* New York, NY: McGraw-Hill, 1935.

Lewis, Clarence I. *An Analysis of Knowledge and Valuation.* LaSalle, IL: Open Court, 1962.

Loevinger, Jane, *et al. Measuring Ego Development,* Volumes I and II. San Francisco, CA: Jossey-Bass, 1970.

Los Angeles City Schools. *The Teaching of Values: An Instructional Guide for Kindergarten, Grades 1-14.* Los Angeles, CA: Division of Instructional Services, Los Angeles City Schools, 1966.

Maslow, Abraham. *Religions, Values, and Peak Experiences.* New York, NY: Viking, 1970.

Maslow, Abraham. *Toward a Psychology of Being.* Princeton, NJ: Van Nostrand, 1962.

Massialas, Byron G., and C. Benjamin Cox. *Inquiry in Social Studies.* New York, NY: McGraw-Hill, 1966.

McDougall, William. *An Introduction to Social Psychology.* London, England: Methuen, 1908.

McPhail, Peter, *et al. Moral Education in the Secondary School.* London, England: Longmans, 1972.

McWaters, Barry. "An Outline of Transpersonal Psychology: Its Meaning and Relevance for Education." In *Four Psychologies Applied to Education: Freudian, Behavioral, Humanistic, and Transpersonal,* Thomas B. Roberts, ed.. New York, NY: Wiley, 1975, pp. 448-452.

Meacham, Merle L., and Allen E. Wiesen. *Changing Classroom Behavior: A Manual for Precision Teaching.* Scranton, PA: International Textbook, 1969.

Metcalf, Lawrence E., ed. *Values Education: Rationale, Strategies, and Procedures. 41st Yearbook.* Washington, D.C.: National Council for the Social Studies, 1971.

Meux, Milton, *et al. Value Analysis Capability Development Programs: Final Report.* Salt Lake City, UT: Granite School District and University of Utah, 1974.

Michaelis, John U. *Social Studies for Children in a Democracy: Recent Trends and Developments.* Englewood Cliffs, NJ: Prentice-Hall, 1972.

Moore, George E. *Principia Ethica.* Cambridge, England: Cambridge University Press, 1929.

Moustakas, Clark. *The Authentic Teacher: Sensitivity and Awareness in the Classroom.* Cambridge, MA: Howard A. Doyle, 1966.

Murphy, Gardner. *Human Potentialities.* New York, NY: Basic Books, 1958.

Murphy, Michael H. "Education for Transcendence." In *Four Psychologies Applied to Education: Freudian, Behavioral, Humanistic, and Transpersonal,* Thomas B. Roberts, ed. New York, NY: Wiley, 1975, pp. 438-447.

Newmann, Fred M. *Education for Citizen Action: Challenge for Secondary Curriculum.* Berkeley, CA: McCutchan, 1975.

Newmann, Fred M. *Social Action: Dilemmas and Strategies. (Public Issues Series).* Columbus, OH: Xerox, 1972.

Newmann, Fred M., and Donald W. Oliver. *Clarifying Public Controversy: An Approach to Teaching Social Studies.* Boston, MA: Little, Brown, 1970.

Oliver, Donald W., and Fred M. Newmann. *The Public Issues Series* (Harvard Social Studies Project). Cambridge, MA: Harvard University Press, 1967-72.

Oliver, Donald W., and James Shaver. *Teaching Public Issues in the High School.* Boston, MA: Houghton Mifflin, 1966.

Palomares, Uvaldo, and Harold Bessell. *Methods in Human Development: Theory Manual.* El Cajon, CA: Human Development Training Institute, 1970.

Parsons, Talcott. *The Social System.* Glencoe, IL: Free Press, 1951.

Pasadena City Schools. *Moral and Spiritual Values.* Pasadena, CA: Division of Instructional Services, Pasadena City Schools, 1957.

Paulson, Wayne. *Deciding for Myself: A Values-Clarification Series.* Minneapolis, MN: Winston, 1974.

Peck, R. F., and Robert J. Havighurst. *The Psychology of Character Development.* New York, NY: Wiley, 1960.

Pepper, Stephen C., *The Sources of Value.* Berkeley, CA: University of California Press, 1958.

Pepper, Stephen C. *A Digest of Purposive Values.* Berkeley, CA: University of California Press, 1947.

Perry, R. B. *Realms of Value.* Cambridge, MA: Harvard University Press, 1954.

Perry, R. B. *General Theory of Value.* Cambridge, MA: Harvard University Press, 1926.

Perry, William G., Jr. *Forms of Intellectual and Ethical Development in the College Years: A Scheme.* New York, NY: Holt, Rinehart and Winston, 1970.

Piaget, Jean. *The Moral Judgment of the Child.* New York, NY: Collier, 1962 (1st ed., 1932).

Porter, Nancy, and Nancy Taylor. *How to Assess the Moral Reasoning of Students.* Toronto, Ontario, Canada: Ontario Institute for Studies in Education, 1972.

Progoff, Ira. *The Death and Rebirth of Psychology.* New York, NY: Julian, 1956.

Radha, Swami Sivananda. "Life Seals." *Ascent: The Journal of Yasodhara Ashram Society,* 5 (Spring 1973) pp. 10-15.

Raths, Louis E., *et al. Values and Teaching: Working with Values in the Classroom.* Columbus, OH: Charles E. Merrill, 1966.

Rest, James. "Developmental Psychology as a Guide to Value Education: A Review of Kohlbergian Programs." *Review of Educational Research,* 44 (February 1974) pp. 241-259.

Rest, James. *Opinions about Social Problems.* Minneapolis, MN: University of Minnesota, 1972.

Roberts, Thomas B., ed. *Four Psychologies Applied to Education: Freudian, Behavioral, Humanistic, and Transpersonal.* New York, NY: Wiley, 1975.

Rogers, Carl. *Freedom to Learn.* Columbus, OH: Charles E. Merrill, 1969.

Rogers, Carl. "Toward a Modern Approach to Values." *Journal of Abnormal and Social Psychology,* 58 (1964) pp. 160-67.

Rogers, Carl. *On Becoming a Person.* Boston, MA: Houghton Mifflin, 1961.

Rokeach, Milton. *Beliefs, Attitudes, and Values: A Theory of Organization and Change.* San Francisco, CA: Jossey-Bass, 1970.

Rucker, W. Ray, Clyde V. Arnspiger, and Author J. Brodbeck. *Human Values in Education.* Dubuque, IA: Kendall/Hunt, 1969.

Samples, Robert E. "Values Prejudice: Toward a Personal Awareness." *Media and Methods,* 2 (September 1974) pp. 14-18, 49-52.

Sarason, Irwin C., and Barbara R. Sarason. *Constructive Classroom Behavior.* New York, NY: Behavioral Publications, 1974.

Sarason, Irwin G., *et al. Reinforcing Productive Classroom Behavior.* New York, NY: Behavioral Publications, 1972.

Sayre, Joan. *Teaching Moral Values Through Behavior Modification.* Danville, IL: Interstate, 1972.

Scriven, Michael. *Primary Philosophy.* New York, NY: McGraw-Hill, 1966.

Sears, Robert R., *et al. Patterns of Child Rearing.* Evanston, IL: Row, Peterson, 1957.

Selman, Robert, *et al. First Things: Social Reasoning.* New York, NY: Guidance Associates, 1974.

Shaftel, Fannie, and George Shaftel. *Values in Action.* New York, NY: Holt, Rinehart and Winston, 1970.

Shaver, James P., and A. Guy Larkins. *Analysis of Public Issues Program: Instructor's Manual.* Boston, MA: Houghton Mifflin, 1973.

Shaver, James P., and A. Guy Larkins. *The Analysis of Public Issues: Concepts, Materials, Research. Final Report.* Logan, UT: Bureau of Educational Research, Utah State University, 1969. ED 037 475.

Simon, Sidney B., and Howard Kirschenbaum, eds. *Readings in Values Clarification.* Minneapolis, MN: Winston, 1973.

Simon, Sidney B., *et al. Values Clarification: A Handbook of Practical Strategies for Teachers and Students.* New York, NY: Hart, 1972.

Simpson, Bert K. *Becoming Aware of Values.* San Diego, CA: Pennant, 1973.

Smith, M. F. *FAIS: The Fusion of Applied and Intellectual Skills, Final Research Report. Project Numbers VTAD-5, 1971-1972.* Gainesville, FL: P. K. Yonge Laboratory School, College of Education, University of Florida, 1974.

Social Studies Curriculum Materials Data Book. Boulder, CO: Social Science Education Consortium, Inc., 1971—.

Sorokin, Pitirim A. "Reply to Professor Weisskopf." In *New Knowledge in Human Values,* Abraham H. Maslow, ed. New York, NY: Harper and Row, 1959, pp. 224-232.

Sullivan, C., Marguerite Q. Grant, and J. D. Grant. "The Development of Interpersonal Maturity: Applications of Delinquency." *Psychiatry,* 20 (1957) pp. 373-385.

Sullivan, Harry Stack. *The Interpersonal Theory of Psychiatry.* New York, NY: W. W. Norton, 1953.

Sulzer, Beth, and G. Roy Mayer. *Behavior Modification Procedures for School Personnel.* New York, NY: Dryden, 1972.

Superka, Douglas P. "A Typology of Valuing Theories and Values Education Approaches." Unpublished doctoral dissertation. Berkeley, CA: School of Education, University of California, 1973.

Suzuki, D. T. "Human Values in Zen." In *New Knowledge in Human Values,* Abraham H. Maslow, ed. New York, NY: Harper and Row, 1959.

Taba, Hilda, *et al. A Teacher's Handbook to Elementary Social Studies: An Inductive Approach.* Menlo Park, CA: Addison-Wesley, 1971.

Tillich, Paul. *The Courage to Be.* New Haven, CT: Yale University Press, 1952.

Tisdale, John R. "Psychological Value Theory and Research: 1930-1960." Unpublished doctoral dissertation. Boston, MA: Boston University, 1961.

Toulmin, Stephen E. *An Examination of the Place of Reason in Ethics.* Cambridge, England: Cambridge University Press, 1950.

Trow, William C. "Value Concepts in Educational Psychology." *Journal of Educational Psychology,* 46 (1953) pp.449-462.

Wallen, Norman E., *et al. Taba Final Report.* Menlo Park, CA: Addison-Wesley, 1969. (Order code #7424.)

Watts, Alan W. *The Book: On the Taboo Against Knowing Who You Are.* New York, NY: Collier, 1967.

Weinstein, Gerald, and Mario Fantini. *Toward Humanistic Education: A Curriculum of Affect.* New York, NY: Praeger, 1970.

Westermarck, Edward. *Ethical Relativity.* New York, NY: Harcourt, Brace, 1932.

Whitaker, Carl A., and Thomas P. Malone. *The Roots of Psychotherapy.* New York, NY: Blakiston, 1953.

White, Earl E., and Hazel I. Smith. *A Guide to Behavior Modification: A Classroom Teacher's Handbook.* Palo Alto, CA: Peak Publications, 1972.

Whiting, John W. M. "Socialization Process and Personality." In *Psychological Anthropology,* Francis L. K. Hsu, ed. Homewood, IL: Dorsey, 1961, pp. 355-399.

Wilson, John, *et al. Introduction to Moral Education.* Baltimore, MD: Penguin, 1967.

Woody, R. M. *Behavioral Problem Children in the Schools: Recognition, Diagnosis, and Behavioral Modification.* New York, NY: Appleton-Century-Crofts, 1969.

Yeomans, Thomas. *Search for a Working Model: Gestalt, Psychosynthesis, and Confluent Education.* Occasional Paper No. 22. Santa Barbara, CA: Development and Research in Confluent Education (DRICE), University of California, 1972.

index of materials

S = Student Material; T = Teacher Material

Douglas P. Superka is a Staff Associate with the Social Science Education Consortium (SSEC) and the ERIC Clearinghouse for Social Studies/Social Science Education in Boulder, Colorado. He has been a high school teacher and guidance counselor in Pennsylvania and California, a consultant to several curriculum development organizations, and a workshop facilitator in values education. In 1973 he received an Ed.D. in Curriculum and Instruction (with a focus on values education) from the University of California, Berkeley.

Christine Ahrens is a former Staff Associate with the ERIC Clearinghouse for Social Studies/Social Science Education in Boulder, Colorado. She received an M.A. in English at the University of the Pacific, where she was a teaching intern. She has been an editor for the Human Sciences Program at the Biological Sciences Curriculum Project.

Judith Hedstrom is a Staff Assistant with the Social Science Education Consortium and the ERIC Clearinghouse for Social Studies/Social Science Education in Boulder, Colorado. She received a B.A. in Urban Studies from North Park College, Chicago, Illinois, and has been a teacher on the Navajo reservation in Arizona, a camp counselor in Wisconsin, and a recreational program director in Chicago.

Luther Ford is an elementary and junior high school social studies teacher in Gary, Indiana. During the 1974-75 school term he was a Teacher Associate at the Social Science Education Consortium. He received an M.S. in Elementary Education from Indiana State University and has been a consultant to the Indiana State Social Studies Advisory Committee and the Urban League of Northwest Indiana.

Patricia L. Johnson is Assistant Professor of Counseling and Human Systems at Florida State University, Tallahassee, Florida. She received a Ph.D. in Education from the University of Michigan and has worked as a values education and interpersonal communications consultant with several public schools and with the National Council of the YMCAs. She has also taught human relations training and group process in the social studies.